CLUELESS IN ACADEME

GERALD GRAFF

Clueless
IN Academe

HOW SCHOOLING OBSCURES THE LIFE OF THE MIND

YALE UNIVERSITY PRESS   NEW HAVEN AND LONDON

Published with assistance from the foundation established in memory of Philip Hamilton McMillan of the Class of 1894, Yale College.

Designed by Rebecca Gibb.
Set in Scala type by Achorn Graphic Services.
Printed in the United States of America.

The Library of Congress has cataloged the hardcover edition as follows:
Graff, Gerald.
Clueless in academe : how schooling obscures the life of the mind / by Gerald Graff.
  p. cm.
Includes bibliographical references (p.   ) and index.
ISBN 0-300-09558-9 (alk. paper)
1. Education, Higher—Social aspects—United States. 2. Learning and scholarship—United States. I. Title.
LC191.94 .G73 2003
306.43—dc21
2002151910

A catalogue record for this book is available from the British Library.

The paper in this book meets the guidelines for permanence and durability of the Committee on Production Guidelines for Book Longevity of the Council on Library Resources.
ISBN 13- 978-0-300-10514-8
10 9 8 7

CONTENTS

ACKNOWLEDGMENTS

I want to give special thanks to Steve Benton, my graduate assistant for the past three years at the University of Illinois at Chicago. Steve went far beyond the call of duty in reading my many drafts and providing constant high-quality feedback, criticism, and encouragement. He also took on much of the work of helping me prepare the manuscript for the press. Some of the ideas and even the words and phrases in this book are as much Steve's as my own.

Two generous grants supported me in writing this book. The first allowed me to spend a fellowship year at the Center for Advanced Study in the Behavioral Sciences in California, where I began the book. The second, from the Spencer Foundation of Chicago, enabled me to finish it. I am grateful to these two organizations, without whose assistance this book would have taken a lot longer to complete.

I am grateful to Robert Scholes, who read two different versions of my manuscript for Yale University Press and offered very constructive advice on how to revise them. The importance to me of Bob's work as a model of how to write about the challenges of English teaching is reflected in chapter 9.

Special thanks also go to Andy Hoberek, who co-authored chapter 10 and whose influence on my thinking runs through the book. I also want to extend special thanks to my longtime friend and now colleague and team-teaching partner, Jane Tompkins, whose ideas and writing figure centrally in this book. Engaging with Jane's work has been crucial to me in forming my own ideas.

I also want to give special thanks to several people who supplied me with information about their creative teaching practices and kindly gave me permission to quote them at length here: Jim Benton, Jack Brereton, Hillel Crandus, Cathy Birkenstein-Graff, Donald Jones, and Ned Laff.

I also warmly thank the many friends and colleagues whose conversations on teaching and learning were instrumental in helping me think out what I wanted to say: Jennifer Ashton, Howard Becker, Jerry Bona, Wayne Booth, Jack Brereton, Marsha Cassidy, Candace Clements, Lennard Davis, Todd DeStigter, Kevin Dettmar, Ann Feldman, Leon Fink, Stanley Fish, Mike Fischer, Bridget O'Rourke Flisk, Steve Flisk, Christopher Freeburg, Howard Gardner, Patty Harkin, Tad Howard, Donald Jones, Steve Jones, Don Lazere, Jo Liebermann, Jo and Larry Lipking, Mark Krupnick, Steve Mailloux, Larry McEnerney, Charlie Newman, Bruce Novak, Karen Mann, Chris Messenger, Walter Benn Michaels, Peter Michelson, Bill Rice, Jeff Rice, Bruce Robbins, Larry Rothfield, Lance Rubin, Cindy Sabik, Dave Schaafsma, Lee Shulman, David Shumway, Herb Simons, Jim Sosnoski, Richard Strier, Steve Tozer, Jeffrey Wallen, Michael Walsh, Jeff Williams, Ellen Winner, Don Wink, Vershawn Young, and the late Tom Samet.

My thanks to the journals and journal editors who kindly gave me permission to reprint parts of this book that they published in different versions in article form: *Arts and Humanities in Higher Education, College English, The Common Review, The Hedgehog Review, Pedagogy,* and *PMLA.*

I want particularly to thank Jonathan Brent, my friend and former co-director at the Northwestern University Press and editorial director of Yale University Press. Jonathan solicited this book and provided me with a penetrating reading of an early draft. Thanks also to my manuscript editor, Jeff Schier, who made many valuable suggestions and eased me through the trauma of online copyediting.

Finally, I express my eternal thanks and love to my wife and collab-

orator, Cathy Birkenstein-Graff, who is writing a textbook with me—
A Short Guide to Argument—that will be a sequel and companion to
Clueless in Academe. Cathy read and commented on many drafts and
patiently talked me through trouble spots. Her patience, support, and
loving guidance contributed much more to this book than I can express.

In the Dark All Eggheads Are Gray

THIS BOOK IS AN ATTEMPT by an academic to look at academia from the perspective of those who don't get it. Its subject is cluelessness, the bafflement, usually accompanied by shame and resentment, felt by students, the general public, and even many academics in the face of the impenetrability of the academic world. It examines some over-looked ways in which schools and colleges themselves reinforce clue-lessness and thus perpetuate the misconception that the life of the mind is a secret society for which only an elite few qualify.

Given the inherent difficulty of academic intellectual work, some degree of cluelessness is a natural stage in the process of education. If cluelessness did not exist, there would be no need for schooling at all. My argument in this book, however, is that academia reinforces cluelessness by making its ideas, problems, and ways of thinking *look* more opaque, narrowly specialized, and beyond normal learning capac-ities than they are or need to be. As I see it, my academic intellectual culture is not at all irrelevant to my students' needs and interests, but we do a very good job of making it appear as if it is.

One way we do so is by obscuring the convergence between acade-mia and the popular media. Too often schools and colleges take intellec-tual conversations that resemble the ones students engage in or encounter in the popular media, and make them seem unrecognizable, as well as no fun. To put it another way, schooling takes students who are perfectly street-smart and exposes them to the life of the mind in ways that make them feel dumb. Why is this? Why in many cases do street smarts not only fail to evolve naturally into academic smarts, but end up seeming opposed to academic smarts, as if the two can't coexist inside the same head? Part of the reason has to do with the legacy of American anti-intellectualism, which elevates hardheaded common sense over supposedly impractical academic navel gazing. But educational institutions themselves contribute to the problem by making the culture of ideas and arguments look opaque and therefore more remote than it actually is from the wisdom of the street.

How this happens, "how schooling obscures the life of the mind," is my central concern. Jargon and specialized terminology, the most frequently blamed culprits, are only the tip of the institutional iceberg. I too am amused by the satires on opaque academic jargon produced by journalists, stand-up comics, and disaffected academics. But blaming the unintelligibility of academia exclusively on jargon and obscure writing prevents us from recognizing deeper sources of obfuscation that are rooted in the way academia organizes and thinks about itself. To appreciate these deeper causes, we need to go beyond spoofs of jargon to the way schools and colleges represent the culture of ideas and arguments.

By the culture of ideas and arguments, I refer to that admittedly blurry entity that spans the academic and intellectual worlds on the one hand and the arena of journalistic public discourse on the other. Not all "academics" are "intellectuals," and intellectuals come in many different types, including academic scholars, journalistic public intellectuals, policy wonks, information managers, media pundits, and legal and government professionals. What these different types have in common, from the research professor to the newspaper editorialist to the mythical educated lay person on the street, is a commitment to articulating ideas in public. Whatever the differences between their specialized jargons, they have all learned to play the following game: listen closely to others, summarize them in a recognizable way, and make your own relevant argument. This argument literacy, the ability to listen, summarize, and respond, is rightly viewed as central to being educated.

For American students to do better—all of them, not just twenty percent—they need to know that summarizing and making arguments is the name of the game in academia. But it's precisely this game that academia obscures, generally by hiding it in plain view amidst a vast disconnected clutter of subjects, disciplines, and courses. The sheer cognitive overload represented by the American curriculum prevents most students from detecting and then learning the moves of the underlying argument game that gives coherence to it all.

The college curriculum says to students, in effect, "Come and get it, but you're on your own as to what to make of it all." As John Gardner has rightly observed, American colleges "operate under the assumption that students know how to do it—or if they don't they'll flunk out and it's their problem."[1] And colleges play hard to get not only with their undergraduates, but with the lower schools. The schools are easy to blame for failing to prepare students for college, and it is indeed a scandal that, aside from a few "star" schools that resemble good colleges,[2] American high schools still don't see it as their mission to prepare all their students for college, even though everybody now agrees that college is a virtual prerequisite for success and a decent life. But it is the failure of higher education to clarify its culture of ideas and arguments that leaves the schools unable to prepare their students for college. The mystification of academic culture trickles down from the top.

Some readers will object that in claiming to know what students have to do to succeed in academia—enter the culture of ideas and arguments—I am really only revealing what they have to do to pass my course. They will say that there's more to being educated than learning to argue, and they are right. In giving priority to ideas and arguments, however, I don't minimize the importance of qualities that can't be reduced to pure rationality—emotional intelligence, moral character, visual and aesthetic sensitivity, and creativity in storytelling and personal narrative. What I do claim is that training in these qualities will be incomplete if students are unable to translate them into persuasive public discourse. To call attention to the educational importance of visual literacy and the body you have to make arguments, not just wave pictures, do a dance, or give hugs.

Argumentation need not be a joyless, bloodless activity, and there is no necessary quarrel between arguments and narratives. Good stories make an argumentative point, and arguments gain punch from imbedded stories. Nor does privileging argumentation in the curriculum necessarily represent the ethnocentric or racist bias that some make it out to be. On the contrary, since effective argument starts with attentive listening, training in argument is central to multicultural understanding and respect for otherness. Respecting cultures different from your own means summarizing others' arguments accurately, putting yourself in their shoes. After September 11 it is all the more crucial that Americans learn to understand the arguments of those who would destroy us, and that the world learn to fight with words rather than with guns and bombs.

I like to think I have first-class credentials for writing a book about cluelessness, having been a university professor for forty years, thereby encountering a great variety of students and others who were often puzzled by things I said and even more by why I said them at all. I have met my own share of incomprehensible academic utterances, which I duly pretended to understand in order to avoid humiliation. Given the genius-worship that runs through our culture, academics are often admired for speaking above other people's heads, but knowing this fact somehow doesn't save me from embarrassment when I fumble painfully to explain what I do to nonacademic relatives and friends.

My experience over the years playing both the baffler and bafflee has made me increasingly curious about the incomprehension, anxiety, and alienation that my academic intellectual world provokes. Finding that no study exists of the root causes of academic befuddlement, at some point I began contemplating a book length analysis, a kind of notes toward a field of clueless studies. I had been unscientifically collecting data on attitudes toward "intellectualism" and what one of my students once called "life of the mind stuff,"[3] data that included notes on classes and office conferences, copies of student papers, and specimens, good and bad, of academic and journalistic writing. I began interviewing—and getting my students to interview—college undergraduates and high school students, probing how they felt about intellectualism and its forms of talk, and I plunged into the extensive scholarly literature on academic literacy and students' problems with it. I also thought back on my own cluelessness as an awkward college student, before the intellectual world had become so familiar to me that I forgot how strange and alienating it had once seemed. I reflected on the divided feelings I still harbor as someone who often feels most like an academic when I am around nonacademics and most like a nonacademic when I am with colleagues.

Since professors are supposed to be smart, sophisticated, and on the cutting edge, making a study of incomprehension can seem oddly retrograde—like giving up an endowed chair in order to reenroll in kindergarten. Professors are trained to think of cluelessness as an uninteresting negative condition, a lack or a blank space to be filled in by superior knowledge. This incuriosity, which helps explain why teaching has been so notoriously undervalued in universities, takes different forms: for some progressive educators, to speak of cluelessness at all is inherently snobbish, elitist, and undemocratic, as if acknowledging students' deficiencies necessarily denigrated their abilities. For some traditionalists, on the other hand, who see cluelessness as a distasteful symptom of cultural vulgarity and a dumbed-down popular culture, the clueless, like the poor, will always be with us, and there is nothing much anybody can do about it except to teach to the best students and let the rest fend for themselves.

These attitudes may explain why the opaque nature of academic intellectual culture, though a common target of jokes, is not a more prominent topic in debates over what ails American education. Though we all now claim to believe in democratic education, as a culture we have never been sure if we think everyone is cut out for the life of the mind or not. Then, too, the topic of academic cluelessness is so fraught with anxieties about class snobbery and inferiority that it is hard to have a frank discussion of it. On the other hand, the topic can often be discerned lurking in the background of discussions of other educational issues, particularly in growing concerns about the achievement gap between high- and low-income students. Recent debates about standardized testing, for example, are really a symptom of the murkiness about what it is that intellectuals do. It's as if standardized tests fill a gap left by our failure to clarify what real intellectual prowess is all about.

But attention to academia's opacity has been further diverted in recent years by the polarized politics of educational debate. In the curricular wars that have raged since the eighties and nineties, we have become so caught up in battles between rival lists of books—the traditional classics versus multicultural and minority texts—that we forget that the chronic problem for the vast majority of American high school and college students has always been *the culture of books and ideas as such,* regardless of which faction gets to draw up the reading list. We become so enmeshed in rivalries between traditional and progressive *versions* of intellectual culture that we overlook the fact that to most students intellectual culture of any kind, whatever its political leanings, is all the same old "school stuff."

This is not to minimize the importance of ideological differences or to avoid taking a stand in the canon wars. It is simply to point out that in order to understand or articulate a political stand you already have to belong to the culture of ideas and arguments, and wield its lingo of "whereas x argues _____, I claim _____." The point was rudely brought home to me in a course I taught at Northwestern in the late eighties: I had asked my class to write responses to essays by traditionalist Allan Bloom and radical black feminist bell hooks. In reading the papers I realized that some students saw little difference between Bloom and hooks. To their eyes, these two writers, who seem ideologically on different planets to me and my colleagues, were just a couple of professors conversing in arcane language about nonproblems. And many of the students who did discern the differences were not able to formulate them articulately or enter the debate. It was not that they lacked interest, but that the language of public controversy that Bloom and hooks commanded eluded them. I concluded that it wouldn't matter much whether Bloom's or hooks's side won the debate if these students remained excluded from the discourse in which it was carried on.

Call it the Law of Relative Invisibility of Intellectual Differences: to the non-egghead, any two eggheads, no matter how far apart, are virtually indistinguishable.[4] With apologies to cartoonist Gary Larson's *The Far Side,* we can picture the situation as follows:

G. Graff

In the dark all intellectual disagreements are gray.

On the other hand, being "in the dark" enables you to notice things that get overlooked by those supposedly in the know. If from a clueless eye view opposing intellectuals look the same, it is because they *are* the same in a crucial way. They share a public language of ideas and arguments that transcends their ideological differences and separates them from many students and other Americans.

As for the battle of the books, my argument cuts both ways in the skirmishes between traditionalists and progressives. Traditionalists are right to insist that not all texts are equal in value and that students should study a significant selection of the world's classics. But what does it profit them to keep the syllabus safe for Plato and Shakespeare if many students need the Cliffs Notes to get a clue about what such authors are up to? Progressives are right that students who are turned off by *Hamlet* may be turned on by Alice Walker's *The Color Purple* (though such results don't necessarily follow predictable racial, ethnic, or class lines). It's foolish not to assign Walker or a popular magazine or film if doing so inspires students to read and study who otherwise would not. Progressives are also right that since every reading list makes a statement about how the experience of particular groups is or is not valued, questions of cultural representation have a legitimate place in decisions about what texts to teach. But what does it profit progressives to get minority writers like Walker and Black Elk into the syllabus if many students need the Cliffs Notes to gain an articulate grasp of either?

In fact, works by Walker and other multicultural writers are now prominently displayed in the Cliffs Notes rack, perhaps the ultimate sign that multiculturalism has made it, but hardly in the way its advocates hoped. Again, then, our intense debates over course reading lists will be academic in the worst sense if students remain outside the academic conversation about books.

But who gives a fig, you ask, about "the academic conversation," which is often a bad conversation, boring, self-important, and dominated by insider orthodoxies? Academic conversations are often all these things, to be sure, but at their best moments they are more valuable and pertinent to students' lives than academic-bashers give them credit for. Even so, you persist, isn't the point of education to produce good citizens, not more academics? Surely it is, but these goals are compatible, for the issues and problems addressed by academic research and teaching are increasingly indistinguishable from the issues we wrestle with as public citizens. The point is not to turn students into clones of professors but to give them access to forms of intellectual capital that have a lot of power in the world.

Those who charge that academic discourse is itself the problem fail to see that *talk about* books and subjects is as important educationally as are the books and subjects themselves. For the way we talk about a subject becomes part of the subject, a fact that explains why we have book-discussion groups to supplement solitary reading, why Trekkies form clubs and hold conferences as well as privately enjoying *Star Trek*, and why sports talk call-in shows and sports journalism have arisen alongside the games themselves. Students must not only read texts, but find things to *say* about them, and no text tells you what to say about it. So our habit of elevating books and subjects over the secondary talk about them only helps keep students tongue-tied.

Seeing academia, then, as these struggling students see it, is a key prerequisite for improved teaching. It is also a key to improving the quality of professorial writing. The sociologist Howard Becker has observed that there is something unfairly circular about the common view that sociologists write badly, since sociological work that is well written is not considered sociology.[5] Becker's witticism holds for academic writing generally: people assume that if they understand it, it must not be academic. Though I have a good deal to say in this book about why academic writing is often bad, I argue against the popular belief that academic writing generally turns its back on nonacademic outsiders or that to make it as a professor you have to envelop your ideas in a cloud of smoke.

The view that academic writing is necessarily insular and obscure props up the overdrawn opposition between research and teaching. We are so used to opposing research and teaching that we overlook the fact that good research is itself pedagogical, often drawing on skills of explanation, clarification, and problem-posing—of asking, "So what?" and "Who cares?"—that are central to good teaching. Indeed, as many academics testify, teaching often helps us sharpen our research writing and thereby advance our careers, a fact that refutes the renunciatory view of teaching that sees it as necessarily sacrificing professional self-interest.

I myself seem to have the most impact on professional audiences when I write in ways that are accessible to lay readers and take their outsider's perspective into account. As I see it, having to explain myself to freshmen or high school students forces me not to dumb my ideas down, but to formulate them more pointedly than I do when I address only my colleagues and graduate students. I agree with the linguist Steven Pinker that "having to explain an idea in plain English to someone with no stake in the matter is an excellent screen for incoherent or contradictory ideas that somehow have entrenched themselves in a field."[6] For again, those outsiders' questions that at first sight seem clueless—"So what?" "What's your point?" "What does it have to do with me?" and "Why does any of this matter?"—often turn out to be the smartest and most clarifying.

It is by making us feel that asking such questions would expose us as naive or foolish that academia gets away with its mystifications. As a recent college graduate put it when asked how well her English major had clarified the issues in her discipline, "The assumption seemed to be that if I was any good I *already* knew what those issues were and why they mattered. I couldn't ask, since I didn't want to look dumb." Academia has its own unspoken policy of "don't ask, don't tell" that prevents clarification from breaking out.

Much of the problem lies in the belief that to *simplify* academic inquiry is to vulgarize it, whereas simplification is a necessary feature of even the most complex kinds of work. Nothing inhibits clarification—and good teaching—more than the professorial fear and loathing of any formulation that seems reductive. In fact, reductions can be harmful or useful, and failing to make the distinction leads us to justify obfuscation and exclusion ("It's just too complicated to explain; if only you were in the field you'd understand what I'm talking about"). As I argue in chapter 7, reductive moments are central not only to teaching but to intramural communication between scholars as well. I am not urging professors, as Gregory Jay recently has, to "complement" our work "with essays and books that translate our fields for the public," though this is certainly a good thing to do.[7] I am arguing that translating academic ideas into nonacademic terms is already *internal* to successful academic communication itself. "Dare to be reductive" is one of my maxims for academics.

In addition to analyzing structures of academic obfuscation, this book suggests ways in which teachers and programs can cut through the curricular clutter to show students how the argument world works. The book draws on strategies I have developed in my own teaching or have borrowed from others that simplify the basic "moves" of public argument for students who have difficulty making them on their own (see the epilogue: "How to Write an Argument: What Students and Teachers *Really* Need to Know"). These include Argument Templates, which I use as training wheels that enable students to get on the argument bike and ride (example: "In the discussion that has followed the September 11 attacks, a controversial issue has been . . ."). Some will object to the formulaic nature of such templates, but all communication is partly formulaic. Formulas can enable creativity and complication as often as they can stifle them. If we refuse to provide such formulas on the grounds that they are too prescriptive or that everything has to come from the students themselves, we just end up hiding the tools of success.

Since it is freshman composition that has been assigned the job of teaching the basic moves of persuasive argument, this book amounts to a plea for making composition and writing across the curriculum programs far more central than they have ever been in high school and college curricula. The low status of composition in universities illustrates the "Law of Academic Prestige" that has been formulated by Deirdre N. McCloskey: "the more useful a field, the lower its prestige. The freshman English course, which is one of the most important things colleges do, is in academic prestige many notches below algebraic topology or medieval philosophy."[8] These priorities are particularly self-defeating for departments of English, which exalt literary studies over writing even though the quality of students' literary experience is registered only through what they say and write. The spread of college "first year experience" courses and "freshman success seminars" is a step in the right direction, but such courses generally stop short of providing intellectual socialization. They need to go beyond teaching study skills, time-management, using computers, and test-taking to give students more help in entering the academic culture of arguments and ideas.

Lastly, a word about the relation of this book to my previous work. In my educational writing, I am best known for the argument that the wisest response we can make to the philosophical and social conflicts that have disrupted education is to "teach the conflicts" themselves, to bring controversy to the center of the academic curriculum. The situation that called forth this argument was the culture wars of the eighties and nineties, which led me to conclude that if disagreements over what should be taught and how are inevitable, the sensible course would be to quit trying to hide these disagreements and start making productive use of them in classrooms so as to bring students in on them. Because my examples of conflicts to be taught were often the debates over the canon and politics in literary studies, some readers have assumed that teaching the conflicts for me focuses only on those debates, whereas teaching the conflicts can be done in any discipline or subject area.

But an even more important point that some readers of my work have missed is that the ultimate motivation of my argument for teaching the conflicts is the need to clarify academic culture, not just to resolve spats among academics or cultural factions. My assumption is that an institution as rife with conflicts as the American school and college can clarify itself only by making its ideological differences coherent. But even if our cultural and educational scene were a less contentious place than it is, the centrality of controversy to learning would still need to be stressed. For there exists a deep cognitive connection between controversy and intelligibility. John Stuart Mill pointed up the connection when he observed that we do not understand our own ideas until we know what can be said against them. In Mill's words, those who "have never thrown themselves into the mental position of those who think differently from them . . . do not, in any proper sense of the word, know the doctrine which they themselves profess."[9] In other words, our very ability to think depends on contrast—on asking "as opposed to what?" This "dialogical" or contrastive character of human cognition has long been a given of modern thought, but the academic curriculum with its self-isolated courses has yet to reflect it. When schooling is bad or dull, it is often because the curriculum effaces this element of contrast or as-opposed-to-whatness from students' view. Thus the academic habit of evading conflict helps obscure the life of the mind.

The problem, however, is that simply throwing inexperienced students headlong into intellectual debates doesn't work. Students won't become engaged in academic debates about ideas unless they have a reason to be interested in them and can gain the rudiments of the public discourse in which these debates are conducted. Whereas my last book, *Beyond the Culture Wars*, was subtitled *How Teaching the Conflicts Can Revitalize American Education*, the present book might be subtitled "How Teaching the Conflicts—or Any Other Educational Approach—*Won't* Revitalize Education as Long as the Culture of Public Argument Remains Opaque to Many Students and Other Citizens."

To put it another way, the most fundamental conflict that needs to be taught in classrooms is the conflict between Intellectualspeak and Studentspeak. I argue that teachers need to be explicit about this conflict and even to sharpen the contrast between academic and student discourse, though their ultimate goal should be to help students discover that these forms of discourse are not as far apart as they seem. My students and I need to meet each other halfway, as they learn the kind of talk that I speak and write and I learn theirs, for the combination of these registers is more powerful than either alone.

This book extends my "teach the conflicts" argument in one further way by seeing conflicts as an internal principle of writing and the teaching of writing. We throw ourselves, as Mill put it, "into the mental position of those who think differently from" us by writing the voices of others into our texts, even trying them on for size. When students are asked to complete a sentence that starts, "At this point you will probably object that . . . ," they begin to move beyond the undivided, one-dimensional voice that is a surer mark of weak student writing than incorrect grammar. And it's by writing the voices of others into their texts that students start learning to produce a public voice.

There are those who argue that the academic obfuscation I examine in this book is no accident. They say that when schooling keeps students mystified it is not failing at all, but working all too well at doing exactly what our culture asks it to, sorting students into cognitive haves and have-nots and therefore into society's winners and losers. As this argument has it, our winner-take-all economy has to find some way to maintain high levels of social inequality, so academic institutions must keep the cultural capital of literate public discourse out of the grubby hands of the riffraff.[10] We academics, then, deliberately withhold our mysteries from the many in order to prop up the power of the cultural elite as well as the fiction that society needs our mumbo-jumbo. I have never accepted this cynical view of education, but I'm afraid we will go on giving it credibility until we change our practices.

PART I: CONFUSING THE ISSUE

1 The University *Is* Popular Culture, But It Doesn't Know It Yet

AN OLD SAYING HAS IT that academic disputes are especially vicious because so little is at stake in them. Behind the sentiment lies the belief that the intellectual culture of academia is arid and self-absorbed, its head in the sand or the clouds, concerned with rarefied stuff that real people don't give a damn about. And there was more than a grain of truth to this view before World War II, when higher education was the privilege of a tiny social elite and the disciplines were dominated by a narrowly antiquarian and positivistic view of inquiry, which was seen as a business of piling up minutely specialized facts regardless of their interest or relevance beyond the scholarly world. In that period, to which many conservatives now look back with misplaced nostalgia, research "scholars" were the opposite of "intellectuals," accumulators of specialized information who left the big picture—the application of the facts to contemporary life—to journalists, the clergy, and other nonacademics.

The narrow pedantry to which scholarship could descend had been a target of satire for centuries, but it reached a kind of culmination with the rise of the modern research university. The philosopher George Santayana, who taught at Harvard from 1889 to 1912, complained that his scholarly colleagues were too busy with their microscopic projects to "form an intellectual society. . . . I never heard of any idea or movement spring up among them. . . . It was an anonymous concourse of coral insects, each secreting one cell, and leaving that fossil legacy to enlarge the earth."[1] William James, Santayana's Harvard colleague, had published similar criticisms of overspecialized scholarship in a 1903 essay entitled "The Ph.D. Octopus."[2] Such broadsides made little impact on the scholars, however, who saw their commitment to solid learning undefiled by controversial—that is, interesting—thought as proof of their integrity as searchers for truth.

Large stretches of academia in which not much has changed can still be found today. But for half a century inward-looking specialization has come under challenge by a counterimpulse toward outward-looking relevance. You need only scan the bulletin boards outside any academic department office or the advertisements for the latest academic books to see that a silent battle for the soul of academia is being waged between clashing conceptions of academic work: between a view that sees such work as inherently esoteric and specialized—and all the better for that—and a view that aspires to "outreach" and to broader influence on the wider society. But because our thinking about academia is still shaped by older assumptions, we tend to overlook the fact that since the end of World War II the tide has actually favored academics who can generalize their specialties and demonstrate their wider applications.[3]

CREEPING INTELLECTUALISM

"Specialized" is one of the most sloppily used words in the lexicon of education, often functioning as code for "politically doctrinaire." But if the word means "restricted in interest to a few experts," then it is misleadingly applied to much current academia. In the wake of the postwar knowledge explosion and the increased cultural diversity of students, faculties, and curricula, the academic specialist and the wide-ranging generalist increasingly merge in the same person, while the writing habits of the so-called public intellectual, once the exception to the rule, begin seeping into academic writing generally. Academia itself has become part of the mass culture industry, which disseminates and popularizes academic theories and trends. Whereas academics were once rewarded for burrowing into a narrow specialty and having nothing to say about the big picture, such habits today are more likely to get one rejected by editors, granting agencies, and hiring committees. If today's academic disputes are still often vicious, it is because *much* is at stake in them, as controversies over bilingual education, evolution, and creationism, the new gender and race studies, grade inflation, and the teaching of literature, mathematics, and history extend far beyond the campus. And as the *New York Times* noted in a report on how "Campuses Across America Are Adding 'Sept. 11 101' to Curriculums," colleges are now much more prone "to tackle current problems" than they were a generation ago, and much speedier in turning those problems into courses, whose existence in turn becomes news in places like the *Times*.[4]

Creeping intellectualism has become pervasive, with the growth of a college-educated audience created by the postwar democratization of higher education, an audience that is fascinated by the culture of teaching and learning. The fascination is reflected in the popularity of films like *Dead Poets Society, Dangerous Minds, Educating Rita, The Mirror Has Two Faces, Good Will Hunting, Legally Blonde,* and countless others, as well as TV series from *The White Shadow* to *The Education of Max Bickford*. Other signs range from cerebral cartoons like Gary Larson's *The Far Side* and *The Simpsons* to ex-commentator Dennis Miller's esoteric allusions on *Monday Night Football* to the use of the word *Theory* as a brand name for a line of women's pants. Academic ideas are increasingly popularized, not only by the media but by academic writing itself, as university presses court the wider audiences of trade houses while trade houses increasingly publish academics. All this refutes the cliché that academia is overspecialized. The University of Chicago Press doesn't boast in its advertisements that its latest titles in the social sciences and Middle Eastern studies are more specialized than those of Harvard University Press. On the contrary, such presses claim their books are paradigm-smashing, pathbreaking, and broad-gauged, and though such terms of praise may have more to do with hype than with accuracy, they show that a shift in priorities has taken place, a pathbreaking shift, you could say.

It's true that in the recent culture wars, academics and journalists have often been at each others' throats. But this very antagonism is now a sign of proximity rather than of distance. Whereas academics and journalists once disdained one another from afar, they now compete for preeminence in the common role of explaining the contemporary world. Then, too, the journalistic bashing of academic stars during the culture wars has been matched by the glorification of many of the same stars in such venues as the *New York Times Magazine*, National Public Radio's *Fresh Air*, or *Night Line*.

The new proximity of the academy and the media has been well described by the academic journalist Ellen Willis, who observes that many of the same theories, terms, and debates now circulate between the university and the media, and back:

> ideas that matter, for better or worse, have a way of spreading as they get picked up, translated, recycled for different audiences up and down the media food chain.
>
> Cultural criticism written by academics influences writers for journals of opinion, who in turn feed the heads of *New York Times* writers and commentators for PBS; eventually every aspect of the culture war finds its way into *USA Today, Roseanne, ER,* and the Movie of the Week.[5]

Not everyone thinks what Willis describes is a good thing, as critics charge universities with selling out to trendiness, faddishness, and disciplinary orthodoxies. Though these charges are often justified, I believe anyone familiar with historical accounts of what academia was like in the supposedly good old days will agree that the gains have been greater than the losses.[6]

Far from being narrow, soulless, and impoverished, then, the content of academic intellectual culture at its best is now rich and potentially compelling. But academia represents and explains this content so badly that one would think it is hiding it, as much from itself perhaps as from its students. Indeed, one of the major facts academia hushes up and hardly recognizes is the one I have just noted, that today's academic culture is less narrowly "academic" than its prewar counterpart, closer in spirit to the pulse of journalism and popular culture, which in turn are increasingly fascinated by academics and their ideas.

In a real sense, the university is *itself* popular culture—what else should we call an institution that serves millions if not an agent of mass popularization? But the university still behaves as if it were unpopular culture, and the anachronistic opposition of academia and journalism continues to provide academics with an ironclad excuse for communicative ineptitude. The damaging effects of this ineptitude were limited as long as only a fraction of the American population went to high school, much less to college, as was the case for much of the last century, and as long as vocational success did not yet depend on a college degree. The consequences have become far more serious, however, as higher education has become a mass enterprise and college credentials are a prerequisite of opportunity and mobility.

So what Willis calls the circulation of "ideas that matter" has its limits, as the opacity of university culture leaves the schools in limbo, preventing them from preparing students for higher education. The university's increased interest in big-picture ideas is not matched by any corresponding effort to clarify those ideas for more than a circumscribed audience. What "feeds the heads," in Willis's phrase, of *Times* writers and PBS commentators (and perhaps even the audiences of *Roseannne* and *ER*) doesn't necessarily enter the heads of college undergraduates or of high school teachers and students.

As a result, the more things change in the intellectual culture of academia, the more they stay the same with regard to what many students and the general public make—or fail to make—of it. On the one hand, the content of the academic disciplines has gone through revolutionary changes, as paradigm-smashing, boundary-crossing, high-wire interdisciplinary scholarship and teaching become the order of the day, and as the line blurs between academia and journalism. On the other hand, the average level of student cluelessness and apathy probably remains roughly what it was, say, in 1910.[7] High-achieving high school and college students become insiders to the most exciting academic conversations, but the majority remain on the outside looking in.

PARLEZ-VOUS ARGUESPEAK?

One of the most closely guarded secrets that academia unwittingly keeps from students and everybody else is that all academics, despite their many differences, play a version of the same game of *persuasive argument*. That this is so may seem obvious, but in my experience many students have not been let in on the news and are surprised when they hear it. The first step toward demystifying academia is to start being more explicit about the academic centrality of persuasive argument, as did a high school teacher with whom I work, Hillel Crandus, and his students, who coined a useful shorthand term for it: "Arguespeak."

To be sure, the Arguespeak of literary studies, philosophy, or history is very different from the Arguespeak of mathematics or chemistry, which is different in turn from the Arguespeak of the social sciences, economics, or computer science. There exist underlying commonalities, however, that are obscured by the divisions between the humanities and sciences and the subdivisions of these fields. Indeed, in obscuring the commonalities across the disciplines, these divisions obscure disciplinary differences as well.

The common persuasive practices to which I refer have been inventoried by compositionists like Mike Rose, who writes in *Lives on the Boundary* of "framing an argument or taking someone else's argument apart, systematically inspecting a document, an issue, or an event, synthesizing different points of view, applying a theory to disparate phenomena, and so on."[8] One could add summarizing the claims of others, sticking with a summary to unpack its key implications and premises, weighing evidence, spotting and identifying contradictions and non sequiturs, telling stories and devising examples that exemplify one's point, generalizing one's conclusions, and many other practices that come into play in every field. Though the sciences communicate in specialized symbolic systems that only other specialists comprehend, even the most brilliant scientists do not advance in their fields unless they can explain to relative nonspecialists—in a grant proposal, for example—what their work does and why it is important.

Even when writing for fellow specialists, scientists have to follow the same rhetorical principles as everyone else if they hope to make an impact. Jerry Bona, head of the University of Illinois at Chicago's (UIC) Mathematics Department and a leader in the field of mathematical modeling, says that mathematics journal editors are impressed by article introductions that define an issue broadly and indicate what is at stake in the writer's argument, what difference it would make to discussions in the field. As Bona puts it, "You can be as technical as you like about integral operators once you get into the body of your paper, but if editors can't understand why you care about your problem in the first few pages you've failed." According to Bona, not only undergraduates, but some professors fail to grasp this fact: "Lots of articles begin, 'Let X be a blotch,' " Bona says. "Their writers are under a misconception about how the game is played."

A second secret is that persuasive argument is not only the *ur*-discourse of academia, but an extension of the more familiar forms of persuasion that drive the public discourse of journalism and often the talk of students themselves. As in academia, journalistic communication involves listening to viewpoints different from one's own, summarizing them in ways others can recognize, comparing and contrasting positions, spotting contradictions and non sequiturs, and coming to conclusions that contribute to a continuing conversation of ideas. These forms of argument literacy connect the academic disciplines not only with each other, but with the public world beyond academia and with student conversations. It is by obscuring these continuities, or at best leaving students to discover them on their own (as a minority do), that schools and colleges make themselves seem opaque.

Here a great opportunity is missed, since "argument" is a term students recognize and connect with their experience (even if they dislike it), whereas equivalent terms like "critical thinking," "rhetoric," and "literate public discourse," seem nebulous unless you are already familiar with them. Children learn to make arguments as soon as they are old enough to lobby their parents to stay up late, go out and play, or not have to eat their vegetables, but schools fail to take advantage of this youthful ability or even discourage it as a form of troublemaking. To be sure, students (and teachers) often confuse argument and debate with fighting, hostility, and confrontation, but this very fact makes the topic of arguing—do you like it or hate it? is it a confrontational or cooperative activity?—a ripe starting point for a class discussion and a first step toward demystifying the academic argument culture.

When students do encounter a culture of ideas and arguments in school (and too often they don't), that culture is often made to appear so remote and artificial that students have trouble connecting it with their own argumentative practices. To take just one example, students are far from clueless about how to argue about the arts, engaging as they do in lively critical discussions about films, music, concerts, and TV shows that overlap at many points with those of published reviewers and critics. Arts education, however, instead of taking advantage of this convergence in order to draw students into adult forms of critical discourse, tends to keep critical discourse of any kind out of sight in order to focus exclusively on primary texts or on exercises that have no relation to the ways critics talk about the arts. Bridging the gap between the discourse of students and teachers starts with the recognition that there is a continuum between the adolescent's declaration that a book or film "sucks" and the published reviewer's critique of it. As I argue in chapter 9, arts education in the schools tends to be poor preparation for college (though so does a lot of college arts education), since art students are not asked to read criticism. In effect, students are expected to produce a kind of critical discourse that is withheld from them and then are graded down when they hand in a poor version of it.

Learning Arguespeak means not simply manipulating a set of mechanical skills, but becoming socialized into a way of life that changes who you are. As Julie Lindquist observes, "when people learn, they don't take on new knowledge so much as a new identity."[9] The educational implications of this personal makeover have been well developed by writers like Mike Rose and the school educator Deborah Meier (whose work I discuss in chapter 14). Meier describes a college sophomore whose education was transformed when he heard a senior classmate saying, "I have a theory about why. . . ." Meier argues that, at its deepest level, being well educated means "getting in the habit of developing theories that can be articulated clearly and then checked out in a thoughtful way." Meier goes on to stress that such habits of mind entail a change in the students' social allegiances comparable to joining a new club. As Meier puts it, "Somehow, somewhere, young people need to join, if only part-time, the club we belong to. That's more critical than the particulars of what they learn."[10]

Like Rose and Meier, I see my goal as a teacher, and the bottom-line goal of education, as that of demystifying the "club we belong to" and breaking up its exclusivity. I want to help students enter this club, which often involves flushing out and engaging their resistance to entering, addressing questions about why as well as how. Demystifying the club, furthermore, means changing the club itself as much as it means changing students. It means widening our notion of who qualifies as an "intellectual" and building on the argumentative talents students already possess.

SIX DEGREES OF OBFUSCATION

What, then, are the specific educational practices, structures, and beliefs that help prevent students and others from penetrating the secrets of academic culture? Here is my list:

1. *Taking Academic Discourse for Granted.* One of the primary causes of academic mystification is the tendency to take academic discourse for granted, as if it were a transparent vehicle of information or ideas. Jim Benton, a teacher of at-risk high school students in Oklahoma and Texas, says that for most of his students the language of academic argument "is as foreign as Latin or Greek would be."[11] It is a language, he says, "whose vocabulary is unknown, whose rules are unspoken and mysterious, and whose underlying thought patterns are unidentified and incomprehensible." Benton argues that teachers need to "acknowledge the foreignness of this language. When they proceed as if it were the same as the language their students already speak, the students are left confused and convinced of their own inadequacy."

What makes academic discourse foreign is not only its jargon, specialized terms, and ten-dollar words, but its ways of posing problems and asking questions—not just its language but its language-games. Questions, for example, like "What does this text mean?" or "What views of love were dominant in the fifteenth century?" contain no jargon or technical terminology, but they are mind-stoppers for students nonetheless. As I suggest in my next chapter on what I call "the problem problem," the difficulty here lies not in the language in which such questions are couched, but in why anyone should want or need to make a *problem* out of them to begin with. The difficulty lies not in the words, but in the habit of posing problems that seem invented rather than real.

And yet, if academic problem-talk were literally as foreign as Latin and Greek, few of us would ever learn it. The compositionist Joseph Harris warns that if we assume that academics and students live in "separate communities with strikingly different ways of making sense of the world," we would not be able to explain "how or why one moves from one group to the other."[12] "Our students," Harris writes, "are no more wholly 'outside' the discourse of the university than we are wholly 'within' it. . . . We are all at once both insiders and outsiders" and should avoid reified distinctions between "us" and "them."[13]

Benton and Harris are both right. Benton is right that the discourse of formal argument is virtually a foreign language to many students, but Harris is right that that discourse overlaps at so many points with student discourse that it is not completely foreign. Every sixteen-year-old has spoken and written sentences that imbed complex thought-processes, but most have never used a formula like "The real issue is not . . . , but . . . ," or "whereas X argues . . . , I maintain that . . . ," much less organized an essay or a paragraph around such structures. A teacher who starts by "acknowledging the foreignness" of a phrase like "the real issue is not" is taking the first step toward showing students that such a phrase is neither as foreign nor as exclusively academic as it looks.

As another compositionist, Kurt Spellmeyer, argues, because languages intersect and overlap, students' entry into academic discourse "must begin, not with a renunciation of the 'home language' or 'home culture' [of the student], but with those points of commonality that expose the alien within the familiar, the familiar within the alien."[14] Student discourse is at once inside and outside the discourse of academia. Adolescents who say "I'm like . . . , she goes," and professors who say "Whereas I contend . . . , she, by contrast, maintains . . ." often fail to recognize that they speak overlapping dialects of a common language. As teachers we need to raise questions explicitly with students about the places where "our" academic discourse overlaps with as well as differs from "their" student discourse. We also need to encourage students to blend these registers in their own writing (as we academics do in our own speaking and writing), to produce what Zdenek Salzmann and other sociolinguists call "diglossia," the use of "two markedly divergent forms" of the same language, "one colloquial (low) and the other formal (high)."[15] Diglossia—a kind of bilingual solution to the problem of low vs. high language—seems preferable to what is often called "code switching," in which African American students, say, are urged to use Black English on the streets and formal English in school while keeping these languages separate.[16] Linguistic integration is preferable to segregation.

2. *The Volleyball Effect*. Academic intellectual culture is a conversation rather than a mere inventory of texts, facts, ideas, and methods. But as I argue in chapter 3, most students experience the curriculum not as a connected conversation but as a disconnected series of courses that convey wildly mixed messages. As students go from course to course and subject to subject, the comparisons that the mind needs to identify points of contrast and common ground between disciplines and subfields are effaced. Deborah Meier writes that "too many kids don't see a connection between their efforts and school success, . . . and have never seen 'academics' played."[17] I claim that students don't see " 'academics' played" because the game is fractured into so many unconnected courses and subjects that it drops out of sight—as if one were to try to learn baseball by watching first basemen, pitchers, and shortstops go through their paces in isolated rooms rather than together on the field. The increased diversity and complexity of today's curriculum—though an unqualified advance in itself—makes it a far more daunting mix of texts, subjects, ideas, and methods than was the relatively restricted curriculum that existed before World War II, or even the one I took in the forties and fifties.

In earlier work I have traced the mixed message curriculum and the confusion it inflicts to the academic habit of avoiding conflicts by keeping teachers in separate classrooms. Insulated by classroom walls that enable them to tune out contentious colleagues, teachers themselves are unaware of the extent to which their methods and assumptions conflict, and there exists no arena for clarifying their differences for students. The illusion that the curriculum is conflict-free is further reinforced by catalog listings that make academic subjects, disciplines, and fields appear uncontroversial—"South American Indians," "The Juvenile Justice System," "Greek Tragedy"—though we know that such seemingly innocuous rubrics paper over the contested nature of the subjects. Cluelessness begins to abate when one gets a sense of what a field's members disagree about. On the other hand, academia's isolated course structure hides points of *agreement* from students as much as it hides disagreements. Since disagreement presupposes a measure of agreement—we can't even start to disagree unless we already share some assumptions and vocabulary—disagreement and agreement are interdependent. A feeling for what insiders agree about or take for granted is as central to becoming socialized into a field as a feeling for their disagreements.

If we deliberately tried to create a system that favored the few and kept the majority on the periphery, we could hardly do better than the mixed message curriculum. For the quicker students manage to cut through the clutter of mixed messages and locate the web of agreements and disagreements that constitute the academic conversation, whereas the rest can only resort to the familiar practice of giving successive teachers whatever they seem to "want" even when those wants conflict. The practice of psyching out your instructors and giving each of them whatever he or she wants was succinctly described by a University of Chicago undergraduate: "In Humanities I bullshit. In Social Science I regurgitate."[18] In such cases, the student becomes a volleyball, batted back and forth between incompatible but noncommunicating assumptions and views. The lesson students learn is that intellectual inquiry is not something you internalize and make part of your identity, but something externally determined by the whims of your successive teachers, though students get used to the experience and many even learn to like it.[19]

The lateral disconnection between courses and subjects in the curriculum is mirrored in the vertical disconnection between levels of schooling, as the nature of the academic game changes abruptly when students go from high school to college. In theory, students learn information in school and then learn to use that information for higher order cognitive activities in college, a process that supposedly corresponds to the natural process of the growing child's mental development. In practice, however, students often experience the switch as a disorienting change of rules that forces you to unlearn at the next stage of education what you learned at the last, usually without any explicit discussion of the extent to which the academic game is one of information or arguments or both.

A UIC freshman wrote that whereas in high school he had learned "to be quiet and listen to the teacher," in college "I'm asked to integrate and give opinions." In this student's experience, high school teachers, for inexplicable reasons, want to see if you know the facts, whereas college professors, for equally mysterious reasons, want you to express your own ideas. Such a system might at least have the advantage of predictability, but it doesn't, since the same inconsistencies may be replayed in college as students go from one course to the next. Consequently, many students never get clear on whether they are supposed to provide information or interpretation and frequently have to ask their instructors, "Do you want my own ideas or just the facts?"

Teachers can always reply, of course, that we want both, just as we want students to be creative and original while mastering the conventions of communication. But such advice often sounds contradictory. Indeed, one reason why it's important to address the mixed messages imbedded in the curriculum is that much of what students need to know in order to succeed in academia has a paradoxical, double quality that will otherwise be confusing:

- Be yourself, but do it the way we academics do.
- There are no right answers, only endless questions; but some answers are better than others and some don't even qualify to get on the map.
- Important issues are endlessly open and debatable; but you need expertise in order to enter the debate.
- Academia wants to hear *your* ideas and arguments, not a mere rehearsal of what others have said; but your ideas and arguments won't be taken seriously unless you take others' views into account.
- Challenge authority, don't just write down what teachers say; but you can't challenge authority unless you know the moves of the game.

The further students are from mainstream literacy, the more likely it is that these paradoxes will come across as flat contradictions.

We all say we want to help low-income students to succeed, but if we were serious we would see elementary, high school, and college educators trying harder to get on the same page with regard to the intellectual rituals they supposedly transmit. To overcome the vertical disconnection between school and college (which replays the earlier disconnection between elementary and high school), school and college teachers need to collaborate to make their worlds one continuous culture instead of separate ones. To overcome the horizontal disconnection of curricular mixed messages, we need a comparative curriculum in which faculties work together to put their courses into dialogue, thereby representing in a visible way how academics, in Meier's phrase, is actually "played." In a comparative curriculum, messages that now clash would become readable as intelligible disagreements, as different dialects of the lingua franca of Arguespeak, or as problem cases for discussion. Though such collaboration would at first entail extra work, in the long run it should save work by putting teachers in a position to help each other and get better results.

As I suggest in chapter 3, making the intellectual world of academia intelligible depends not just on individual teaching, but on moving beyond the privacy of "the classroom" to organizing the curriculum in a more connected and coherent way. Curricular mixed messages are the result of a system in which teachers know little about what their colleagues do in their classes. Students' cluelessness about academia is rooted in teachers' cluelessness about each other.

3. *The Overrating of Fact.* A third source of obfuscation is a belief that has come under increasing criticism but still maintains a stubborn hold: that before students can progress to higher-order forms of thinking they need a foundation of factual information. E. D. Hirsch's 1987 best-seller, *Cultural Literacy,* gave new life to this view just as it seemed to be dying out. The problem is not simply that knowledge of facts is useless unless students can use such knowledge in relevant conversations. The problem is that for many students knowledge of information is virtually *unlearnable* unless it is tied to conversations that those students see some point in entering. Hirsch himself formulates the prob-

lem clearly in summarizing the objection to his own view: "You can't expect students to remember . . . a mere catalogue of information. Nobody remembers information unless it is embedded in interesting material." Hirsch quickly dismisses the objection, however, arguing that it does not apply to "young children," who "like to pick up adult information before they can make sense of it."[20]

Hirsch may have a point about the curiosity of some very young children. But for students of any age, trying to learn pure information "before they can make sense of it" has a notoriously poor track record, so poor that the famous satire of the fact-crazed teacher Mr. Gradgrind in Dickens's *Hard Times* does not seem a completely unfair caricature. As Barbara Herrnstein Smith argues in a critique of Hirsch, our ability to store and recall information is tied to our interests and purposes: we tend not to remember facts unless they are connected to contexts and discussions we care about.[21] Displaying pointless information for its own sake—the activity rewarded by many standardized tests—is the mark of a bore, not an educated person.

To put it another way, facts are dependent on arguments for engaging our interests and thereby getting into circulation. Whether in a freshman theme or in the public marketplace of ideas, the heavy cargo of knowledge needs the wings of argument in order to travel and have an impact. To take one example, in a post–September 11 op-ed piece in the *New York Times*, Nicholas D. Kristof argues that the fate of Middle Eastern societies may ultimately depend on the education of women. Kristof cites economic historian David S. Landes's "magisterial" book, *The Wealth and Poverty of Nations*, which argues, in Kristof's words, that "the best clue to a nation's growth and development potential is the status and role of women."[22] In order for Landes's magisterial scholarship to make it into Kristof's article and reach readers (like me) who haven't read it, his work had to have the authority of scholarly fact, but his facts had to have an argument on which to fly.

The problem lies in the familiar two-stage model in which learning information is seen as separate from, and preliminary to, learning what the information means or how it may be used. In effect, such a model says to students: "First study the facts about the educational level of women in developed vs. undeveloped countries; then, when you've got the facts down, you'll be ready for prime time, for adult discussions of what the facts mean for the future of nations." Unfortunately, the process of learning facts in a vacuum tends to be so boring and alienating that when the curtain finally parts to disclose the adult discussion, it's too late—the class is asleep.

Furthermore, far from helping you enter higher-order discussions, learning lots of facts in a vacuum may actually prevent you from doing so. I have had students whose minds seemed so cluttered by the disconnected bits of information they had crammed that they were unable to locate the issues that could have organized their information. As David K. Cohen and other advocates of "teaching for understanding" argue, covering masses of decontextualized information is subject to diminishing returns; it is better to reduce the quantity of information being taught in order to improve the quality of students' understanding of it.[23] Instead of imparting facts in a vacuum, teachers are likely to be more successful when they introduce information as it becomes necessary for students to make sense of an issue or a set of arguments. Such a process more closely approximates real life, where we usually learn information not from prepackaged sources, but by inferring it from our reading and conversation. Just as few of us would try to learn baseball by first studying the *Baseball Encyclopedia* and only then playing in a game or attending one, we shouldn't withhold the culture of ideas and arguments from students until they've learned supposedly foundational facts. But once schooling has programmed students to confuse learning with knowing decontextualized facts, de-programming them in college can be very difficult. At the least we should be bringing the facts vs. arguments debate into our classes and discussing it with students: how far does doing well in academia depend on what you know or on what you do with what you know? What does it mean to do something with what you know? When we fail to discuss such questions with students, we put them at the mercy of the mixed messages from their teachers.

4. *The Mystification of Research.* A fourth way American education perpetuates cluelessness is by maintaining a sharp separation between both high school and undergraduate study and the domain of university research. As an undergraduate in the fifties, I knew vaguely that my

professors and their graduate students carried on something called "research," but whatever that meant was assumed to be of no concern to me and my classmates. Nor did I have any idea where my professors fit on the intellectual map of their fields, or indeed that such a map existed. I later realized that I was meant to be ignorant of these matters, lest my innocence be compromised by cold professionalism, specialism, and careerism. Consequently, when I went on to graduate school I was exceptionally naive about what academic research was all about and probably took years longer to learn the ropes than I otherwise would have.

To be sure, only a small percentage of college undergraduates are interested in going on to graduate school, much less in becoming research scholars. Some esoteric and specialized forms of academic research should not be thrust on undergraduates unless they volunteer an interest in them. But it is not necessary to turn undergraduates into clones of research specialists in order to bring them more fully into the culture of research. When universities fail to do so, they again withhold the rules of their inner game from students and then punish them for not knowing how to play it.

There is something bizarre about the assumption that undergraduates will be able to make intellectual sense of their professors when they are screened from the work that those professors presumably care most passionately about. As long as undergraduates are expected to be ignorant of the research done by their teachers, they have little chance of grasping what an academic discipline or field is all about. Yet most undergraduate major programs offer students information and skills that are considered preliminary to entering the discipline but rarely bring students close to it. Thus humanities majors study works of art but not criticism, and mathematics and biology majors do equations and calculations but gain little sense of how mathematicians and biologists think and converse.

When we wall off undergraduates from the culture of research, in effect we invite them to be alienated from the intellectual life of the faculty. Not surprisingly, many undergraduates accept the invitation, feeling little identification with the questions that animate their instructors, with the familiar result that students and teachers live in separate mental worlds that rarely meet. The visible emblem of these separate worlds is the stark contrast between the ivy-covered buildings on one side of the campus and the rowdy bars and sports arenas on the other. And as if to make sure that high school students will be oblivious to research when they get to college, university teacher education programs often keep future high school teachers in the dark about research in their content areas.

Promisingly, things are changing, as the term "undergraduate research," once a contradiction in terms, becomes a significant trend in college education. Indeed, as high school science fairs proliferate, it no longer sounds completely odd to speak of high school or even elementary school students as engaged in research. On the other hand, undergraduate research still tends to be reserved for grad-school-bound honors students and restricted to the hard sciences (as it is for several of the national organizations that sponsor such research). At my own university, however, an annual student-run Undergraduate Research Symposium sponsored by the College of Arts and Sciences draws increasing participation from undergraduates across the humanities and social sciences.

Without a doubt, involving undergraduates in research can increase the already excessive pressures on students to rush prematurely onto the career track: will ten-year-olds soon feel pressure to publish books and articles, as children now reportedly feel pushed to start preparing for their SAT tests at age six? Despite such dangers, I believe American education can only benefit if undergraduate research turns out to be the future whose time has come. In my experience overseeing the Undergraduate Research Symposium at UIC, undergraduate research transforms the student-teacher relationship, turning students and teachers from strangers or adversaries into collaborators playing on the same team for common purposes. Once undergraduates are treated as collaborators in research, the old conflict between research and teaching abates, as does the division of the professorial cerebral cortex into separate research and teaching compartments—between "my own work," as we say, and the presumably alienated labor of my teaching.

And since the alienation of students from their academic work is often matched by the alienation of faculty members from the publish-

or-perish demands of theirs, faculty members may have as much to gain as their students from undergraduate research. Much research in the humanities and social sciences that is considered unfit for undergraduates would not need to be if it were better written and more interestingly conceived, as it might be if we had to share it with undergraduates under proper conditions of quality control. As I suggested earlier, it would not be a bad thing for the prose style of our academic publications if professors had to explain our research to undergraduates. It is reported that at the University of Chicago in the forties, Enrico Fermi "insisted that every faculty member teach basic physics to undergraduates every year. Having to explain the science in relatively plain English helped clarify their thinking, he said."[24] If Fermi is right, we need to rethink the assumption that the career interests of research scholars are best served when those scholars are released from undergraduate teaching.

5. *Anti-intellectualism.* When we academics feel ashamed of our intellectual culture, we naturally hesitate to explain it—who, after all, cares? And not surprisingly, academics often internalize America's love-hate attitude toward intellectualism, which is still associated with nerds, geeks, control freaks, and uptight, "judgmental" misfits. To modify Groucho Marx's famous maxim, academics would not stoop to explain the mysteries of any club that would have them as members. These self-flagellating attitudes result in a kind of professional antiprofessionalism that has been shrewdly analyzed by critics like Stanley Fish and Bruce Robbins,[25] an antiprofessionalism whose bad effects on teaching Andrew Hoberek and I examine in chapter 10. This antiprofessional self-loathing leaves academics in no position to change the minds of students who are already suspicious of the intellectual club as a haven of class snobbery or as a threat to their image of masculinity or femininity, or to their class, ethnic, or racial identity.

Though I believe these anti-intellectual attitudes are waning—in some quarters anyway, it has become downright hip to be square—their residual influence is still widespread. They have even gained a second wind as old-fashioned varieties of American anti-intellectualism have been overlaid by new ones from the counterculture of the sixties and the New Age therapeutic culture. According to these new political versions of anti-intellectualism, Arguespeak is a male thing, a white thing, an upper middle class thing, a Western thing, or some other version of ethnocentric bias. To make argument central in the curriculum, according to this view, is to impose a repressive dominant culture on the marginalized, the disenfranchised, and the disempowered. It follows that instead of making the culture of ideas and arguments more accessible so that more students can join it, teachers should encourage students to realize their own authentic voices.

One of the best retorts I know to this countercultural anti-intellectualism comes from a defender of multicultural pedagogy, the compositionist Victor Villanueva, Jr. Villanueva concedes that teachers should "give students the means to find their own voices, voices that . . . speak of their brown or yellow or red or black skin with pride and without need for bravado or hostility," and he urges teachers to be alert to the cultural prejudices that still infuse thinking about standard English and its relation to Black English and other dialects. But Villanueva goes on to argue that students can better realize their own voices if they "recognize and exploit the conventions we have agreed to as the standards of written discourse."[26] In other words, we can teach and use these standard conventions without necessarily buying into the social prejudices and biases that have historically accompanied them. That is, Arguespeak is not only separable from any dominant ideology, but an indispensable tool for criticizing it. Elaine Maimon makes the point well: "Rebels are people who know the landscape and who can move easily through it. Those who would keep students ignorant of the academic landscape in the name of helping them find their own rebellious voice do not understand much about guerilla warfare."[27] Then, too, as Lisa Delpit argues in *Other People's Children,* minority students are ill served by attempts to protect them from standard forms of literacy that they desperately need in order to gain a measure of power in our culture. Like Villanueva and Maimon, Delpit rejects the conclusion that teaching argumentative literacy is intrinsically racist or ethnocentric.[28]

Indeed, it's about time we turned this disabling conclusion on its head by questioning the idea that the economically disadvantaged are necessarily less skilled than the privileged at argumentation. William

Labov, a pioneering scholar of black working class speech, concluded after extensive interviewing that "in many ways working-class speakers are more effective narrators, reasoners, and debaters than many middle-class speakers, who temporize, qualify, and lose their argument in a mass of irrelevant detail."[29] When disadvantaged students fail to channel their reasoning and debating abilities into academic work, the fault probably lies with schools that fail to encourage student debaters or treat them as troublemakers. The fault also lies with teachers who so overemphasize surface correctness in spelling, grammar, and punctuation that they ignore the quality of students' thinking.

Consider the following excerpt from Labov's conversation with a fifteen-year-old African American named Larry, who was asked by Labov if he thought God was white or black:

Larry: He'd be white, man.
Labov: Why?
Larry: Why? I'll tell you why. 'Cause the average whitey out here got everything, you dig? And the nigger ain't got shit, y'know? Y'understan'? So—um—for—in order for that to happen, you know it ain't no black God that's doin' that bullshit.[30]

I do not think I romanticize Black English when I find Larry's way of expressing himself more powerful, cogent, and interesting than many of the more formally correct but turgid public statements made by official religious leaders. The point is not that Larry should be given a college scholarship or made director of a religious studies program, but that to dismiss Larry's language as subliterate is to miss not only his potential, but the large area of convergence between low and high forms of discourse. As our literary tradition since *Huckleberry Finn* demonstrates, power of expression does not always correspond to educational level and command of surface correctness.

6. *The Contrast of Academia and Popular Culture.* A final factor that contributes to the mystification of academia is one I mentioned at the start of this chapter: the habit of defining academic culture by contrasting it with popular culture and the media. In a sense, the modern American university and American popular culture are estranged twins. Both institutions emerged at the same historical moment after

the Civil War, each being a product of modernization, industrialism, and liberal progressivism. From the outset, however, the university and popular culture have defined themselves against one another and therefore failed to notice what they have in common. Academia and popular culture have been defined as everything the other is not, particularly in their supposedly characteristic ways of communicating. Whereas academic communication, reputedly, is immensely complex, sophisticated, and accessible only to specialized experts, media communication is facile, vulgarly reductive, given to cheap sensationalism, and dominated by sound bites. Or, reversing the value judgments, academic communication is hopelessly opaque, jargon-ridden, and rarefied, whereas media communication is down-to-earth and democratically accessible. The academic/popular culture contrast still structures our thinking in ways that not only rationalize bad habits of academic communication, but lead us to pose educational questions poorly.

For example, one form the academic/popular culture contrast still takes is the complaint that schools and colleges fight a losing battle with popular entertainment for the hearts and minds of the young. The culture of ideas and arguments, so the complaint runs, is constantly overwhelmed and negated by visceral experience and spectacle. How can Socrates, Mill, and Henry James hope to compete for students' attention with "Survivor," the Spice Girls, the World Wrestling Federation, and the latest Schwarzenegger/Stallone action hero blockbuster?

The complaint makes sense up to a point, but it is misleading in two ways: first, from an educational point of view, the real opposition should be not between Henry James and the Spice Girls, but between intellectual and nonintellectual discussion of Henry James *and* the Spice Girls or any other subject. As I have noted, it is not the object in itself that creates problems for students but the public, academic ways of analyzing, arguing, and talking about the object. Members of the Spice Girls fan club do not read academic analyses of the Spice Girls (though if they were students, asking them to do so would be a way to draw them into academic culture).

Second, when popular culture and the mass media beat out academia in the battle for youthful hearts and minds, this happens not only because they are more sensational and immediately gratifying than is schooling, but also because they are far better thought through and organized for achieving their objectives. If educational institutions hope to compete with the media for students' attention—and to attract their share of public dollars—they need to devote at least as much serious thought to how they organize their representations as do the media managers who produce a ninety-second TV commercial. This means asking questions that academics rarely ever ask about intelligibility conditions: how do particular texts, ideas, and problems figure to become intelligible to those who don't already understand them?

Though academia has lately produced an amazingly sophisticated body of thought about the dynamics of representation, it remains at a remarkably rudimentary and incurious stage in thinking about how it represents itself. New forms of electronic communication may be changing this situation, but what still passes in universities for thought about the curriculum rarely goes much beyond the level of: get a bunch of good teachers together who are well trained in their fields and turn them loose on students with as little interference as possible. Unfortunately, even the best set of teachers and courses may not add up to anything intelligible, much less meaningful, without the kind of planning and teamwork that goes into producing a play or an ad for Miller Lite beer. Though teaching will always be an art of improvisation, it is not clear why an academic semester should not be almost as carefully scripted and orchestrated as a theater performance, a film, or a concert—or as a college orientation week. As journalist Hubert B. Herring reported after attending his son's college orientation, the event "had the qualities of a polished, entertaining show."[31] Unfortunately, the same can rarely be said of the academic year itself.

If I am right that teachers and journalists are part of a common explanation business, then it makes increasing sense to bring them together in classrooms. My university recently offered a couple of courses that did so. One, on "Studying the Media *With* the Media," was co-taught, with the help of a small internal grant, by Barbara Ransby, a UIC professor of history and African American studies, Gretchen Helfrich, a local FM radio talk show host, and Salim Muwakkil, a *Chicago Tribune* columnist. Another course on "The Public Intellectual," co-taught by Stanley Fish and Cary Nathenson, featured guest appearances by the cultural journalist Barbara Ehrenreich and the lawyer and mystery writer Scott Turow. Visits to these courses confirmed my hunch that such collaborations help academics and journalists to learn complementary lessons from each other. It is not just that the academics help the journalists think in more sophisticated ways about their topics, while the journalists help the academics learn clearer and more succinct and effective ways of communicating. At a deeper level, the collaboration changes the way both groups think by counteracting the different kinds of professional insularity to which each is prone, forcing them to confront how their pet ways of thinking and speaking look to outsiders. This is the kind of insularity check that can be achieved by teaching with colleagues from other disciplines and with those whose views challenge ours.

THE REVENGE OF THE NERDS

I have suggested that there is less excuse today for the forms of academic mystification I have been cataloguing, since intellect, so long despised in America, has been rising in esteem. This is not to say we can declare the end of American anti-intellectualism and pronounce Richard Hofstadter's classic book, *Anti-Intellectualism in American Life,* obsolete.[32] We need only consider George W. Bush's electoral victory in 2000 over Albert Gore, Jr., which was reminiscent of Dwight D. Eisenhower's victories over egghead Adlai Stevenson in the fifties, for evidence that American anti-intellectualism is not in danger of extinction. When Bush mispronounced the word "subliminal" in responding to charges that his campaign had run deceptive attack ads, the columnist Maureen Dowd wondered if Bush would gain votes from his inability "to pronounce the crime he was accused of."[33] On the other hand, the very closeness of the 2000 election, by contrast with Ike's landslide victories over Stevenson, suggests that the eggheads have gained ground. So do the debates that emerged over whether Bush's apparent dim-wittedness is a ruse that cleverly disguises a keen intelligence. As Jonathan Chait noted in the *New Republic,* some observers reason that "if Bush bamboozled much of the public and virtually the entire news media, . . . how dumb can he be?"[34] However we might answer Chait's question, our very fascination with the intelligence of our leaders suggests that intellect is taken more seriously than it was in the Eisenhower era.

Perhaps even more significant is the fact that conservatism, which was unabashedly anti-intellectual in the populist versions chronicled by Hofstadter, has taken on an egghead cast. Unlike the McCarthyite know-nothings Hofstadter described, current conservatives like Irving and William Kristol, William Bennett, David Brooks, Roger Kimball, Ralph Reed, Dinesh D'Souza, Pat Buchanan, and Newt Gingrich are more prone to claim the label of intellectual than to disavow it. (To be sure, there are exceptions: for Fox News's Bill O'Reilly, "intellectual" still is a term of abuse.) Even a Rush Limbaugh, whom many academics dismiss as a lightweight, probably thinks he has as much claim to the label as they do. (To my mind, Rush is a *bad* intellectual but an intellectual.)

When I was in high school in the fifties there was a vast gulf between the nerds and the popular crowd or the jocks (though these terms did not yet exist). In many schools today the nerds have so infiltrated the popular crowd and the jocks that the words may be losing their meaning. "Nerds rule," declares Stephen S. Hall in a recent *New York Times Magazine* article, featured on the issue's cover as "The Triumph of the Braniac." Though Hall concedes that such a claim is an exaggeration, he presents evidence that in some high schools at least it has become cool to be good with books and booktalk.[35] Popular films today are often allegories of intellectualism, as if our culture were struggling to sort out the gains and losses of reading books and arguing about ideas. In these films the intellectuals often come off quite well—in *Good Will Hunting* and *The Revenge of the Nerds* they get the girl, beating out jock frat boys. Even apparent counterexamples, productions that exalt stupidity like the movie *Dumb and Dumber* and MTV's *Beavis and Butthead,* seem closer in spirit to postmodern irony than to old-fashioned anti-intellectualism.

To be sure, the triumphant nerds in these films, like the subjects of the *Times Magazine* article, are usually computer geeks and technical scientists, not philosophical or cultural thinkers. Our image of the intellectual is closer to the policy wonk or the technocrat than to the man or woman of ideas, closer to a Henry Kissinger than a Hannah Arendt.

Filmmakers who do try to represent the world of ideas often betray a shaky familiarity with it, as in the case of *Finding Forrester*, in which, as a reviewer noted, we are supposed to know the film's novelist hero is a genius because of his "exhaustive familiarity with *Bartlett's Familiar Quotations*."[36] As the success of Hirsch's *Cultural Literacy* showed, our culture still confuses intelligence with possession of quiz show information. We equate the life of the mind with narrowly functional forms of thinking, with lab-coated, clipboard-carrying technicians and teenage computer wizards. This narrow way of defining intellectualism is reflected in the popular formula, "You don't have to be a rocket scientist (or a brain surgeon) to know that. . . ." It seems no accident that we have no formulas like, "You don't have to be a feminist film critic to know . . . ," or "Hey, it's not constitutional law," even though the concerns of these fields can be as challenging and even as technical as those of rocket science or brain surgery.

You don't have to be a rocket scientist, however, to see that the habit of equating advanced thought with brute information and technical genius is itself a symptom of what I have been talking about: the nebulousness that is felt to surround the intellectual world. We know what it takes to answer quiz show questions, but our picture is less clear of what it takes to analyze gender in films or to problematize the legal distinction between public and private. And though the technical aspects of rocket science, brain surgery, and computer circuitry are over our heads, we are confident that we at least know what rocket science, brain surgery, and computers are *for*, whereas the aims of academic film criticism and legal theory are evidently so opaque that these fields don't even qualify to be proverbial examples of opacity.

2 The Problem Problem and Other Oddities of Academic Discourse

AS TEACHERS WE OFTEN PROCEED as if the rationale of our most basic academic practices is understood and shared by our students, even though we get plenty of signs that it is not. We take for granted, for example, that reflecting in a self-conscious way about experience— "intellectualizing"—is something our students naturally see the point of and want to learn to do better. If they don't, after all, why are they in school? At the same time, we cannot help noticing that many students are skeptical about the value of such intellectualizing. When students do poorly, the reasons often have less to do with their lack of ability than with their reluctance to become the introspective type of people who relish and excel at such tasks.

Aversion to the apparent pretentiousness of intellectual ways of communicating is often central to this reluctance. In *The Unschooled Mind* Howard Gardner observes that the problems students have in comprehending texts are often magnified by their "insensitivity . . . to the vocabulary of argument—'contend,' 'hypothesize,' 'refute,' 'contradict'. . . ."[1] Gardner is right about the connection between poor reading comprehension and students' lack of a "vocabulary of argument." The problem, however, often lies not in the students' "insensitivity" to this vocabulary but in their disinclination to acquire it. In some high schools and colleges, students would risk ostracism if they used expressions like "hypothesize" or "I contend." As the saying goes, nobody likes a smart-ass.

Hillel Crandus, a teacher of eleventh-grade English, asked his class to write short papers (which Crandus shared with me) expressing how they felt about analysis, especially the kind of close interpretive reading of texts that's the staple of literature courses. One student, call her Karen, wrote, "Personally, I don't like analyzing everything that happens to me. Some of it would be a big waste of time. I sometimes find myself analyzing dreams that I've had, but it's usually pretty pointless. To me a lot of things happen for a very obvious reason that does not need a lot of discussion or insight." Another stated flatly that "the only thing that overanalyzing leads to is boredom."

In my experience, the distaste Karen feels for "analyzing everything that happens" to you, and the belief that some things "happen for a very obvious reason" and therefore need no further inquiry, don't necessarily disappear once students move on to college, though by then students have become more guarded about betraying such views in the presence of their teachers. As a University of Chicago undergraduate put it, " 'Academic' type people take life too seriously and don't let themselves read for enjoyment. There's more to life than intellect . . . you can read for fun." A UIC freshman told his composition instructor that "I don't want to dig deeper into the meaning of something. What I say is what I mean." Whenever I survey students on the question, many admit they have a problem with academia's tendency to turn everything it touches into grist for the analytical mill, almost as if teachers were deliberately trying to spoil everybody's fun.

In this chapter, I look at some standard academic practices that often seem second nature to teachers and A-students but come across to many students as bizarre, counterintuitive, or downright nonsensical. These perceptions of the absurd nature of intellectual practices underlie the familiar stereotypes of the educated: eggheads, nerds, sissies, snobs, braniacs, know-it-alls, brown-nosers, control freaks, ideologues, and manipulative propagandists. These characterizations may be rooted in misperceptions of the life of the mind, but ones that are unlikely to be dispelled unless teachers flush them out and address them.

1. The Problem Problem

Nothing better exemplifies the apparently counterintuitive nature of intellectual practices than their preoccupation with what often appear to be bogus "problems." Academic assignments ask students not only to become aggressive know-it-alls, but to cultivate problems to an extent that seems perverse or bizarre. I call this syndrome the "problem problem."

One reason why students often resist the academic fixation with problems is suggested by Wayne Booth, Gregory Colomb, and Joseph Williams in their valuable primer on academic writing, *The Craft of Research*. Booth, Colomb, and Williams discuss the difficulties inexperienced students have with the conventions used to set up the problems that form the starting point of most expository essays.[2] Yet the difficulties students have in constructing the kind of problem that launches an essay stem not only from their unfamiliarity with the conventions of problem-posing, but from deeper uncertainties about the "problematizing" role itself.

Booth, Colomb, and Williams do not mention these uncertainties, but they provide a clue to them when they distinguish between problems that are recognized to be such and those that are not.[3] Problems of the first kind, like earning a living, finding a mate, curing diseases, preventing air pollution, or eliminating poverty and homelessness come to us with an apparently *pre-given* quality. These problems are already so widely acknowledged that writers can usually take them up without having to make an argument for seeing them as problems, though there are situations in which they might have to (for example, talking about poverty with an audience of Social Darwinists). Many of the problems with which academics deal, however, lack this pre-given quality, as when they concern the meanings of words, abstract concepts, and texts, or the actions of people long dead. In such cases, where we can't assume that others will see the problem we are taking up *as* a problem, we have to work to sell them on its reality and importance. Academics not only cultivate problems that are unrecognized as such, they like to *invent* problems that most people are unaware of, or look for new ways to describe already recognized problems.

In this penchant for problematizing, academic research scholars resemble avant-garde artists who "defamiliarize" previously familiar subjects, using alienation effects to make what seems obvious and unproblematic look strange. But despite the lip service given to Socrates' maxim that the unexamined life is not worth living, searching out new problems can seem profoundly counterintuitive: are there not already enough problems in the world without our straining to invent new ones? From a certain commonsense point of view, academia's cultivation of problems looks manufactured, perverse, and silly, and academic problem-posers resemble the dotty scientists on the island of Laputa in Jonathan Swift's *Gulliver's Travels,* who grapple earnestly, for instance, with the problem of turning excrement back into its original food.

A good example of the perceived absurdity of many of the problems addressed by academics is reported by Vivian Gornick in her memoir, *Fierce Attachments,* in which Gornick describes how her immersion in the intellectual life as a student at New York's City College alienated her from her mother in the Bronx. Gornick relates how her sentences "got longer within a month of [my] first classes. Longer, more complicated, formed by words whose meaning she did not know, . . . It made [my mother] crazy. . . . 'What are you talking about?' she would shout at me. 'What *are* you talking about? Speak English, please! We all understand English in this house, Speak it.' "[4] When Gornick tried to explain the thesis of the book she was reading, "a comparative history of the idea of love over the last three hundred years," her mother would have none of it: "That's ridiculous," she said slowly. "Love is love. It's the same everywhere, all the time. What's to compare?"[5]

The academic faith in the singular virtue of finding problems in subjects—love, in Gornick's case—generally thought to be unproblematic seems especially bizarre and forced when the problems have to do with the meanings of texts. The idea that, below their apparent surface, texts harbor deep meanings that cry out for interpretation, analysis, and debate is one of those assumptions that seems so normal once we are socialized into academia that we forget how counterintuitive it can be. In fact, this assumption has probably never been comprehensible, much less convincing, to much of the general population or even to some academics. (A certain college dean is said to have wondered aloud why entire departments were needed to study the books he has no trouble reading on the train to work every day.) An exception might seem to be scriptural texts, whose meanings have been picked apart and debated for so many centuries that the practice does not seem odd— except to sects that see even scriptural interpretation and theological debate as coming between the believer and God.

In their written responses, many of Crandus's eleventh-graders confess that most classroom analysis of texts and interpretations seems tedious and pointless, an infinite regress that goes nowhere. As one student, Elaina, put it, "A student will make a comment that, maybe to me, seems straightforward, yet we still seem to dig deeper into just what that comment meant." Karen, the student whose reservations toward "analyzing everything that happens to me" I quoted above, wrote as follows about a class discussion of Richard Wright's autobiography, *Black Boy:*

> [I]t seems to me that we analyzed things that didn't seem to have much to analyze. For instance, the fire episode in the beginning of the book. In my opinion, Richard started the fire out of curiosity and boredom. The discussion we had in class got into things like it symbolizes his imagination or internal impulses, or even how he feels about his racial impression. I'm not saying that these aren't good ideas, but I think it's making something out of nothing. . . .
>
> Another reason I do not like [to] analyze, though this may sound arrogant, is because it is not important to me. I don't care what the fire in *Black Boy* symbolizes. It doesn't really make [any] difference to me. To some people, it does make a difference, and that's fine with me. But I don't really see how this helps me out in my life, the past, the present, or the future. It could end up helping me a lot, you never really know. I know it will at least help me out in college English classes.

Karen suspects that the symbolism attributed to works like *Black Boy* is simply not *there* in the text—in any case, she can't see it. Just as for her "a lot of things happen for a very obvious reason that does not need a lot of discussion or insight," what a text means is apparent on the surface and therefore needs no analysis. But even if deeper meanings are indeed present in the text, Karen adds, she doesn't care, though she acknowledges that such things do matter to some people and might some day to her, if only to help her get through college English courses.

Another student, Eileen, complains that

> during our classroom discussions, we tend to pick and pick at every single aspect of a paragraph until there is nothing left. I don't even remember half the time what the discussion started off about. . . . That is why I think that when we have our classroom discussions, they need not to be SO indepth. . . . In my past, I have never really enjoyed reading, so that I am sure may be a factor in this. But I still feel that I am not alone on this one. Many students have agreed with me on my thoughts. In one paper a student described our classroom discussions as, ". . . beating a dead horse. . . ." I think that we have a great class that is a lot of fun, but sometimes, things just get way too deep for me.

A third student, Laura, who also dislikes being forced to analyze, writes that "I have talked to some students that I know feel this way. They dislike the thought of being forced to pick apart why things went a certain way. One, they don't see the point, two, they sometimes have no clue what's going on, and three, they could care less why it happened."

Again, from these three students' commonsense perspective, asking what texts mean is superfluous since texts are self-interpreting. Either they mean what they say or they are obscure, but either way there is little point trying to decode them. It is tempting to ascribe these beliefs to adolescent naivete, but their view is probably shared by most adults in our culture. Indeed, the belief that texts and other things speak for themselves and therefore do not require interpretation has deep roots in Western philosophy, as Jacques Derrida shows in a commentary on Plato's *Phaedrus*, a dialogue in which Socrates indicts writing for undermining the self-evident meaning that presumably becomes immune to misunderstanding in face-to-face oral communication.[6] From this Platonic point of view, the meaning of a text, say, on the nature of love is simply whatever the text itself says. To find out what the text has to say about love, you just read the text. To make a *problem* out of what the text means, then, as teachers do in discussing the text in class, is to make a mountain out of a molehill. After all, if the author had really intended the hidden meaning ascribed to him by interpreters, why didn't he come out and say it? In short, what's the big deal?

The problem is exacerbated by uncertainties about *intention*—a concept that has itself been endlessly debated by aestheticians and philosophers of language. Jay, another of Crandus's eleventh-graders, finds classroom analysis of textual intentions "not interesting": "Like when we are asked to think about the way an author would respond to our responses, how are we supposed to know? As far as I know most of us are not close personal friends with any of the authors we have read so far. So why would we know what the author would think?"

Laura writes that, when asked why something happens the way it does in a text, "I would have trouble analyzing why it happened because I wasn't there, I have never personally talked to the author. . . ." A tenth-grader at another school expressed a view similar to Jay's and Laura's in a symposium on Shakespeare's *The Tempest*, when I asked her if she thought Shakespeare shared the preference she had expressed for Caliban over Prospero: "I wouldn't know," she replied. "I never met the man." As these students see it, either a text's intention is obvious on the face of it or it isn't. If it isn't, we can phone the author and ask what his or her intention was, but if the author is dead or otherwise unavailable, there is nothing much to be done. So again, where's the problem?

If what authors intend does not seem a genuine problem, then making a problem of *unintended* psychological or social meanings in texts seems all the more patently a waste of time. A college teacher reports the following exchange with a freshman student on Mark Twain's *Adventures of Huckleberry Finn*. The teacher, hoping to get her class to see the ambivalent treatment of racial injustice in the novel, called attention to the apparent discrepancy between the novel's satire on slavery and racism and the many passages in which the slave Jim is made a comic butt of Huck and Tom Sawyer's pranks. One student, however, offered an explanation of the discrepancy that seemed more plausible to him than the presence of cultural contradictions.

Teacher: So what do you all make of the apparent contradiction here?

Student: Hey, maybe Mark Twain was having a bad day. Or maybe he just didn't care.

Teacher: How's that?

Student: I mean, maybe he was just lazy, or he had to make a deadline.

The teacher retorted that even if we assume that Twain was lazy, indifferent, or in a hurry, this fails to explain why these qualities expressed themselves in such a racially coded way. She realized, however, that her response was convincing neither the student nor many of his classmates. They resisted entertaining the kind of richly symptomatic reading that she, as a good intellectual, was angling for, one in which textual anomalies betray deeper, more interesting problems.

This instructor reflected that she had not prepared the class for looking at contradictions in texts, or even mentioned the topic. She also reflected that it had only been in graduate school that she herself had discovered that texts might be all the more interesting and valuable for the contradictions they contained. In both high school and college she had been taught that great works of art are unified, and she had learned to write papers that discovered the principle of unity in the works' themes, language, or symbolism. If there were contradictions in a work, it presumably was second-rate. In her future classes, she resolved to introduce the issue of textual contradictions and discuss it with students rather than expect them to watch for such contradictions or to know what to say about them.

If it seems dubious to make a problem out of the meanings even of canonical writers like Shakespeare, Plato, and Twain, it has to seem doubly preposterous to find problems in the meanings of popular romances, films, and TV shows, not to mention events like the O. J. Simpson trial. (Teachers have long complained about students who, when asked to interpret popular culture, respond with the comment, "Hey, it's just a movie.") At the symposium I just mentioned on *The Tempest*, some college as well as high school students rolled their eyes conspicuously when a college student unpacked the assumptions about the nuclear family in an episode of the TV series *Home Improvement*. The students could grant the possibility of hidden depths in Shakespeare, but in a TV sitcom—give me a break!

Again, such doubts about intellectual overreading would not be so pervasive among students if they were not widely shared by educated adults. The view that popular culture products either have no meaning or none that is worth discussing is pervasive among academics as well as journalists, who periodically issue derisive editorials whenever an academic is caught attributing gender attitudes, say, to a performance of popular music star Madonna or to an episode of the TV series *Friends*. To be sure, the elaborate allegories academic critics claim to find in popular or high culture do sometimes stretch the reasonable limits of credibility. Nevertheless, analysts of popular culture seem to me right that such works influence our beliefs and behavior all the more powerfully because they come imbedded in seemingly innocuous entertainment that is not thought worthy of close scrutiny. There is a difference, in other words, between legitimate critical skepticism toward over-the-top symbolic readings that fail to justify themselves with reasons and evidence, and the anti-intellectual dismissal of any reading that challenges the received understanding of a text or event. That said, however, it is important that teachers not dismiss students' skepticism of the academic obsession with the problem of hidden meanings. Unless those doubts are respected and fairly aired and discussed, students will feel they have no choice but to play along with an interpretive game whose validity they do not accept.

When this happens, students repress their anxiety and alienation and some end up resorting to Cliffs Notes—or increasingly nowadays to the Internet. In his recent book, *The Crafty Reader*, Robert Scholes quotes a sampling of recent internet postings by desperate students who have been asked to produce accounts of what something in a text means:

> 1. Subject: Huck Finn symbolism of river.
> I am writing a paper on the symbolism of the Mississippi River in Huck Finn. How is the river a symbolic mother to Huck? I need examples from the book too. Please help fast.
> 2. Subject: Oedipus Rex—Irony
> I need help finding Irony in Oedipus Rex. There's supposedly a lot in there but I've been assigned Scene II and there's only so much.
> 3. Subject: symbolism: gardens
> what do gardens symbolize? are there any sexual innuendos? anything one could dig up on the symbolism of gardens would be of great help. thanks.[7]

What is striking here is that the writers of these posts see interpretation as an occult process rather than one that might be mastered by learning disciplined reading. As they see it, rivers and gardens in themselves have some fixed but secret meaning that you either get or don't get; if you're one of those who doesn't, you can only get on the Web and try to find one of those who do.

Some, of course, would argue that this kind of student desperation only shows what a serious mistake it has been to put the interpretation of hidden meaning at the center of the academic humanities, thereby turning texts into crossword puzzles and trivializing reading. To me, however, these student postings demonstrate not the folly of asking students to search for deep meanings in texts, but the failure to give students the help they need to conduct the search well, with a sense of how and why it can be useful. As Scholes comments, "These students are crying for help."[8] Students who run to the Web to find out what gardens and rivers symbolize have no other recourse when their teachers treat such questions as self-evident. The practice of searching out and inventing "problems," whether posed by texts or other objects of study, needs to be discussed with students, with an open invitation to air their doubts about the practice and its value.

2. Negativism and Oppositionality

For many students, academia's fixation on seemingly superfluous problems seems linked with another off-putting trait, its relentless negativ-
ism and oppositionality. In *Errors and Expectations,* her classic book on
the problems of basic-writing students, Mina P. Shaughnessy touches
on this trait in describing the problem novice writers have when they
are "expected to make 'new' or arguable statements and then develop
a case for them."[9] To make "a case" for yourself, to make statements
that are "arguable," you must be oppositional and defensive, if not can-
tankerous. Furthermore, the value academia places on making "arguable" statements can seem not only needlessly embattled, but flatly il-
logical. Why would any sane person go out of his or her way to say
things that are "arguable"? Just as common sense suggests that it is
foolish to invent problems that did not previously exist, it also suggests
that the point of writing and speaking is to make statements that *nobody* is likely to dispute, so that provoking disagreement is a sign that
the writer has failed. A sound essay, according to this way of thinking, consists of uncontroversially true statements. In fact, this way of
thinking once dominated the academic disciplines, where knowledge
was seen not as a conversation or debate but as an accumulation of
positivist truths, a sort of pyramid of discrete facts built up brick by
isolated brick.

As often, however, common sense has things wrong, which explains why we do not find many essays with titles like "Human Beings
Have Elbows," "Breathing Is Possible," and "Washington Is the Nation's Capital," though all these propositions are perfectly true. As
Booth, Colomb, and Williams point out, "Readers think a claim significant to the degree that it is contestable,"[10] or, in Shaughnessy's term,
"arguable." Precisely because nobody disputes them, uncontroversially
true statements are by definition inarguable and therefore not worth
making, at least not as an essay's main thesis. The reason why official
prose sounds notoriously banal is that it goes out of its way to be uncontroversial. A college of education mission statement I have seen declares, "We are committed to preparing individuals to become out-
standing teachers, who understand and teach students in thoughtful,
caring, and intelligent ways." The College here takes a courageous

stand against those who would prepare teachers to be thoughtless, un-caring, and unintelligent.

Paradoxically, claims that are arguable and solicit disagreement are a sign of an argument's viability, not its failure. A completely uncontro-versial proposition does not even qualify as an "argument"—we would not say, "The man argued that Washington, D.C., is the nation's capi-tal." Unless this paradox is explicitly addressed, however, many stu-dents will labor under the misapprehension that the goal of an essay is to string together a series of uncontroversially true statements. A student who turns in such an essay will—and should—draw an in-structor's comment of "So?" or "Who disputes it?"

On the other hand, imagine such a student, chastened by such comments, trying to do as he or she is told. Instead of making an un-controversial and therefore negligible claim, our student goes to the other extreme and offers a claim that is outrageously controversial. Now the instructor's response shifts from "Who disputes it?" to "Surely not," or "What's your evidence for that?" Clearly, formulating a tenable point is a tightrope act in which students have to court controversy, but only as much as they can anticipate and deal with. Here is why finding a makable "point," as Shaughnessy points out, can be harder than it looks.

Expert players of the game of public discourse know that the easiest way to set yourself up to make a tenable point is to contest a point somebody else has made or, even better, has taken for granted. Such experts have acquired an inventory of formulaic templates for this kind of contestation. In *Lives on the Boundary* Mike Rose cites fellow compositionist David Bartholomae's suggestion that "when stuck, stu-dent writers should try the following 'machine': 'While most readers of _____ have said _____, a close and careful reading shows that _____.' "[11] According to a walker's guide to the city of Chicago, freshmen at the University of Chicago are given the following advice: "If someone asserts it, deny it; if someone denies it, assert it."

Rose observes that this reflexive negativity "perfectly expresses the ethos of the university," though "university professors have for so long been socialized into this critical stance, that they don't realize how unsettling it can be to students who don't share their unusual back-ground."[12] Rose is right, but it also needs to be added that some profes-sors find this contentious ethos as "unsettling" as students do and perhaps for that reason fail to call students' attention to it. As students go from teacher to teacher and from subject to subject, they often re-ceive confusingly mixed signals about the value of controversy: Mr. B the physicist regards it as a distraction from the uncontroversial truths of science, whereas for Ms. J the chemist the clash and warfare of com-peting hypotheses is at the center of science; Mr. R the embattled mor-alist philosopher and Ms. C the feminist political scientist love to stir up debate and they reward contentious students, but Ms. A the feminist art historian regards debate as an unfortunate expression of macho ago-nism (I discuss such curricular mixed messages in chapter 3).

To the confusion created by these mixed messages add the fact that what counts as a wildly controversial statement in one course or discipline may be seen as uncontroversial or old hat in another. As a consequence, students are often left unsure whether controversy is to be courted or avoided, and since their teachers' different views on the question are screened from one another in courses that do not commu-nicate, the question is rarely posed in an overt way. No wonder, then, that many students end up opting for docility. Whereas high-achieving students intuit the conventional templates of contestation and contra-vention ("While most think X, I argue Y . . .") from their reading, others won't acquire them unless such templates are explicitly supplied. When this doesn't happen, students are forced to play the academic game with one hand tied behind their backs.

3. Persuasion as Aggression

When the academic penchant for problematizing and negativity goes unexplained, the intellectual energy expended on academic tasks tends naturally to look like mere aggression rather than reasonable behavior. There is thus a connection between the impenetrability of intellectual practices and the tendency to associate intellectualism with bullying and other unattractive personal qualities, especially those involving per-suasion. To argue persuasively, you have to have an axe to grind, to want others to do something they are not already doing, if only to think differently about something than they do. Such an attitude will seem at best presumptuous, and at worst arrogant and coercive.

In her autobiography, *A Life in School*, Jane Tompkins gives a vivid description of how it feels to be this sort of person, so bursting with the passion to persuade that it hurts: "There are situations that set going in me an electric current that has to discharge itself in words. I sit in meetings, and before I know it, I've spoken, passionately, sure there's some point that *has* to be made, which no one can see but me. If the meeting lasts long enough, I have to speak twice, three times. It's got nothing to do with the topic, or very little; the dynamic is almost physical; if I don't talk I'll explode. . . . When talking is being, and being is being listened to, not talking drains your life away."[13] Though Tompkins writes lyrically in passages like this one about her passion for argument, she fears that such a passion may have more to do with showing off, exerting control, and gratifying her ego than with a commitment to truth. Tompkins here expresses vividly the reasons why many students are ambivalent about their persuasive abilities.

For many students, the very word "argument" (like "criticism") conjures up an image not of spirited conversational give and take, but of acrimonious warfare in which competitors revile each other and make enemies yet rarely change each other's minds. Disputes end up producing winners and losers or a stalemate that frustrates all parties; either way they are useless except for stirring up bad blood.

This tendency to equate persuasion with aggression is especially rife among students who grow up in liberal pluralist surroundings, where "Live and let live" is a ruling maxim and "whatever" the popular mantra. As students often put it, "You have your opinions, I have mine, so what's the point of either of us trying to persuade each other? Everybody's an individual, so nobody has the right to tell anybody else what to do or think." There seems little value to them in becoming the type of people solicited by academic writing assignments—in other words, those who seem guided by the arrogant premise that everyone should think the way they do or that they have the right to generalize about or speak for others.

On the other hand, students from more traditional backgrounds often share their liberal classmates' dim view of persuasion. To Christian fundamentalists, the secularized society may seem too far gone to be open to persuasion, just as the culture of persuasion and argument seems in league with a Godless secular humanism that views moral issues as endlessly subject to debate. Whether from secular or religious backgrounds, then, American students are often trained to regard persuasion as a waste of time at best and asking for trouble at worst.

This student attitude toward persuasion is tied up with a deeper refusal to become the sort of *public* self that schooling assumes we all naturally want to be. Often when I am struggling unsuccessfully to help students master sentence structure or paragraphing, I realize that what I'm up against is not the students' inability to perform these operations, but their aversion to the role of public spokesperson that formal writing presupposes. It's as if such students can't imagine any rewards for being a public actor or even imagine themselves in such a role.

This lack of interest in entering the public sphere may in turn reflect a loss of confidence in the possibility that the arguments we make in public will have an effect on the world. Today's students' lack of faith in the power of persuasion reflects the waning of the ideal of civic participation that led educators for centuries to place rhetorical and argumentative training at the center of the school and college curriculum. Underlying the centrality of this training was a classical conception of public citizenship that has come to seem unreal as the small town has given way to urban massification and as the ideal of the citizen has been displaced by that of the consumer. If even successful adults find it hard to imagine themselves influencing public policy through their rhetorical and argumentative skills, students figure to find it all the harder to visualize themselves in such public roles.

The standard theme assignment that asks students to take a stand on public issues like homelessness, poverty, or abortion rests on the increasingly hollow pretense that what we think and say about such issues can actually make a difference. Given the notoriously widespread cynicism about the chances that our opinions (or votes) will influence public policy, it is hardly surprising if students are fatalistic too. These doubts about the payoff of persuasion underlie much of the student relativism that has been so widely deplored for half a century now.

When students say that value judgments are merely matters of subjective opinion, what looks like philosophical relativism may actually be an inability to imagine a world in which one's arguments might have consequences.

The emergence of the Internet, the electronic town meeting, and talk-back radio hold out promise that this cynical fatalism can be reversed. We may also be witnessing a revival of student idealism and activism, qualities that may not have completely disappeared. The same student who claims at one moment that all beliefs are subjective can often be found a moment later arguing passionately for a cause. Adolescent cynicism and fatalism frequently mask uncertainty, as if students were challenging their elders to talk them out of it. Again, these are important issues to be raised in class.

4. Elaborated Codes

Another counterintuitive feature of academic intellectual discourse is its seemingly superfluous degree of self-explanation and elaboration, especially when we compare that discourse with casual conversation. Shaughnessy observes that conversation accustoms students to feeling "free to express opinions without a display of evidence or [to] recount experiences without explaining what they 'mean.'" Students so trained, according to Shaughnessy, tend to assume that "the reader understands what is going on in the writer's mind and needs therefore no introductions or transitions or explanations."[14] Instructors' comments like "needs further explanation," or "what's the context here?" seem simply obtuse, since to the student the explanation and the context seem self-evident. Novice writers often have trouble generating much quantity of text, since to unpack and elaborate on their points would make them feel they are laboring the obvious.

Shaughnessy's point is reinforced by the work of British sociolinguist Basil Bernstein, who argues that expository writing and other forms of public communication make up an "elaborated code," in which assumptions and arguments are explicitly unpacked for anonymous audiences who cannot be assumed to already know them, in contrast to the "restricted code" of conversation between intimates, where many things can go without saying. According to Bernstein, elaborated codes characterize the more abstract and distanced interactions of middle class and professional life, whereas restricted codes are characteristic of the face-to-face communication of working class culture.[15] Shirley Brice Heath cites Bernstein in her comparative analysis of working class and middle class cultures in *Ways With Words*, showing how restricted codes prevent working class students from entering the distancing—and often alienating—conventions of written discourse.[16]

Linguists like Rosina Lippi-Green and William Labov have challenged Bernstein's distinction, especially his overly neat identification of working class culture with restricted codes, when the same codes can often be found among middle class speakers and writers as well.[17] Labov rightly points out that what Bernstein regards as the superior elaborated code of middle class communication may simply be "turgid, redundant, bombastic and empty."[18] Though these criticisms do point up blind spots in Bernstein's view, Bernstein's distinction between restricted and elaborated codes seems to me to shed useful light on many problems students have with public discourse.

For example, the concept of restricted code helps account for students' difficulties with the convention of summarizing others' views before responding to them and that of anticipating and formulating possible objections to one's arguments, conventions that can seem pedantic and affected. I stumbled on this problem in the project to which I referred earlier that involved teaching Shakespeare's *The Tempest* to college and high school students: I noticed that though the eleventh-graders in the project often stated their interpretations of the play very forcefully, they almost never mentioned, much less summarized, the opposing interpretations of classmates or teachers, even when they were responding directly to those interpretations. Asked to take sides in the play's conflict between Caliban and Prospero, here is how two students, Dorothy and Chris, responded:

Dorothy: We believe that Prospero's actions [against Caliban] were justified because Caliban attempted to rape Prospero's daughter. Caliban feels absolutely no remorse for attempting to "violate the honor" of Miranda. When Caliban was confronted by Prospero, he says, "O ho, O ho! Would't have been done!"

Chris: Prospero is an evil, manipulative, racist, slaver, a murderer, a liar, and a tyrant. Caliban is an innocent, a victim of Prospero's cruel manipulations.

Dorothy and Chris express themselves with passion and force, and they have read the text with admirable closeness, but since they make no mention of what those who oppose them say or might say, they sound as if they are merely making counterassertions rather than engaging others in debate. They state their ideas in a vacuum rather than grapple with ones that are different from theirs.

Dorothy and Chris are apparently used to the restricted code of conversation, in which the physical presence of interlocutors relieves you of the need to summarize their views. Since in conversation their classmates are present to them and surely know what they have just said, why bother to summarize them? As for their teacher's views, it would seem even more superfluous, if not presumptuous, to restate them, since if anyone knows what he or she thinks, it is your teacher. Nobody has told Dorothy and Chris that in the more distanced conditions of writing (and of rigorous oral argumentation), we often need to summarize others (even when they are physically present) in order to make sure we are on the same page, to establish the degree of common ground necessary for advancing the discussion.

Theorists of psychological development, like the influential William Perry, might see the self-centered quality of Dorothy and Chris's thinking as a reflection of the developmental stage typical of twelve-year-old minds.[19] This kind of developmental theory can readily become a self-fulfilling prophecy, however. Dorothy and Chris may fail to restate opposing views not because they have yet to reach the developmental stage for recognizing opposing views, but because nobody has ever suggested to them that they need to make such restatements, why they need to do it, and how they could do it. Even at their ages they can probably do better, but we won't find out unless they are challenged to do so and given help. I would start by asking them to complete the following template: "In response to my defense of Prospero [Caliban], Dorothy [Chris] would object that . . ."

In this chapter I have inventoried some of the main features of academic discourse that seem odd or counterintuitive when left unexplained. I have suggested that the best way to deal with these apparent oddities is not to duck them, but to build classroom discussions and writing assignments around the questions they pose and to let students debate these questions. What is the point of looking for hidden meanings in everything you read? Why must expository writers have a "point" all the time? How do you know if the meanings a reader ascribes to a text are really there or not, and how can you debate the issue? Do works of entertainment have hidden meanings as the acknowledged classics do? Why summarize and restate other people's views even when those people are present? Does academia reward or punish students who are aggressively argumentative? Is it in fact arrogant to try to persuade other people that you are right? Is debate about ideas a form of warfare or a way of getting beyond warfare? Do you want to intellectualize, and why or why not? All these challenging questions are central to education, yet they have been allowed to fall through the cracks between courses and disciplines.

Whatever side students come down on for these questions—and students will divide on them as much as most of us do—opening these questions for discussion has the educationally desirable effect of positioning students as anthropologists, intellectual analysts, of their own academic lives. Even if some students end up rejecting academic roles, they at least may discover that their rejection will be more powerfully expressed if they draw on the resources of academic discourse to formulate it. This tactic may not eliminate student anti-intellectualism, but it can give it a more intellectual cast, and for teachers this is more than half the battle.

3 The Mixed-Message Curriculum

IN THE LAST CHAPTER, I looked at some of the features that make the culture of academic argument seem baffling, strange, and alienating to many students. I argued that teachers need to identify and isolate these features, to bring them into the open for classroom discussion and clarification, and to flush out and address student confusions and doubts about them. But student confusions about academic argument (and public argument generally) are rooted not only in the conventions and habits we have examined, but in the disconnected way the curriculum represents academic culture to students. In this chapter, I show how the disconnection of the curriculum not only obscures the issues and arguments that give coherence to academia, but compounds the problem by sending students confusingly mixed messages about how academic work is done.

To put it another way, academia's *external* impenetrability is a result of its *internal* disconnection, particularly the disconnection between academic courses. Recent educational discussion is rife with criticism of curricular incoherence, which is blamed on the so-called cafeteria-counter curriculum of unrelated courses and subjects.[1] But what has not been widely discussed is how curricular incoherence prevents students from being socialized into intellectual culture. I've written on this topic before, but I need to tell the story again since it is crucial to this book's diagnosis of how the academic argument culture gets obscured.[2]

About a century ago, universities imagined the world of knowledge as a kind of immense pyramid that was built by a process in which each scholarly specialist added a small brick or two to the growing edifice of objective truth. With the collapse of this positivistic view of knowledge in the early twentieth century, scholars and educators have increasingly come to see the world of knowledge as resembling a dynamic conversation rather than as an accumulation of discrete bricks of fact. Yet we still are left with a curriculum composed of separate bricks, which we call courses.

THE STUDENT AS DOUBLE AGENT

At the University of Chicago in the fifties, I happened to take a course in romantic literature and an introductory sociology course back-to-back one semester. The romantics course was taught by a colorful humanist of the old school who freely aired his prejudices, including his contempt for the social sciences, whose quantitative ways of thinking he blamed for draining the color and romance out of modern life and reducing it to banality. The professor ridiculed the "spreading blight of statistics worship," he approvingly quoted Wordsworth's line that "we murder to dissect," and he exhorted us to trust imagination, intuition, and feeling as the only reliable guides to truth. But the professor's most withering scorn was reserved for depersonalized social science prose, and it was woe to any of us who used the passive voice or an impersonal construction like "It is argued that," when we meant "I think."

In my sociology class the next hour, however, the statistical conception of knowledge and the depersonalized passive voice were unashamedly alive and well, as if generations of literati had never objected to them. Whereas in literature class we were encouraged to offer personal interpretations, in sociology a claim was suspect if it was not backed up with statistical support or other "hard" empirical evidence. Indeed, what counted as evidence was different in the two courses: in literature, for example, the evidence for what "the reader" should see in a text was the language of the text itself analyzed in the privacy of your room, whereas if you made a claim about readers in sociology you were expected to have gone out and interviewed some.

I soon realized that to please either professor I would need to tune out the teachings of the other. I must have managed the feat pretty well, for I ended up with an A in both courses. What still sticks in my memory is how painlessly I was able to negotiate the clashing mental universes of the two disciplines. For three days a week from ten to eleven I consorted with Blake, Shelley, and other visionaries who rebelled against what Shelley had called "the selfish and calculating principle" of science and commerce. Then, without skipping a beat, from eleven to twelve I became one of the coldly rationalistic Lockeans or Cartesians against whom I had conspired an hour earlier. I must have been aware of the clash between the philosophies and methods, but I ignored it, since neither course offered any incentive to take seriously the challenge represented by the other. On the contrary, there were strong reasons not to, since the quarrel between "Lit" and "Soc" was not part of either course's subject and would not be on either final exam, and since confronting either instructor with the other's objections would have been foolishly risking trouble. The prudent move was to forget how Lit and Soc might be in dialogue and get on with the separate courses' demands, which were taxing enough.

None of this is to say that the experience I've described had no educational value. Being bounced back and forth between the world views of literary romanticism and scientific empiricism probably gave me a healthy experience of what it feels like to move around inside different systems of thought and provisionally try on opposite ways of seeing the world. You could even argue that being forced to make sense of completely disjunctive perspectives was good preparation for living in a fragmented postmodern culture in which we have to sort out the conflicting judgments of experts on our own. In exposing me to dramatically opposed ways of thinking, the curriculum I experienced in the fifties was surely an improvement over pre–World War II, when the culture of the educated classes had been more homogeneous but for that reason more artificially sheltered from what went on around it. Arguably, the cognitive dissonance to which I was exposed was a good thing, forcing me to figure things out for myself instead of waiting for my teachers to feed me pat answers.

What is striking about my experience, however, as I have already suggested, was how *little* cognitive dissonance there actually was. Since the perspectives of the literature and sociology courses never came together to be compared and contrasted, they remained in separate mental compartments, leaving my exposure to divergent viewpoints incomplete and unconsummated. My experience points up a fallacy in the theory of curricular pluralism, which assumes that exposing students to diverse viewpoints stimulates critical thinking. It may, of course, which is why I feel no nostalgia for the monolithic core curriculum that was superseded by postwar curricular pluralism. When the plurality of course-perspectives do not meet, however, the student's exposure to diversity is as likely to switch critical thinking off as on. Mere exposure to diverse perspectives, with no engagement with what is at stake in the differences, can be as thoughtless a process as surfing TV channels or flipping through a discount catalog.

THE STUDENT AS VOLLEYBALL

The college experience I have described came back to me recently on reading Brent Staples's autobiographical memoir, *Parallel Time: Growing Up in Black and White*, in which Staples recalls his doctoral work in psychology at the University of Chicago in the seventies. Whereas the mixed messages I had experienced as a Chicago undergraduate reflected differences between disciplines, those Staples encountered were within the same discipline of psychology. His psychology courses, Staples writes, were an odd "smorgasbord of the old and the new": "In the morning I studied Rorschach's Ink Blot Test with an old German gentleman who believed that the test told all about the mind. In the afternoon I sat with a young statistician who treated ink blots as meaningless toys to be used in statistical games. Erika Fromm held fast to psychoanalysis as the true and only gospel. The philosopher Paul Ricoeur taught that Freud's version of mind was one version among many."[3]

Staples does not mention any bad effects these discrepancies may have had on his graduate education, and since he has gone on to become a successful columnist—though not a psychologist—they cannot have been too damaging. Maybe no great harm was done in my case either, though I now believe I would have had a far more satisfying and meaningful educational experience had I been encouraged to see my courses in conversation with each other. And when I look today at my own students, who are exposed to a vastly more diverse and conflicted range of assumptions, texts, and methods than I experienced in the relatively placid and stable campus life of the fifties, I have to conclude that such curricular mixed messages are a major cause of stunted education that widens the gap between student insiders and outsiders.

Consider that a student today can go from one class in which it goes without saying—and therefore will probably not be explicitly said—that the traditional humanities canon is a noble heritage to be unproblematically passed on, to another class in which it equally goes without saying that that same canon is compromised by ideological domination. On another level, students can go from a class in which knowledge is assumed to be "out there" and objective to another class in which knowledge is assumed to be a social construction actively produced by the knower; or from a class in which the teacher lectures from the front of the room, the students take notes, and knowledge is considered something to be handed down by authority, to a class in which the instructor sits in a circle with the students and acts as a nondirective "facilitator," and knowledge is seen as something students themselves construct through dialogue and collaboration. As I noted in my introduction, the student becomes a kind of volleyball, batted back and forth in an intellectual game whose rules change without notice from course to course. Who wouldn't be dazed when the beliefs that were pronounced dead in one's morning class turn up alive and well after lunch?

Granted, students often cope very well with this Volleyball Effect, doing an excellent job on their own of connecting what their teachers do not, making up individual versions of the academic conversation out of noncommunicating courses. Some students tell me they like the do-it-yourself curriculum, which leaves them free to put the pieces of the puzzle together as they like. And why shouldn't students like a system to which they've experienced no alternative? As a puzzled UIC freshman remarked when I referred critically to the practice of doing whatever one's teachers want, "I've been doing whatever my teachers want since first grade!" Often, however, students who flourish under the do-it-yourself curriculum are of the minority that arrives at college already socialized into the club of academia by home, church, or other prior experience. Those who lack this edge generally have to cope by giving each instructor whatever he or she seems to want even when it flatly contradicts what the previous instructor wanted.

For such students, the curriculum represents not a coherent intellectual world with conventions and practices anyone can internalize and apply to the specific challenges of each discipline, but an endless series of instructors' preferences that you psych out, if you can, and then conform to, virtually starting over from scratch in each new course. Some instructors want you to recall and give back information without interpretation or judgment, whereas others want you to express your own ideas. Some instructors think there are clear-cut answers to questions, whereas others (often in the same discipline) think there are no right answers and that those who think so are naive or authoritarian.

Teaching freshman composition at UIC the last three years has given me a palpable sense of the destructive effect this disjunctive experience has on our students, many of whom fail to survive the first year. When I organized one course around the theme of "academic intellectual culture," I realized early on that to most of the students this concept seemed nebulous or meaningless. I began to understand why when I asked them what other courses they were taking and what they were doing in them. I realized that to many UIC freshmen a term like "academic intellectual culture" is an empty abstraction. As they experienced it, the challenge of college was how to get through first-year chemistry, social science, English, and so on. In theory, my composition course would give these freshmen the meta-language, the tools of reading, writing, and argumentation, that would help them in other courses and disciplines. But as many of them saw it, "English" was one more hurdle among others, with no apparent relation to anything else they studied. I was one more incomprehensible prof to be humored and circumvented.

CONTRADICTION AND COMPARTMENTALIZATION

The mixed-message curriculum helps explain a phenomenon that has been noticed by literacy researchers—the difficulty many students have recognizing and acknowledging *contradictions*. After teaching literature for several years, I began to notice that whenever my students encountered a contradiction in a literary work, they almost always either ignored it or found a way to rationalize it, as if the author of the work had intended it. The better the students, the more ingeniously they contrived to find a "deeper underlying unity" in seemingly contradictory texts. I realized that the students had imbibed the assumption that great writers don't make mistakes (and if a text is assigned in school, it must be great), so if textual contradictions appear, they must have been deliberately planted in order to force readers to use their ingenuity to resolve them. Then it occurred to me that as an undergraduate I had myself performed this rationalizing operation in many papers, and had been rewarded for it.

Kathleen McCormick, in *The Culture of Reading and the Teaching of English,* describes participating in a fascinating experiment in which Carnegie Mellon University undergraduates were asked to read and respond to a short text on time management "that was designed to contain contradictory information" in views by several experts on the subject. For example, one expert quoted in the text advised readers to "work through one's fatigue," whereas another urged "the importance of resting 'at the least sign of fatigue.' "[4] The research team found that in their written responses two thirds of the students "did not mention that contradictions existed in the text," while another 20 percent "noted that the experts disagreed but mentioned this only in passing in summary form and, for most of their essay, ignored this fact." One student addressed "the disagreements and contradictions" in the time management text "by keeping each in an isolated paragraph" of her paper.[5]

McCormick traces these results to two factors: first, students are so trained to accept the word of experts at face value that when the experts disagree students contrive not to notice it; and second, students are led to think that writing a unified essay requires eliminating contradictory views. McCormick quotes one Carnegie Mellon student who told researchers he "felt that the only way he could resolve contradic-

tions was 'to use only the information that fit together' " and leave out
whatever did not.[6] These reasons are certainly convincing, but I have
to think that part of the explanation also lies in the students' exposure
to conflicting course-perspectives that never engage, inducing students
to compartmentalize clashing views and thereby fail to learn how to
deal with contradictions. The isolated paragraphs of the student paper
in which the text's conflicting views of time management were kept
separate seems a perfect mirror of students' compartmentalized experience of isolated courses.

If the mixed-message curriculum prevents students from recognizing or dealing with contradictions, it also makes their learning so
course-specific that it loses its application beyond the course. What you
learn, that is, seems so tied to the course in which you learn it that you
hardly think about applying it even to your other courses, much less
to your life beyond school. Such an effect would help explain a curious
syndrome described by Howard Gardner in *The Unschooled Mind,* in
which students who have seemingly mastered sophisticated ways of
thinking in school abruptly regress to primitive, "unschooled" beliefs
as soon as they are asked to apply what they have learned to situations
and contexts outside the course. For example, students "are able to repeat back accurately the principal claims of relativity theory, according
to which temporal and physical properties must be considered in light
of a particular frame of reference." Yet when queried outside the
course, the same students revert back to their earlier "belief in absolute
space and time." Similarly, Gardner notes that elementary and middle
school students revert to flat-Earth thinking after passing a course in
which they have shown they know the Earth revolves around the sun.[7]
I suspect that in such cases what such students learn is so tied to the
specifics of the course that it remains in a "for school only" compart-
ment in their minds.

To be sure, some students encounter a turning point or Eureka-
moment course, one that equips them with an overview or meta-frame-
work that enables them to connect, synthesize, and pull together their
otherwise dissociated set of courses. Often one discipline—philosophy,
anthropology, cultural history, women's studies—supplies the unifying
lens that allows students to "read" their other courses and subjects

through a coherent perspective. Providing such a meta-discourse is often the aim of newly developed interdisciplinary courses and programs—gender studies, disability studies, law and economics—whose emergence represents an attempt to counteract the fragmentation of the mixed-message curriculum. Though interdisciplinary courses and programs have been effective in the schools (the spirit of innovation seems to decline incrementally as one goes from kindergarten to doctoral study), in the colleges they have fallen far short of counteracting the centrifugal pull of the curriculum, at worst reproducing the curricular fragmentation that they aim to counter. Since the new interdisciplinary units are simply *added* to the existing disciplines, they tend to remain disconnected from each other as well as from the disciplines themselves.[8]

REDUNDANCY LOST

To put my point in the jargon of information theory, a disconnected curriculum tends to be low in redundancy, the reinforcement of convergent messages that enables us to map our environment and gain confidence in our ability to negotiate it. The problem is by no means new—complaints about curricular fragmentation date from the earliest emergence of the elective system that was pioneered by Harvard president Charles William Eliot after the Civil War. Indeed, as W. B. Carnochan has shown, modern-day critics of the cafeteria-counter curriculum have said virtually nothing different from what President James McCosh of Princeton and other nineteenth-century critics of Harvard's elective system noted more than one hundred years ago.[9] But though curricular incoherence has long been with us, in degree it is measurably greater today than in the past in the wake of the postwar knowledge and cultural diversity explosions I described in my introduction.

In literary studies, for example, though the methods of approaching literature had begun to diversify in published academic criticism by the fifties, students were generally exposed to only two, chronological literary history and New Critical textual analysis, and one could do quite well by mastering only the latter. Despite the disjunction I described between my sociology and romantic literature courses, my classmates and I experienced a vast amount of unspoken agreement among our professors when we went from a class taught by an old-fashioned literary historian to one taught by an upstart formalist critic. Today, by contrast, in addition to old-fashioned historicists and formalists, any moderately ambitious literature department is likely to include new historicists, feminists, deconstructionists, Lacanians, queer theorists, English as a second language specialists, race and ethnicity scholars, and pragmatists. Such departments may also harbor film specialists, creative writers, compositionists, and analysts of popular culture. With the proliferation of methods and genres there is correspondingly less common ground in terminology, in assumptions about what "literature" is or can be, and in what constitutes legitimate evidence for a literary claim or an acceptable argument.

Some critics blame the confusion on something peculiarly arcane about the reasoning of literary critics. In a 1976 article that contrasts "How Critics Write and How Students Write," David Carkeet observes that

> prior to his exposure to literary methods, the average student will have a pretty clear idea that some things are true and some are false, while a range of things is in the middle. As for this middle ground, people normally have an intuitive sense about evidence—how to stack it up, how far it can be taken, where to draw lines, and so on. But the conventions of argument are substantially different in literary circles, and there is no way for a neophyte to know a priori what a good literary argument is, or to know what kind of bad arguments are treated as good arguments.[10]

Carkeet here accurately and wittily describes the "neophyte's" confusion in the face of literary-critical reasoning, which indeed tends to be presupposed rather than explained in literature courses. I suspect, however, that an equally important factor is the increased proliferation of critical approaches to which literature students have been exposed since the sixties, without any corresponding increase in the cross-factional discussion of assumptions that might help students sort things out by clarifying points of comparison, contrast, and agreement. In fact, since

tradition and inertia exert a strong residual pull, even today college literature students who resist the temptation to panic will usually still do
well if they master old-fashioned formalist close-reading. The bombard-
ment of dissonant approaches, however, often prevents students from
making this discovery. The multiplication of methods, vocabularies,
and -isms combined with the lack of a coherent conversation in which
they can be compared and contrasted increases the likelihood of students' feeling intimidated and of talking themselves into the belief that
"I'm just not cut out for this stuff."

WHO CARES?

Curricular disconnection, then, widens a gap between teachers and students that was already wide because of the marginal status of intellectual culture in the United States. The problem has been described by
the literary scholar David Richter, who, while interviewing undergraduates as part of an accreditation team, was struck by "the great gap . . .
between [undergraduates] and their teachers." Richter observes that the
gap "was not just a matter of age or experience." The students "felt
isolated from the ideas and questions that their teachers argued among
themselves. There was an enormously interesting conversation swirl-
ing around them, of which they were able to catch brief words and
phrases. The students felt like children in unhappy marriages who have
to be protected against hearing the bickering of their parents." Richter's
comment gets at the connection I have been trying to show between
the internal disconnection of academic institutions and their external
unintelligibility. When the "parents" are not in conversation with each
other, their relations are obscured from the "children," who are further
infantilized.

Richter goes on to suggest a link between curricular disconnection
and student apathy and relativism. If the professorial conversation was
not "enormously interesting" to the students as it was to their teachers,
the subject matter may have been only part of the reason, for any subject tends to elicit apathy and indifference when experienced in a disjunctive way. As Richter puts it, "Like such children, students are hard
to fool. They learn, sometimes in cynical ways, to accommodate the
seemingly contradictory ways of instructors. They learn that, just as

Professor Jones likes papers to be folded while Professor Smith likes them flat, Professor Jones sees the self as lonely and agonized while Professor Smith views the subject as socially constituted. The problem is that they are likely to view the question of personal identity as being in the long run of equal importance to that of folding papers."[11]

I argued in chapter 2 that much of the oft-lamented relativism of today's youth actually stems from the difficulty of imagining a world in which their arguments would make a difference. I would now add that this relativism is reinforced by students' exposure to clashing course perspectives that never meet. The curriculum sends an implicit message that the institution does not care strongly enough about the intellectual differences between instructors to bother engaging them, so why should students be expected to care, either?

A link between student apathy and another kind of disjunction— that of the school day—has been incisively pointed out by the high school educator and critic John Taylor Gatto:

> Suppose that you and I . . . decided to create some struc-
> tural way to make young people indifferent to everything.
> And suppose we came up with the idea that we would enthu-
> siastically launch them on an hourly basis on one or another
> project of art or thinking and then we would ring a bell and
> say you must stop and move immediately away from this.
> And we did that for year after year after year after year.
> Would that not produce an internal mechanism that said
> nothing is worth finishing? And if nothing's worth finish-
> ing, isn't the next logical step that nothing's worth begin-
> ning?[12]

In school as in college, repeatedly changing the subject without making the necessary connections and transitions is a prescription for apathy.

If the mixed-message curriculum forces students into an undue dependence on psyching out what teachers want, it can also make it hard for students to discern what those wants actually are. If Richter's Professor Jones refers to "the self" while his Professor Smith calls it "the subject," or if Jones refers to "the great books" while Smith refers to "Western hegemonic discourse," their students may not recognize that the two instructors are actually talking about the same thing, that is, that they disagree. And even if it is apparent that the instructors disagree, how they would talk to each other about their differences will not be, though by then the students will probably have lost interest anyway.

In addition to keeping students confused about academic usages and conventions, the mixed-message curriculum also makes it difficult for students to know which kinds of competence figure to matter from one course or subject to the next. Another writing across the curriculum theorist, Art Young, describes the case of an undergraduate named Mary who got a solid B in Young's English composition courses but was marked down as "semiliterate" by her biology professor, who angrily complained to Young about the poor quality of her writing. The problem, Young discovered, lay not, as he at first guessed, in the different writing conventions of the English essay and the biology report. Rather the problem was that Mary assumed that "because this was a biology course and not an English course, concerns for a focused introduction, purposeful organization, and attention to spelling and punctuation would not matter." Mary, Young writes, "knew perfectly well how to perform [these] basics, she just didn't think scientists 'cared about this stuff,'" as was probably often the case in her experience.[13]

CURRICULAR SUBURBAN SPRAWL

I have elsewhere traced the mixed-message curriculum and the Volleyball Effect to the add-on system of curricular formation that came in with the modern departmentalized school and college. In this system, new courses and subjects are assimilated by simply being added to the aggregate, a tactic that conveniently avoids conflicts and dispenses with the need to rethink the curriculum as a whole.[14] The American curriculum has evolved in much the same way as the American city: when threatening conflicts have erupted, they have been relieved by adding a new "suburb"—a new course, a new program, a new department, eventually (for universities) a new building. Whenever a threatening innovation appears—feminist history and literary criticism, creative writing, econometrics, psychohistory, structuralism, multiculturalism—it is assimilated by adding a new instructor, course, or program, a process that appeases both the old guard and the innovators by giving each a portion of the curricular turf and insulating them from each other so they won't bicker.

The add-on method of assimilating change goes hand in hand with an ethos of pedagogical laissez-faire: I promise not to interfere with what you want to teach or study if you promise not to interfere with me. The vacuum left by the absence of open debate is filled by academic administration, conceived as an art of crisis-management whose aim is to put out fires as they occur and neutralize departmental turf wars rather than exploit their educational potential. Administrative "conflict management" comes to mean conflict avoidance or suppression, usually by keeping clashing factions in separate buildings, offices, departments, and courses to maintain peaceful coexistence.

To give the add-on method its due, it has enabled academic institutions to assimilate a tremendous degree of change and diversity, making American education wonderfully receptive to innovation and able to reconcile it easily with tradition. It allows the old guard to go on doing what it has always done in its sector of the curriculum even as young turks shake things up in theirs. A high educational price is paid, however, when the increased diversity that results leads to conflicts, which are evaded instead of confronted. As these conflicts become more polarized and ideologically loaded, hatreds that have no way of being channeled into open discussion tend to fester, erupting finally in shouting matches at faculty meetings or campus demonstrations. And finally, another kind of price is paid as shrinking budgets deprive administrators of the former luxury of avoiding conflicts by adding new academic "suburbs" and expanding the playing field.

The irony of such curricular compromises is that though all factions may win concessions, they ultimately defeat their own educational interests by isolating themselves from the opposing positions they need in order to make their own values intelligible to students. For example, the separation of Western and non-Western cultures in noncommunicating courses deprives students of the cross-cultural comparisons they need in order to understand what may be distinctive about either culture. In turn, the isolation of factions in separate courses increases the likelihood of students' feeling coerced by political correctness of the Left or the Right. For when the classroom walls enable teachers to tune out objections from their colleagues that they would rather not hear, everyone is given a license to dogmatize without fear of being contradicted except by the rare courageous student. Teachers often brag that they urge their students to disagree vigorously with them, and not accept their word on authority. I have no doubt that these teachers are sincere, but they unwittingly send students the opposite message when they are content to stay sheltered from those colleagues across the hall or the quad who would be in the best position to disagree with them and provide a model to students of how to disagree in public. Students would figure to be more prone to disagree with their teachers if they had more chance to see those teachers disagreeing with each other.

If the mixed-message curriculum cheats students, it may cheat their teachers even more. For when our classroom walls enable us to tune out colleagues who disagree—or even agree—with us, we teachers are robbed of the peer challenges and the intellectual community that we need in order to avoid going brain-dead. I am reminded of this fact whenever I give a talk at another campus or a professional conference. At home my pet assumptions may be contradicted by the occasional contentious student, but such occasions are rare, whereas on the road I am routinely forced to explain and defend myself.

Away from home, I become part of an intellectual community again, as I am when I write and publish, whereas at home I am expected to teach my classes and attend faculty meetings but otherwise to mind my own business and keep my ideas to myself. On the road I am encouraged to assert myself intellectually—that is why I have been invited to give the lecture or attend the conference—whereas asserting my ideas at home would evidently threaten too many others who have their own ideas. Campus culture is governed by a tacit code of democratic silence, whereby we all agree to muzzle ourselves so that no individual or group gets their way. Again, this mutual nonaggression treaty preserves short term peace, but in doing so it shuts down intellectual community or pushes it to the margins. It also deprives faculty members of the public sphere of ideas that we need in order to grow intellectually, to influence students and other publics, and to defend our economic interests in a shrinking market. No wonder academics communicate badly, seeing that the isolation from colleagues in which we teach is the poorest possible training for representing ourselves in public.

My critique of curricular isolation should not be confused with accounts that attribute curricular incoherence to disciplinary specialization. Frank H. T. Rhodes, for example, complains that "faculty members have added courses that reflect their own, increasingly specialized interests" rather than "a commitment to common educational goals." I agree with Rhodes that fragmentation and incoherence are the product of a curriculum that is produced by "adding" courses that randomly reflect faculty interests rather than serve the educational needs of students. I don't agree, however, that these faculty interests are "increasingly specialized," a claim Rhodes himself belies when he goes on to say that knowledge has been "compartmentalized" by "the rapid spread in most universities of freestanding programs . . . devoted to specialized studies as well as a host of cultural issues—poverty, peace, ethnicity, gender, and sexual preference." Clearly, poverty, peace, and the other issues in Rhodes's list do not exemplify specialization, but rather the move toward broader outreach that I noted in my introduction. The problem is not the proliferation of studies that are so specialized that they can't communicate, as Rhodes implies, but rather the existence of entities that he calls "freestanding"—programs and courses that have potential interests in common but no means of coming together.[15]

TOWARD A COMPARATIVE CURRICULUM

Clearly, it is crucial to begin providing students with a more connected view of the academic intellectual universe, one that lets them recognize and enter the conversation that makes that universe cohere and relates it to the wider world. This task is not easy, for American schools and colleges have been wonderful at adding exciting new components— subjects, courses, fields, and intellectual perspectives—but pathetically inept at connecting and integrating these rich materials so that those not already at home in academia can make sense of them.

Two strategies are needed. First, we need more centrally placed composition courses—preferably in writing across the curriculum programs that involve professors and graduate assistants from across the disciplines, not only English. Since writing is central to all disciplines, all departments have to take responsibility for it, not fob the task off on the English department and walk away. Then, too, only if writing is taught by instructors from all disciplines are students likely to get a sense of the contrasts and convergences between disciplinary conventions of communication. An excellent model is the composition course taught by Donald Jones that I describe in chapter 13, which focuses not only on the contrasts and convergences between writing in different disciplines, but also on the opposition between academic and personal writing. However the job is done, it is crucial that students come away from basic writing courses with the understanding that entering the public argument culture is the name of the academic game.

Second, we need to explore ways of putting courses into conversation. In the last chapter of *Beyond the Culture Wars,* I discuss a number of strategies for connecting courses, including "teacher swapping" (instructors visit or teach each other's classes), student symposia based on common texts taught in different courses and departments, and visiting lectures and lecture series that bring together courses around common issues and problems. I also described the "learning community" programs that have been developed at numerous schools and campuses, in which the same cohort of students takes several courses that are linked by a common theme, the instructors of which meet regularly with the students and each other.[16] (Jane Tompkins and I have recently co-written a dialogue in which we elaborate on the benefits of the learning community model.[17]) I cited the book *Learning Communities* by Faith Gabelnick, Jean MacGregor, Roberta S. Matthews, and Barbara Leigh Smith, which describes programs based on such thematic clustering, expounds the educational rationale for the tactic, and addresses some of the practical challenges of putting it into effect at large urban commuter campuses (which need it most) as well as small colleges.[18]

Students and teachers in these programs report that the more connected and focused experience provided by the thematically linked courses results in a higher proportion of students becoming insiders to the intellectual club, identifying with intellectual roles and becoming more independent and motivated. Students are no longer reduced to slavishly conforming to whatever individual instructors "want," since authority has been shifted from the individual instructors to the community of instructors and students, as in real-world intellectual communities in which experts are answerable to other experts and lay people. Learning community teachers report that they are able to "demand more" from their students and "get more in terms of student perseverance and quality of performance."[19] Another way to put it is that, unlike the standard curriculum in which many students drift listlessly from one course to the next, the learning community model does not offer students the option of being alienated from the intellectual life. Because the learning community constitutes a real intellectual conversation, the task of the student is no longer just to get through a series of subjects but actually to join the conversation.

The University of Illinois at Chicago initiated a pilot program of learning clusters for 250 freshmen in the fall of 2002. Cohorts of twenty-five students chose among ten clusters, each consisting of three courses—a freshman seminar taught by faculty members across the disciplines, a section of English composition, and a third course that fulfils general education requirements. The writing assignments in the cluster's composition course were especially important in ensuring that the disciplines brought together in each cluster cohered for the students. If we did our jobs well, the freshmen who took our clusters should come away measurably better socialized into academic culture and its discourse than those who don't.

Clearly, collaborative teaching in learning communities or other models is no panacea. In collaborating with colleagues, instructors give up the luxury of doing as they please, and they risk making things more confusing for students rather than less. Merely coming together with colleagues does not automatically make academic work more exciting or clear—it takes considerable effort, planning, and trial and error. In the long run, however, the pedagogical payoff of collaborative teaching should be greater than that of teaching in isolation, for collective teaching can be self-policing in a way that solo teaching is not. Finally, an advantage of the learning community model is that it enables instructors to enact a new kind of curriculum instead of talking about it in endless faculty meetings that only result in a superficial reshuffling of what existed before.[20]

Whenever I urge these ideas, I am told that academics are too temperamental or too much a bunch of loners to collaborate in their teaching, and even if they are not, their departmental turf wars and ideological battles have made them too polarized to make this idea realistic. Or it is said that academics have become too highly specialized to converse with one another.[21] These objections are logically circular: as long as we academics tell ourselves we are too far apart to have a common discussion within the curriculum, our failure to have that discussion forces us further apart. Again, it is notable that we academics regularly (if not always gracefully) engage in collective discussions when we leave our campuses to attend conferences and when we respond to each other in print. We have learned to take for granted an immunity from collegial disagreement in our teaching that we would never expect in the real world of intellectual work. It would be wrong as well as futile to try to force unwilling teachers to teach with their colleagues, but it doesn't follow that we have to organize education for the academic Greta Garbos who want to be alone. If I am right that students need to experience an intellectual conversation in order to join it, then the curriculum needs to represent that conversation in a more connected way.

PART II: INTELLECTUALISM AND
ITS DISCONTENTS

4 Two Cheers for the Argument Culture

IN THE PREVIOUS CHAPTERS, I have discussed confusions that can be traced to academia's ways of fogging over its conversations. Some observers, however, complain that what characterizes the academic scene is not "conversation" so much as smash-mouth combat. I have taken flak myself for arguing that conflict and controversy should be made more central in the curriculum. My critics object that today's academia, like today's popular media, is all too rife with conflict of a distinctly ugly and unedifying kind. The critics point to talk-show violence, political attack ads, and other signs of a pervasive "Gotcha!" spirit that aims at humiliating opponents rather than achieving consensus and cooperation.

These objections often come from feminists, some of whom see patriarchal gender bias in the adversarial forms of debate favored in such academic fields as law and philosophy. According to these critics it's increasingly hard to tell the difference between the debates of academics and the trash-talking and taunting that occurs in various professional sports or the kind of media pseudo-debate that was satirized in a celebrated *Saturday Night Live* segment of the seventies in which Dan Ackroyd opened his weekly news commentary rebuttal to his counterpart Jane Curtin with the line, "Jane, you ignorant slut."

TANNEN VS. THE ARGUMENT CULTURE

One of the most articulate critics of this culture of demonization, insult, and macho combat is Deborah Tannen, who surveys its many defects in her recent book, *The Argument Culture: Moving from Debate to Dialogue.* Tannen objects to a "pervasive warlike atmosphere that makes us approach public dialogue, and just about anything we need to accomplish, as if it were a fight."[1] Like George Lakoff and Mark Johnson in *Metaphors We Live By,* Tannen questions the metaphors of war and combat that all too automatically shape our thinking about how we think and converse.[2] The argument culture, Tannen writes, "urges us to approach the world—and the people in it—in an adversarial frame of mind. It rests on the assumption that opposition is the best way to get anything done: The best way to discuss an idea is to set up a debate; the best way to cover news is to find spokespeople who express the most extreme, polarized views and present them as 'both sides'; the best way to settle disputes is litigation that pits one party against the other; the best way to begin an essay is to attack someone; and the best way to show you're really thinking is to criticize" (3–4). Though Tannen properly warns against reaching too quickly for simplistic gender stereotypes that would deny women's ability to argue on a par with men, she points out what is hard to deny, that men are more likely than women to engage in "ritual opposition," to "take an oppositional stance toward other people and the world," and "to find opposition entertaining—to enjoy watching a good fight or having one" (166).

Tannen sees academia as especially prone to ritualized combativeness. As she puts it in a recent article based on her book, "Many aspects of our academic lives can be described as agonistic. For example, in our scholarly papers, most of us follow a conventional framework that requires us to position our work in opposition to someone else's, which we prove wrong. The framework tempts—almost requires—us to oversimplify or even misrepresent others' positions; cite the weakest example to make a generally reasonable work appear less so; and ignore facts that support others' views, citing only evidence that supports our own positions."[3] In the same vein, Tannen complains that "the standard way of writing an academic paper is to position your work in opposition to someone else's, which you prove wrong." Students, she notes, "are taught that they must disprove others' arguments in order to be original, make a contribution, and demonstrate their intellectual ability." Such teaching leads them "to oversimplify at best, and at worst to distort or even misrepresent others' positions, the better to refute them" (268–69). Tannen cites the case of a professor who confided to a colleague whom he had attacked that "he actually agreed with him, but of course he could not get tenure by . . . simply supporting someone else's work; he had to stake out a position in opposition" (269).

Tannen's critique is often persuasive. Many of the vices and excesses to which she refers are instantly recognizable, and it is hard to disagree with her objections to the incivility, abusiveness, and bullying that pass for public disagreement today. The compositionist Sharon James McGee has observed that "many students see argument only through the lens of the *Jerry Springer Show*—as a shouting match broken up by bouncers."[4] Anyone concerned about school violence has to be aware that verbal abuse can escalate into physical abuse, which in turn can become psychotic and murderous. Tannen is right that we need a lot more open-minded "dialogue" and a lot less crudely polarized "debate" both in academia and the media, and that we need forums for disagreement that do not lock us into rigid "positions" but allow us to change our minds and concede our mistakes.

Nevertheless, I trust I do not simply exemplify the ugly behavior Tannen objects to if I take issue with her negative verdict on the argument culture. Though Tannen is right that bad versions of the argument culture often dominate the social and academic scene, to me this seems an argument not against the argument culture but for a better one. For debate is unavoidably central to the life of democratic educational institutions and democratic societies. To restore the civility Tannen and the rest of us want in American public discourse, we need more keen debate, not less. Here we could generalize the point that political theorist Michael J. Sandel has made about senatorial confirmation hearings: "The way to restore civility to the confirmation process," Sandel writes, "is not to avoid ideological debate but to engage in it more openly."[5] And as I argue in this book, when we academics shrink from acknowledging the centrality of argumentation, we end up hiding our secrets from our students and force them to play the academic game at a disadvantage.

At times Tannen writes as if she herself agrees with such sentiments. Tannen concedes that "conflict can't be avoided in our public life any more than we can avoid conflict with people we love" (4). She acknowledges that conflict, debate, and disagreement are unavoidable aspects of human experience, and she grants that a degree of oppositionality is inherent in the process of differentiating ourselves as individuals. As she puts it, "Even saying 'I agree' makes sense only against the background assumption that you might disagree" (26).

At these conciliatory moments, Tannen seems to grant the positive potential of productive disagreement as the basis of democratic community. She calls attention to the deep forms of agreement and cooperation that underlie disagreement but get ignored when we wall ourselves up in polemical positions and fear losing face by conceding a point. She argues sensibly (273) that to balance our proneness to what compositionist Peter Elbow calls "the doubting game," we need to try out Elbow's "believing game," in which, before we attack a belief, we imagine what it would feel like to hold it.[6] In such passages, Tannen's quarrel seems to be not with debate as such, but with the kind of reductively binary debate encouraged by the point-counterpoint format of the media, where every issue is presumed to have only two sides. (As Alex Jones observed in the aftermath of the Florida presidential vote controversy, journalism often confuses fairness "with the unsatisfactory practice of quoting one strident voice and then its opposite in every story."[7]) As Tannen puts it, her objection is not to contentiousness as such, but to "programmed contentiousness—a prepatterned, unthinking use of fighting to accomplish goals that do not necessarily require it" and are often prevented by it (8). At these moments, Tannen seems to want only a kinder and gentler version of the argument culture, moving it from sensationalized, hotheaded antagonism to respectful negotiation of differences.

At other moments, however, Tannen seems to adopt an abolitionist view of debate and oppositionality, writing as if these things should be made to wither away and be replaced by something else. At these times, Tannen implies that debate *as such* is the problem, that what is needed is not more productive and respectful debate, but the cessation of debate. This more radical version of the argument is suggested by Tannen's subtitle: "Moving from Debate to Dialogue." (It may or may not be indicative of her ambivalence that in the paperback edition Tannen's subtitle is changed to *Stopping America's War of Words*, subtly shifting the emphasis to ending "war" rather than debate.[8]) When Tannen writes in this "end it, don't mend it" mode, she seems to wish for some alternative to debate in which we would no longer have to "stake out a position in opposition" or "position ourselves in opposition to someone else's [view], which we prove wrong." It is this antidebate message, I believe, that most readers take away from her book.

ARE WE DEBATING OR CONVERSING?

Again, there is no doubt that academic and journalistic polemicists are often more prone to score debater's points than listen to what opponents have to say, and that a strong dose of Elbow's "believing game," in which we make an effort to inhabit the opponent's belief before leaping to refute it, would be salutary for everybody. But it doesn't follow that we can simply desist from staking "out a position in opposition" or from positioning "ourselves in opposition to someone else's [view], which we prove wrong." For some measure of contrast or againstness, some "as opposed to whatness," is inherent not only in the process of writing, but of being an individual. To be sure, our reasons for writing and reading have as much to do with establishing common ground as with differentiating ourselves from each other.[9] But it is not wrong that works of scholarship and opinion journalism do not get published if they merely agree with what others have said and don't "stake out a position in opposition."

The problem is that in the very act of warring against polarization, Tannen herself falls into a needless polarization of "debate" versus "dialogue," as in her book's original subtitle. The mistake here lies in setting up debate and dialogue as polar opposites, when they are better seen as complementary moments in the process of social exchange, which constantly alternates between the adversarial and the consensual. (This slippage between "debate" and "conversation" is my excuse for my tendency to use these terms interchangeably in this book.)

Tannen writes as if we always *know* whether a given discussion is "debate" or "dialogue"/"conversation," as when she draws a sharp contrast between academic courses that privilege debate over those that encourage "conversation" or "discussion." But which mode we are in—debate or dialogue?—is not always self-evident, a fact that explains why parties to an exchange often disagree about how to classify what they are doing: "Hey, don't take it personally—I'm not *arguing* with you, I'm just stating a fact." Or, "Take it easy, I'm not putting you down, I'm just trying to find out where we stand."

This ambiguity—are we debating or conversing?—is amusingly illustrated by one of my favorite Monty Python sketches, "The Argument Clinic." A man appears at the clinic and announces that he is looking for an argument. He is directed to office 12, whereupon opening the door he is met with a stream of insults and invective from the functionary behind the desk:

"You snotty-faced piece of parrot-droppings. . . . Your type makes me puke. You vacuous, toffee-nosed, malodorous pervert."

"What's this? I came here for an argument."

"Oh, I'm sorry. This is Abuse. You want 12A next door." Going to the office next door, the client asks the man at the desk if this the Argument Department.

"I told you once . . ."

"No, you didn't."

"Yes, I did."

"Did not."

"Did . . ."

Finally, the client objects that "this isn't argument, just mere contradiction."

"No, it isn't."

"Yes it is. An argument is a connected series of statements leading to a definite proposition."

"No, it's not . . ."

"Argument is an intellectual process, not an automatic gainsaying of anything the other person says."

"Not necessarily."[10]

Though it's easy to spot the differences here between abuse, argument, and "mere contradiction," the sketch forces us to reflect on how slippery these distinctions can be. Veteran teachers know that a discussion that some students experience as a healthy airing of differences is experienced by others as "mere contradiction," even abuse.

Indeed, the word "argument" is itself ambiguous, sometimes being used to denote adversarial dispute ("Let's not get into an argument over this"), sometimes to refer neutrally to anything that has been stated or proposed ("As I understand it, your argument is . . ."), though even this neutral usage hints faintly at controversy, for there would be no need to propose at all if the proposal were not controversial. Though students are often confused by these ambiguities in the word "argument," they are rarely brought up by teachers. Mea culpa: I must have used the word thousands of times in class, but only recently have I begun to stop and unpack its different meanings.

But perhaps the most telling refutation of Tannen's thesis in *The Argument Culture* is the confrontational quality of the book itself. At those moments when Tannen questions the legitimacy of oppositional debate, she traps herself in a performative contradiction in which what she *says* is undermined by what she *does*. In the act of warning readers against the adversarial, agonistic, oppositional stance, Tannen cannot help becoming adversarial, agonistic, and oppositional. In complaining that we clear a space for our views by positioning "ourselves in opposition to someone else's," Tannen enacts the behavior she objects to, positioning herself in opposition to debate lovers. Tannen anticipates this objection, calling her book not "a frontal assault on the argument culture"—which would "be in the spirit of attack that I am questioning"—but an attempt to "expand our notion of 'debate' to include more dialogue" (25–26). But Tannen's pages do often border on "frontal assault," with their hard-edged, disputatious style—which I take to be a virtue—that seems closer to the abrasive rationalism she opposes than to the soft-focus New Age mentality with which she identifies ideologically. (In this respect, Tannen resembles my colleague Jane Tompkins, another aggressive polemicist who is ambivalent about polemics.)

Furthermore, is it really true that bullying tactics get you ahead as an academic? In my experience, students who attack for the mere sake of attacking or who caricature their targets are readily spotted and corrected. And scholars who earn reputations as hatchet men and women tend to lose credibility among their peers. Polemics tend to be more persuasive with uncommitted audiences when they avoid abusive gestures, accord their opponents a measure of respect, and make due concessions. Tannen sees as typical the professor who admitted to his colleague that he had attacked him in order to get tenure, not because he really disagreed with him. To me the professor sounds like someone with a self-destructive delusion about how his profession works.

By the same token, how accurate is Tannen's picture of today's classrooms as rife with rancorous contention? I would bet that most American students go through their entire high school and college careers without ever witnessing a debate between their teachers, and extended disagreements between classmates are probably only slightly more frequent. To be sure, there is no shortage of classroom *competition,* but very little of that competition gets channeled into sustained intellectual debate. On the faculty side, there is no lack of disagreement, but what debate there is takes place behind the classroom scenes in faculty meetings and private conversations, or (for college faculty) in publications and conference presentations.

A UIC graduate student, Steve Benton, put the point well in a letter responding to Tannen in the *Chronicle of Higher Education:* "The operative metaphor in the classes I've been in has not been . . . a battleground of ire-raising debate, but a hot tub of sleep-inducing consensus. Gunslingers though they may be at professional conferences and in faculty lounges, the teachers of the classes I've sat in have, for the most part, done an excellent job of keeping their own classrooms safe from critical controversy." Benton concludes that the "fact that students . . . are not adept at constructively negotiating intellectual disagreement . . . seems to me a very good reason for giving us more practice at it."[11]

Perhaps only in their publications do professors open up. Jeffrey

Wallen's caustic account of the quality of discussion at academic public events is right on the mark:

> In our profession, our ways of disagreeing with each other are often pathetic. You sit through a fifty-minute talk, and at the end someone will sheepishly raise a few points that obscure rather than convey what the questioner really finds objectionable in the paper: it would be impolite to state forthrightly why one objects to what was said or to challenge the fundamental premises of the speaker. Or someone else, less restrained and more hostile, will blow off steam quibbling about some of the details of the talk in an effort to demonstrate her own greater learning and insight, but she will leave untouched the real ideas of the paper and whatever might be important in the line of thought that was developed: it would be professionally uncool to genuinely contest the spirit of the talk or to act as if there really were a lot at stake in what we say to each other.[12]

In my experience, the avoidance of disagreement Wallen describes here is more common among literary academics (many of whom grew up hearing that there is something inherently anti-literary about propositional discourse) than among their colleagues, say, in philosophy departments. But the attitude he describes—contestation is "uncool"—is certainly at least as pervasive as the combativeness deplored by Tannen.

When Tannen complains that college students are advised to look for someone to attack in order to generate a paper topic, I can only say, "Would it were so!" As I argue in several later chapters (especially 9–11), standard high school and college paper assignments tend to ask not for polemical opposition, but for rehearsals of information or for textual interpretations in a vacuum. My own students' writing seems to improve dramatically when I encourage them to "stake out a position in opposition" and provide them with help on how to do so. Once students are let in on the secret that most influential intellectual work— Tannen's included—springs from having something to contest, they can proceed with a clearer sense of their task. And once it is made clear that such contestation is necessary, teachers can then help their students learn to engage in it in ways that are not crudely abrasive and antagonistic.

Far from the excess of contentiousness that Tannen sees in today's classrooms, then, I find much too little. Classroom disagreement rarely moves beyond the trading of opinions and observations—Pythonesque "mere contradiction"—to enable differences to be worked through. Even the angry recent confrontations over differences of race, ethnicity, and gender have taken place mostly outside classrooms, where these differences are usually expressed in a noncontroversial airing of "alternative perspectives" and in the choice of assigned authors. The compositionist Joseph Harris rightly describes this evasive celebration of differences as "a kind of multicultural bazaar, where [students] are not so much brought into conflict with opposing views as placed in a kind of harmless connection with a series of exotic others."[13]

Learning becomes even more of a conflict-free zone when we move from the colleges to the schools. According to Arthur Powell, Eleanor Farrar, and David K. Cohen in their classic book *The Shopping Mall High School,* "conflict is rarely the way [high school] classroom participants come to terms with one another. . . . Agreement is far more common than antagonism . . . because peaceful coexistence seems preferable to outright conflict. . . . Teachers and students have . . . subtle ways of accommodating either differences or similarities: they arrange deals or treaties that promote mutual goals or that keep the peace." As one school administrator quoted in the book observes, "Interpretation, analysis, inference, main ideas are not part of our educational curriculum." Powell and his colleagues conclude that "avoiding those things was the essence of the treaty that students and teachers had willingly, if tacitly agreed upon."[14] This kind of classroom, which steers clear of disagreement, "main ideas," and other potential sources of trouble, seems far more recognizable and typical to me than the embattled classroom war zones described by Tannen.

Underlying the critique of the argument culture by Tannen and other feminists is a reaction against aggression and its excesses that has become all the easier to understand and sympathize with in a post–September 11 world. The question, however, is whether aggression can be successfully dealt with by disparaging conflict and the kind of debate in which there are winners and losers. In a fallen world, arguably, conflict and win/lose debate are inevitable. If I believe my government's policies are mean and destructive, I want my side to *win* the election—throw the rascals out—and I see no reason why I should be made to feel ashamed of this desire. (And if you think I should be ashamed of it, you will want to win this point of dispute with me.) Instead of trying to eliminate or repress the aggression that wells up in us when we fight for our beliefs, recognizing the unavoidability of such aggression might enable us to get it under control and prevent it from becoming violent and misdirected.

THE PEDAGOGICAL VALUE OF CRUDE DEBATE

Tannen's contradictory way of exemplifying the polemical spirit that she deplores suggests again that there is something unavoidable about the cultural centrality of argumentation and debate. This claim, which echoes a tradition of thought back to classical rhetoricians such as Aristotle and Quintilian, has been reasserted by many recent thinkers. One is Michael Billig, whose recent book, *Arguing and Thinking: A Rhetorical Approach to Social Psychology,* calls disagreement "the root of thought" itself. Thinking, writes Billig, "is a form of internal argument, modeled on outward dialogue; attitudes are rhetorical stances in matters of controversy. . . . To hold an attitude is to take a stance in a matter of controversy," "to make an argument *against* counterviews."[15]

The point is even more succinctly made in the title of a recent composition textbook: *Everything's an Argument,* edited by Andrea A. Lunsford and John J. Ruszkiewicz. As the editors put it: "All language, including the language of visual images or of symbol systems other than alphabetical letters—is persuasive, pointing in a direction and asking for response. From the morning news to the AIDS ribbon, from the American flag to the Nike swoosh, we are surrounded by texts that beckon, that aim to persuade. In short, we walk, talk, and breathe persuasion very much as we breathe the air: *everything* is an argument."[16] Lunsford and Ruszkiewicz distinguish between respectful disagreement that leads to shared explorations and mere fighting. They warn that argumentation need not be "agonistic or combative," nor need its goal be "to win out over others." Unlike Tannen, however, they see contentious debate as an unavoidable and normal state of affairs.[17]

Tannen might still object that the argument culture is too crudely polarized to be a positive force in education. She might argue, for example, that the Left/Right dualism that structures so much of our public debate is often a pseudo-opposition that conceals as much as it enlightens. In *Culture of Complaint,* a recent book on the culture wars, Robert Hughes describes the clash of cultural Left and Right as a "sterile confrontation," one that disguises the fact that "the two PCs—the politically and the patriotically correct"—need each another in order to justify their existence.[18] Hughes is right to point out the limits of the dualism, but his point would be lost on anyone who has not yet grasped the dualism to begin with. The opposition of Left vs. Right that sophisticated critics like Hughes justifiably want to get beyond may be one to which students and others have not yet been exposed.

To take another suspect dualism, the *New Republic* art critic Jed Perl has recently argued that "High-versus-low is a shopworn intellectual debate," one that is "of little interest to anybody who really cares" about the arts. Debating Mozart vs. the Beatles, for example, is "for the pedants who can't wait to turn off the music, all the better to hear the sounds of their own voices. The more that you're engrossed in different kinds of music (or different kinds of art), the less you're going to care for comparisons that are by their very nature too crude to tell you much of anything."[19] Perl may be right about the crudity of the High vs. Low dichotomy, but he can afford to dismiss it because he takes for granted its history and import. The high/low dualism that bores Perl is grasped only shakily by many students. When we disdain the crude binary oppositions of the culture war, we ignore the heuristic value of these oppositions for those who haven't yet mastered them.

For this reason, I would make a case for the pedagogical value even of "crude" debate, if only as a precondition of advancing subsequently to more nuanced, less reductively polarized conversations. Some debates are not worth entering, but if we shrink from entering debates generally because their quality never seems up to our standards, we are unlikely ever to produce better debates. In order to have good debates, we probably have to start by having bad ones and learn from the experience how to make them better.

Letting students in on the dirty little secret that they will do well in school if they learn to join the argument culture is just a beginning. Learning to play the game well is still an arduous task that won't seem at all gamelike to many students. At the least, however, educators will have cleared the air about what the game of schooling is ultimately about and what students need to do to survive it and flourish in it. And with luck, getting the argument game out in the open and acknowledging its inevitability will help us start playing it the way Deborah Tannen rightly wants—with less egotistical competition and more mutual respect.

5 Paralysis by Analysis?

FOR DEBORAH TANNEN, the trouble with contemporary intellectual life is that it is excessively angry and adversarial. For others in our culture, however, the trouble with contemporary intellectual life is that it is intellectual. Contemporary culture, it is said, has become so cerebral and analytic that it alienates us from our bodies, our pleasures, and our true selves. The problem is not too much polemical debate but too much analysis and dissection—not the argument culture but, as it might be called, the analysis culture.

The argument and analysis cultures are twins, however. Critiques of the two often overlap, as when certain feminists oppose "women's ways of knowing" to the alleged maleness both of adversarial debate and analytic thought. The eleventh graders I quoted in chapter 2 who expressed distaste for "overanalyzing" and "analyzing everything that happens to me" reflect an outlook that is pervasive among their elders as well. Like athletes who blame missed two-foot putts, batting slumps, and dropped touchdown passes on "paralysis by analysis," many of us fear that excessive self-consciousness prevents us from the peak performance we could achieve if we could get in touch with ourselves and go with the flow.

In this chapter, I take up three sources of discontent with the analysis culture, which is accused of inducing (a) calculating cold-bloodedness; (b) long-winded and pretentious explanation; and (c) the curse of secondariness or estrangement from firsthand experience. In each case, I suggest, the culprit is not analytical rationality but its mis-use. In the end I argue that it is futile to rebel against the analysis culture, a fact that may explain why we are so ambivalent about it. For the more insistently we worry about becoming too analytic and hyper-conscious about our lives, the more analytic and hyperconscious we become.

The failure to confront this ambivalence about analysis contributes significantly to bad education, either by letting anti-intellectualism in schools and colleges go unchallenged or by causing mixed signals about intellectualism to be sent to students who are already distrustful of it. Though students are told that it is good to analyze and criticize, they also infer that it's not good to wade in too deep and that the waters of analysis can be corrosive. At best, schools and colleges fail to make a convincing case for intellectualism, while at worst they reinforce the disastrous misconception that what makes schooling boring and alie-nating is not too little intellectual challenge, but too much.

HAIL TO THEE, NO-BRAINER

The revolt against the analysis culture in the twentieth century enlists a vast range of modern and postmodern artistic movements, bohemian and countercultural lifestyles, therapeutic cults, and New Age mysti-cisms. One of the popular poets and gurus of the anti-analytic attitude is Bob Dylan, particularly in his lyrics of the sixties. In "Love Minus Zero—No Limit," for example, Dylan contrasts his loved one with peo-ple who "Read books, recite quotations, / Draw conclusions on the wall. . . ." Unlike these members of the chattering classes, Dylan's lover "does not bother, / *She knows too much to argue or to judge*" (emphasis added). In "The Gates of Eden" Dylan sings of a lover who "tells me of her dreams, / *With no attempt to shovel the glimpse / Into the ditch of what each one means*" (emphasis added).[1] She doesn't fight against the analysis culture, which would only be to play its dirty rationalistic game. She is indifferent to it and therefore above it.

Paradoxically, though, to sing along with Dylan's celebration of his unselfconscious lover is not to be unselfconscious as she is, but to adopt an intellectual attitude. She may "know too much to argue or to judge," but we who idealize her, including Dylan himself, are inevitably caught up in arguing and judging, as Dylan is in arguing that her silence speaks volumes and in judging her superior to the chatterboxes around her.

None of this is to pick a quarrel with the jocks, who are probably often right that in their world too much conscious analysis prevents one from "staying focused" and who call a player who is doing everything right "unconscious." My own best performance in an organized basketball game—twenty-one points in a park league—occurred the one time I was able to hypnotize myself into pretending that the game was only practice. Normally I was so acutely aware of the importance of the game, the presence of the crowd, the presence of my father in it, and other distractions that I would choke and fire air balls. Unfortunately I was never again able to trick my mind into this state of indifference.

In an intriguing case of apparent paralysis by analysis, during the 2000 baseball season New York Yankee second baseman Chuck Knoblauch became unable to execute a short toss to first base that any little-leaguer could make with ease. Knoblauch's throwing problem became so acute that he was moved to the outfield and eventually traded. According to Stephen Jay Gould, some observers blamed Knoblauch's problem on "the intrusion of unwanted consciousness," an athletic equivalent of "writer's block."[2] Conversely, when such great football running backs as Gayle Sayers and Walter Payton were asked how they made their amazing open-field cuts and moves, they invariably answered that they had no idea, that instinct had taken over; had they had to think consciously about what they were doing they could never have done it.

Michael Jordan usually gave a similar answer when asked how he made such split-second court decisions as whether to drive to the hoop, to pull up for a jump shot, or to pass to an open teammate. Jimmy Johnson, coach of the Dallas Cowboys' back-to-back Super Bowl champions of 1992–93, credited the book *Flow: The Psychology of Optimal Experience,* by my former University of Chicago colleague, psychology professor Mihaly Csikszentmihali, for the theory that enabled the Cowboys' players to overcome their inhibitions and play more instinctually and effectively.[3] In his "Zen Christian" book, *Sacred Hoops: Spiritual Lessons of a Hardwood Warrior,* Phil Jackson, coach of the National Basketball Association champion Chicago Bulls and Los Angeles Lakers, describes stressing the importance to his players of "being fully present in each and every moment," blocking out thoughts that might distract them from the immediate play at hand.[4] These examples all suggest that top athletic performance tends to be, in an expression that has now migrated beyond sports, a no-brainer.

On the other hand, an opposing school of athletic thought maintains that sports success is not a no-brainer at all, but the result of intelligent planning and diligent practice. (The maxim that "luck is the residue of design" is often invoked here.) Gould ultimately sides with this cerebral view in the debate, arguing that "we surely err in regarding sports as a domain of brutish intuition," for the greatest athletes "must also perform with their heads."[5] Jordan had no peer because he was not only the most talented basketball player ever, but also one of the smartest and most hard-working. Jordan's ruthlessly driven behavior in practices became part of his legend. Jimmy Johnson and Phil Jackson may have won because they got their teams to go with the flow and stay present to the moment, but Johnson was noted for his shrewd evaluations of talent and Jackson for brilliant game preparation and strategy.

When Tiger Woods joined the professional golf tour at the age of twenty-one, the editors of *Golf Digest,* who had signed Woods to do instructional articles, did not expect so young a player to possess great understanding of swing mechanics, much less the ability to put those mechanics into words. The editors were amazed to find that Woods's "grasp of fundamentals was complete. His understanding of cause and effect in the full swing was astonishing and would grow even richer through time. What's more, his explanations were expansive, articulate and ordered perfectly. He quickly displayed a knack for phrasing his advice in a way that embraced the widest range of golfers possible."[6] It seems that for every instinctive Muhammad Ali or Willie Mays, there is a Tiger Woods, a Joe Louis, or a Pete Rose, stars who have also been students of their sport, or a Ted Williams, who combined raw talent with intense study. Williams is generally regarded as the greatest natural hitter in baseball history, but he also literally wrote the book—at least a well-known book—on hitting.[7]

But though paralysis by analysis afflicts intellectual workers as well as athletes—as the phenomenon of writer's block demonstrates—the differences ultimately stand out. No matter how much intelligence goes into it, superior athletic performance involves something different from composing arguments, analyses, sentences, and paragraphs. There may be instinctive expository writers, but expository writing is never a complete no-brainer. Gayle Sayers, Walter Payton, and Michael Jordan did not have to write books and essays on their athletic feats, and if they did have to the kinds of intelligence they showed on the field and the court would not have been much help to them. Even the books by Phil Jackson and Ted Williams had to be ghosted for them.

DOWN WITH CALCULATION?

A long tradition of thought, however, finds the analysis culture oppressive in every realm of behavior and desperately seeks to escape it. In the Dylan lyric, the saving alternative to rational thought is a woman, but it may also be children, peasants or other primitive types, Gypsies, bums, and other vagabonds, non-Westerners, dumb animals (preferably birds), bullfighters, outlaws, artists, and anyone lucky enough to have lived before the coming of modern industrial civilization. This idealization of the pre- or nonintellectual is a major theme of the European romantics. Shelley railed against "the selfish and calculating principle" and longed for the unpremeditated happiness of the skylark; Wordsworth complained that with "our meddling intellect. . . . We murder to dissect"; Friedrich Schiller in *Naive and Sentimental Poetry* half-longed for the "naive" prereflective bliss of premodern societies.[8] Even as the romantics longed to be primitive, however, they bitterly recognized that their very longing only betrayed how far they were from true primitives, who have no need to romanticize what they already are. George Santayana summed up the double bind of romantic primitivism when he tartly noted that "the notion of recovering innocence is a contradiction in terms. . . . Savages were never rudimentary on purpose."[9]

In denouncing selfish calculation and murderous dissection, romantic literati like Shelley and Wordsworth were striking back against the twin juggernauts of modern science, with its arrogant claim to superior knowledge and cultural authority, and industrial commerce, with its habit of making utility and profit the measure of all things. This revolt against the alienating effects of science and commerce focused on what twentieth-century social critics of the Frankfurt School have called "instrumental" rationality, a type of thinking that is so exclusively concerned with means, technique, and efficiency that it washes its hands of any concern with moral ends.[10] This critique of instrumental reason was clearly directed at amoral *misuses* of reason that were not really rational at all. But, by a kind of philosophical guilt by association, the critique readily became broadened into a sweeping condemnation of rationality itself, which was seen as inherently instrumental and therefore evil.

Instrumental rationality, in other words, and its identification with amoral science and commerce, gave intellectual analysis itself a bad name. Shelley, for example, in calling the calculating principle "selfish," implies that it is not only narrow economic calculation that is egotistical, but the reasoning intellect itself, whereas Wordsworth's "we murder to dissect" implies that there is something murderous about all analytic dissection, not just some amoral misuses of it. For many romantics, then, the remedy for instrumental reason was not a more morally enlightened use of reason that takes ends as well as means into account (this was the moral rationality that had been admired from Plato and Aristotle to Samuel Johnson), but the poetic imagination, which was celebrated for having severed diplomatic relations with science and commerce. When W. H. Auden wrote that "poetry makes nothing happen,"[11] he was reflecting this romantic tradition that defines poetry negatively as everything the degraded utilitarian world of practical action is not.

Among the results of this romantic battle between poetic creativity and scientific-industrial reason was the now conventional bifurcation of the academic disciplines into sciences and humanities. The split has often been harmful to both arts and science education, to say nothing of modern culture, especially when it dissociates both art and science from critical rationality, leaving art to be seen as a kind of vacation from rigorous thinking while science becomes a moral imbecile with a calculator. The arts and humanities are defined as soft, antiintellectual, and "caring," while the sciences are defined as hard, value-free, and devoid of conscience and feeling.

Still another product of this bifurcation of fact and instrumental reason vs. "values" is the conflict between "traditional" and "progressive" educational philosophies, an opposition that is especially disabling when it severs the teaching of disciplined critical thought from the teaching of imagination and creativity. The most notorious classroom embodiment of the rationalistic side of this dichotomy is Charles Dickens's schoolteacher Thomas Gradgrind in *Hard Times,* whose credo goes: "Teach these boys and girls nothing but Facts. Facts alone are wanted in life. Plant nothing else, and root out everything else. You can only form the minds of reasoning animals upon Facts: nothing else will ever be of any service to them." Gradgrind sees his students as "little pitchers . . . to be filled so full of facts" that they become "a kind of cannon loaded to the muzzle with facts." As Dickens's narrator comments, Gradgrind sees students as "a galvanizing apparatus, . . . charged with a grim mechanical substitute for the tender young imaginations that were to be stormed away."

Gradgrind's compulsion is to stamp out imagination wherever it threatens to break out. Asking his students for the definition of a horse, he disallows the answer of Sissy Jupe, "girl number twenty" in his classifying system, who defines the word by evoking the personal meaning of horses for herself and her family. "Girl number twenty unable to define a horse!" Gradgrind declares, praising instead the answer given by young Bitzer, who knows how to give the teacher what he wants:

"Quadruped. Gramniverous. Forty teeth, namely, twenty-four grinders, four eye-teeth, and twelve incisive. Sheds coat in the spring; in marshy countries, sheds hoofs, too. Hoofs hard, but requiring to be shod with iron. Age known by marks in mouth."

"Now girl number twenty," says Mr. Gradgrind. "You know what a horse is."[12]

As a representative intellectual, Gradgrind is clearly a *reductio ad absurdum*, having no interest whatsoever in ideas, arguments, or analysis. But anyone who recoils against the grim regimen of modern schooling can easily be tempted to identify Gradgrind's positivistic hatred of creativity and imagination with any form of education that emphasizes intellectual rigor. Dickens's caricature thus helped pave the way for those versions of twentieth-century progressive education that see intellectual rigor as inimical to the heart and the feelings.

I say "those versions" of progressive education because, contrary to recent critics like Sandra Stotsky, Rita Kramer, and Diane Ravitch, not all forms of progressive education have been anti-intellectual.[13] Many commentators have pointed out that John Dewey consistently warned his followers against confusing child-centered education with the abandonment of intellectual standards and the assumption that anything children think or do is correct.[14] As Laurence Cremin comments in his standard history of progressive education, *The Transformation of the School,* "One wonders at the incredible distortions that have marked contemporary assessments of Dewey's role in the development of progressive education."[15]

But Dewey's warnings against mindless forms of child-centeredness went unheeded by progressive educators like Hughes Mearns, who in the twenties developed a "theory of permittings" that regarded the child as a natural creative artist who hardly needed instruction at all. "The modern discovery of the child as artist, . . ." Mearns wrote, "is coincident with the realization of the beauty of primitive art generally. The child is a genuine primitive. He needs little or no instruction."[16] As Cremin observes, "in too many [progressive] classes license began to pass for liberty, planlessness for spontaneity, recalcitrance for originality, obfuscation for art, and chaos for education. And thus was born at least one of the several caricatures of progressive education."[17] Cremin is right to call the equation of progressivism with anti-intellectualism a caricature: not all educational progressivism has been anti-intellectual, and some is better described as ambivalent.

An instructive recent example of this ambivalence is found in Jane Tompkins's recent autobiography, *A Life in School.* Tompkins, whose eloquent description of the excitement of intellectual passion I quoted in chapter 2, laments the complete absence of that kind of passion in her early schooling. She observes, for example, that in her elementary school, though she had been assigned to a class for the "Intellectually Gifted," she and most of her classmates "were not challenged or stimulated."[18] In graduate school at Yale, she was disappointed that "there was no intellectual debate to speak of. . . . Scholars had vendettas against other scholars, . . . [b]ut there were no critical debates that cut across periods and specialties" (81). On the occasions when Tompkins does encounter intense intellectual passion, she revels in it, as she describes doing when one exceptional teacher allows her to experience "the pure joy of thinking," and another provides her with an attractive model of "powerful intellect, moral idealism, and strength of will" (57–58). Later, at the School of Criticism and Theory (with her future husband, Stanley Fish), "the sheer excitement of it was unlike anything I'd ever experienced; it was intellectual and it was visceral at the same time" (101).

At these moments, Tompkins sees no incompatibility between being fully intellectual and fully "visceral." In her words, it is "not a question of repressing or cutting back on intellectual inquiry in school, but rather of acknowledging and cultivating wholeness" (213). At this point a reader might think that Tompkins's remedy for bad or nonexistent intellectual community in schools and universities would be a *better* intellectual community. As Tompkins moves through her story, however, she comes increasingly to wonder if intellectuality is reconcilable with emotional and physical wholeness. She becomes convinced that intellectual engagement is necessarily vitiated by ambition, professionalism, competitiveness, and what she feels in her own teaching to be egotistical showing off. Tompkins identifies intellectual distinction with the professional success rat race and the pressures on students "to perform in a way that would get them approval from their parents and their peers" (209). In the end, then, instead of seeking to replace bad forms of intellectual life with more authentic ones, Tompkins winds up locating her alternative in transcendental meditation, massage, walks in the woods, and the self-help books of Hugh Prather and others (117).

By the end of her book, Tompkins is writing as if intellectual passion and emotional "wholeness" were a zero-sum game in which one can advance only if the other retreats. Tompkins describes feeling oppressed, for example, by "a hypertrophy of the intellect and will" in the university that leads to "an undernourished heart" (212). It is not surprising, then, when she concludes that assuming intellectual authority as a teacher silences her students. Tompkins says she tries to "curb my impulse to correct the students, to show them the way, because when I do it shuts them up" (146). Tompkins is surely right that the forms of intellectuality that dominate educational institutions are often arid, narrowly competitive, and alienating. But it is unfortunate that she decides that intellectuality is part of the problem rather than part of the solution.

DOWN WITH EXPLANATION?

As I noted above, the postromantic backlash against analysis is often a reaction against the cold-blooded rationality ascribed to science, commerce, and technology. For those who would blame cultural malaise on excessive intellectualism, however, the advance of the mass media and what Frankfurt School critics called the culture industry provides another set of targets. These include editorialists, media pundits, talking heads, policy wonks, academics, and other experts whose theories and methodologies claim to explain everything from global warming to road rage. The popular media have done much to give analysis and explanation a bad name.

The antipathy toward explainers expresses a weariness with the sociological, psychological, and philosophical profundities that in a media society inexorably follow in the wake of news events and cultural trends. As early as the thirties, James Thurber satirized the newly popular vogue of psychoanalysis and self-help therapies in a book significantly titled *Let Your Mind Alone*.[19] In the sixties the protagonist of Saul Bellow's novel *Herzog* (1965) jeered at the twentieth-century "dream of intellect, the delusion of total *explanations*,"[20] and Jules Feiffer, the cartoonist of neurotic urban life, titled one of his satiric collections *The*

Explainers.[21] Bellow continues to fulminate against explainers in his recent novel, *Ravelstein,* whose hero (based on the late Allan Bloom) complains that "the gray net of abstraction covering the world in order to simplify and explain it . . . has *become* the world in our eyes."[22]

The backlash against media pseudo-explanation has intensified in the nineties, as the growth of cable TV has increased the volume of media analysis that surrounds a given event. One need only mention the avalanche of coverage directed at events such as the O. J. Simpson trials, the slaughter of the Branch Davidians in Waco, Texas, the deaths of Princess Diana and John F. Kennedy, Jr., the Oklahoma City bombing, the Clinton/Lewinski scandal, the Florida election controversy of 2000, the Gary Condit/Chandra Levy scandal, and of course the September 11 terrorist attacks on the World Trade Center and the Pentagon. The appearance of an essay collection by academics on "the cultural meanings of Monica" elicited a sardonic *New York Times* headline: "You Knew This Was Next: Monica 101."[23] The saturation coverage of such events has intensified the mounting reaction against "the natterati," "the chattering classes," "bloviators," the "punditariat," and "punditocracy," in the new coinages that reflect this reaction.

An interesting example of the backlash against the hypertrophy of explanation was a short opinion piece, entitled "Don't Mean Diddly," that appeared in the *New Yorker* in 1994, at the height of the furor over the Simpson trial. The author of the piece (which was unsigned) complained of the growing tendency of the media to attribute profound cultural meanings to ephemeral events like the Simpson case. It went on to see this trend as a symptom of our culture's insatiable hunger for deep meanings even when they are bogus. As the writer put it, we Americans "no longer believe in the integrity of events; that is, we are no longer able to accept events at their own value . . . but must see them as episodes in a drama, by some unknown author." The writer continued: "The growth of a paranoid style of explanation—the belief that the truth is hidden beneath the surface of events—has become absolute. Everybody accepts the idea that the truth is hidden. The prizes, in the academy and on the cable box alike, now go to people who can claim, however absurdly, to have detected the real complexion of events behind a mask of particulars that are mere cosmetics."[24] Having taught literature for more than thirty years, I could not help recognizing something eerily familiar here. I had long been used to hearing students grumble about the "hidden meanings" that my colleagues and I dug from—they would say forced on—novels, plays, and, more recently, advertisements and TV sitcoms. What was novel about the argument of "Don't Mean Diddly," however, was the suggestion that the main perpetrators of dubious hidden-meaning talk were no longer academics and highbrows, but the media.

What was new, that is, was the writer's conflation of "the academy" and "the cable box." Indeed, the writer put the blame for the media's overinterpretation of the Simpson case on the academic "cultural-studies business,"[25] as he or she called the loose confederation of feminists, queer theorists, semioticians, deconstructionists, and media analysts that makes up today's academic vanguard. I confess that having lately become used to seeing trendy professors abused in the press for trying to emulate media stars, I felt a cheap satisfaction at seeing media stars abused for emulating professors.

Pundits will dispute whether academics have sold out to the media or the media has sold out to the academy, or whether the issue is really one of selling out at all. What seems clear is that the anonymous *New Yorker* writer was onto something in pointing out the new convergence between the media and the academy around a common interest in cultural generalizations. As I suggested in chapter 1, if journalists and academics are increasingly at each other's throats—as they have been in the culture war—this is because they are now more than ever in the same business, competing for the role of explaining the culture to itself.

I am not persuaded, however, by the sweeping charge of "Don't Mean Diddly," that facile and meretricious explanations are the only results of the new academic/journalistic alliance. Not that such charges are never justified, but distinctions need to be made. It does not seem obviously foolish to think the Simpson case harbored important meanings for a range of issues including domestic violence, police brutality and racism, the American deification of athletic stars and other celebrities, the proper responsibility of the media in reporting trials, and the disturbing discrepancies in the confidence felt by many whites and blacks in the fairness of the American legal system. The article's suggestion that we somehow accept events like the Simpson case "at their own value" instead of looking for meanings in them sounds rather like an injunction to shut up and go along with the conventionally accepted meanings, that is, to quit thinking. In this connection, there was something disconcerting about the essay's folksy title—"Don't Mean Diddly"—with its echoes of good-ol'-boy populist anti-intellectualism, presumably answering back the pontifications of fancy-pants, pointy-headed elitists.

Indeed, the folksy title obscured the fact that the piece went on to indulge in the very intellectualism that it railed at. In arguing that deep-think readings of the Simpson case are symptoms of "a paranoid style of explanation" and a sign that Americans "no longer believe in the integrity of events," the essay only added one more deep-think explanation to the glut. As the passages I have quoted clearly indicate, "Don't Mean Diddly" is written not in the down-home idiom of its title, but in an intellectual register that is indistinguishable from that of the over-analyzing eggheads it satirizes. I verified this observation when I circulated "Don't Mean Diddly" to a class of college undergraduates and found that for many the essay was not significantly less opaque than writings by cultural studies theorists like Michel Foucault. Several, for example, were at a loss to decode phrases like "paranoid style of explanation" and "the cultural studies business." I bet that any reader who wants to try my test that "Don't Mean Diddly"—like most academic writing—will look much the same to students and parents for whom such intellectual discussions *really* don't mean diddly because they are incomprehensible. The point, however, is that even an essay that objects to the overintellectualized talk of academia and the media ends up exemplifying the power and prestige of that talk. Slams at "pundits" and "punditocracy" may often be deserved, but it takes another pundit to slam one.

Just as the information economy and the culture industry increasingly reward the skills of abstract verbalization and argumentation, cultural power is more and more wielded by those who can speak and write cogently—in venues like the *New Yorker*—on the hidden meanings of texts, trials, and cultural trends. Precisely due to the increasing saturation of both the media and the academy with power talk about hidden meanings, it seems more important than ever that schools and colleges train citizens who can detect the difference between genuine versions of such talk and pseudo-intellectual blather, and who can convey their judgments persuasively.

DOWN WITH SECONDARINESS?

I observed above that since the romantic period, the arts have often been defined as an alternative to the culture of instrumental rationality and media overexplanation. I also suggested that this way of thinking about art suggests why arts education is often anti-intellectual, conceived as it is as an oasis from the kind of analysis and intellectuality that otherwise supposedly dominates our culture. An unfortunate split runs through arts education, reflecting the romantic culture war between creators and critics, between the teaching of art "itself" and the teaching of art criticism.

Ambivalence toward the critical analysis of art reappears on both sides of today's culture war. For many traditionalists, the assumption is that a great masterpiece is so powerful that it cannot help making an impact on any student who can be brought to read it carefully. If students do not read or read poorly, the argument goes, it is not more exposure to criticism they need, but more attention to the great texts themselves. On the progressive side, the assumption often is that the students' spontaneous responses should be celebrated even if they are not—or especially if they are not—expressed in literate terms. If students are alienated from argumentation and analysis, the remedy is to switch to more personal and autobiographical assignments. Though opposed, these views agree in emphasizing the need to keep students' encounters with artworks as unmediated as possible.

The grain of truth in this view is that good reading does have to be rooted in a student's primary experience of a text or work. But if that experience is to mature and be stretched beyond the place where it already is, it needs a critical vocabulary in which to express itself. It is therefore misleading to oppose the firsthand experience of reading to secondhand critical analysis *about* our reading. How we talk about books shapes how we read the books themselves.

The recognition that book-talk fulfills a need helps explain the fast-growing popularity of organized book discussion groups as well as the success of Borders and Barnes and Noble as gathering places. At a time when the public conversation about books has become attenuated, people feel a special need to share their reading experiences with others. Brian Hall makes the point in a recent essay on the reading-group trend: "Talking with friends about books harks back to the original impulse behind storytelling, the forging of human bonds. We have told ourselves stories not just, in Joan Didion's phrase, in order to live, but in order to live with one another."[26] As Hall's comments suggest, primary storytelling itself is insufficient for the "forging of human bonds," for audiences need to talk about the stories they read and to compare their interpretations in order to be sure that they have read the same story. The more isolated from one another readers feel, the more they need such secondary conversations in order to establish a bond with other readers.

As an example of the attraction of reading groups, Hall cites David Denby's book *Great Books,* an account of Denby's return to Columbia University in 1991 to reenroll in the humanities core courses he had taken as a freshman thirty years earlier. Hall quotes Denby's explanation that he returned to college because he was "sick at heart," sick of "that immense system of simulacra" of a modern media society, what he later calls, discussing the Bible, "the aureole of second-handedness that gathers around memory in the late twentieth century and finally replaces it."[27] There is something odd, however, about Denby's dissatisfaction with the "aureole of second-handedness" around his reading experience, which resembles the "Don't Mean Diddly" author's impatience with Americans' unwillingness to accept "events at their face value." Just as it is strange to think you can counter a cultural explanation glut by explaining it in a magazine essay, it is strange to think you can dissolve an aureole of second-handedness about your reading by enrolling in college courses, where reading is inevitably steeped in second-hand discussion. If Denby really wanted to avoid second-handedness, he would have done better to read the books at home.

Yet even had Denby locked himself in his room at home, his "primary" reading experience would still have been adulterated by all the "secondary" reviews and critical essays and conversations to which he

had been exposed in his life. And luckily so, since, without that secondary experience and the models it provided, Denby would never have
been able to write *Great Books,* which is not only a powerful evocation
of how it feels to reread the classics, but a thoughtful intervention in
current culture war debates over humanities study, the canon, and
other topics. Again, this is not to minimize the importance of Denby's
primary experience of the great books, but rather to point out that such
experience is necessarily impure, already contaminated by critical discourse. That is why it's a mistake to oppose the primary experience of
reading to secondary book-talk, especially if you are yourself producing
more secondary book-talk like Denby's *Great Books.*

The increasing inability of a media-saturated culture to shelter any
area of experience from secondary forms of self-consciousness calls
into question the old opposition between intellectuals and the unculti-
vated mass. Harold Rosenberg made the point over thirty years ago in
a provocative essay that he titled "Everyman a Professional" but that he
might have titled "Everyman an Intellectual." "In actuality," Rosenberg
wrote,

> there exists no such thing as an "uncultivated mass." If
> there is anyone in America who has managed to elude being
> educated by free compulsory schools and by the millions of
> pictures and written and spoken words poured into every
> crevice of this country hourly, he is so hard to catch he may
> be written off as prospective audience material. Today, every-
> body is already a member of some intellectually worked-over
> group, that is, an audience. And in the sense that it is liter-
> ate, selective, and self-conscious in its taste, every audience
> is an audience of intellectuals. Science fiction, tabloid sports
> columns, rock 'n' roll gab, the New Criticism, presuppose
> various levels of technical preparation and familiarity with
> terminology on the part of their readers.[28]

Granted, Rosenberg exaggerates. Though there is indeed a sense in
which followers of sports columns and rock 'n' roll gab are intellectuals,
they would not all answer to the label. Nevertheless, Rosenberg's

deeper point is valid, that to live in today's culture is to be "a member of some intellectually worked-over group" and to speak a version of its language.

The title of a well-known poem by Wallace Stevens, "Not Ideas About the Thing But the Thing Itself," concisely sums up our cultural weariness with analysis, secondariness, and "aboutness."[29] Yet Stevens's eloquence notwithstanding, it is time to call a truce in the old warfare between primary experience, seen as supposedly separable from intellectual interference, and secondary talk about experience, seen as devoid of creative and personal qualities. Like its twin the argument culture, the analysis culture is here to stay.

PART III: COMMUNICATIVE DISORDERS

6 Unlearning to Write

ANY ACCOUNT OF THE STUPEFYING feeling of cluelessness academia induces in many people needs to address the state of academic writing, where academic habits of communication appear in full dress. For those who are aware that it exists, academic writing—the writing professors publish—tends to mean bad writing—turgid, pretentious, jargon-ridden, and humorless, stuff nobody would write or read who wasn't trying to get tenure. To be sure, a lot of academic writing (not yours or mine, of course) richly merits these scornful epithets. Many academics themselves will tell you that you compromise your career if you write in ways that nonacademics can understand.

Once upon a time there was surely more than a grain of truth in this view, and if you think there still is you can easily find plenty of examples of current academic writing to prove you right. Those examples, however, will no longer represent the whole story. Not only has accessible writing become permissible in today's academia, but it actually gives one an edge, I believe, in being heard and exerting influence.

Does anyone think, for example, that Henry Louis Gates compromised his academic career by writing lucid prose like the following in this passage from his book *Loose Canons*? Gates is discussing the academic theory that terms like "black" and "homosexual" are "socially constructed" concepts with no real referent:

> Now, if there's no such thing as a homosexual, then homophobia, at least as directed toward people rather than acts, loses its rationale. But you can't respond to the discrimination against gay people by saying, "I'm sorry, I don't exist; you've got the wrong guy." The simple historical fact is, Stonewall was necessary, concerted action was necessary to take action against the very structures that, as it were, called the homosexual into being, that subjected certain people to this imaginary identity. To reverse Audre Lorde, *only* the master's tools will ever dismantle the master's house.[1]

The passage presupposes an academic audience that knows who Audre Lorde is and is familiar with her ideas, an audience accustomed to usages like "the very structures that, as it were, called the homosexual into being." Yet it also draws vitality from colloquialisms like "you've got the wrong guy."

I wrote in my first chapter that a battle has been raging for the soul of academia between a view that sees academic culture as inherently esoteric and specialized and a view that aspires to "outreach" and greater influence on the wider society. In current academic writing, this battle is reflected in a division between academic and vernacular voices, a division to which many academics respond, as Gates here does, by sensibly refusing to choose, and having it both ways.

"Oh sure," you say. "But Gates was a tenured full professor, not to mention an academic superstar when he wrote that. It's easy for established academics like you to tell your junior and part-time colleagues and your grad students to lighten up, but if they wrote the way Gates does (assuming they could find the time in their killer teaching schedules to write), they would be ostracized." Perhaps this is the case, but then one can be ostracized for writing turgidly as well as in the vernacular. There's a danger of talking ourselves into the belief that we can't get away with writing accessibly when the old prohibitions against doing so are actually dissolving.

Gates's passage is just one example of a new vernacular voice that has been creeping into academic prose, the kind of voice academics have often used when not on the job but up to now have tended to keep out of their writing. Jeffrey Williams has provided a useful overview of the recent turn of some academics toward autobiography, personal narrative, and writing that seems closer to journalism than to traditional scholarly prose, a trend that Williams calls "the *journalization* of academic criticism."[2] He cites a range of examples, including books such as Michael Bérubé's *Public Access: Literary Theory and American Cultural Politics* and *Life as We Know It: A Father, a Family, and an Exceptional Child*, Cornel West's *Race Matters*, Laura Kipnis's *Bound and Gagged: Pornography and the Politics of Fantasy in America*, Richard Rorty's *Achieving Our Country: Leftist Thought in Twentieth Century America*, Andrew Ross's *The Celebration Chronicles: Life, Liberty, and the Pursuit of Property Value in Disney's New Town*, Nancy Miller's *Getting Personal*, James Phelan's *Beyond the Tenure Track*, Alice Kaplan's *French Lessons*, Cathy Davidson's *36 Views of Mount Fuji*, Frank Lentricchia's *The Edge of Night*, Gates's *Colored People*, Marianna Torgovnick's *Crossing Ocean Parkway*, bell hooks's *Born Black: Memories of Girlhood* and *Wounds of Passion: A Writing Life*, Jane Tompkins's *A Life in School: What the Teacher Learned*, Tobin Siebers's *Among Men*, and Eve Kosofsky Sedgwick's *A Dialogue on Love*.[3] Williams also mentions the collection *Confessions of the Critics*, edited by H. Aram Veeser, and one could add Lennard Davis's *My Sense of Silence: Memoirs of a Childhood with Deafness* as well as Davis's novel *The Sonnets*.[4] As we'll see in the next chapter, the new vernacularism isn't limited to literary academics either.

THE MYTH OF ACADEMIC SPECIALIZATION

All this is well and good, you say, but let's face it, isn't most academic research even more *overspecialized* than it ever was? Not really: if academic research is *over*-anything, it is *overgeneralized*, seeing that the highest rewards now go to scholars who make big, ambitious, interdisciplinary claims, leaving only the crumbs for those do creditable work that has a more modest agenda.

Though research still rules, what counts as "research" has changed dramatically over the last century in ways that elevate generality and downgrade specialism. A history of academic research since the turn of the century would be a story of progressive enlargement in the definition of research.[5] In 1916, the state-of-the-art research topic in the humanities was something along the lines of "The Syntax of *at* and *ana* in Gothic, Old Saxon, and Old High German," the actual title, in fact, of a University of Chicago Ph.D. dissertation completed that year. This situation changed with the expansion and democratization of universities after World War II. Most of the research done in today's humanities departments would not have qualified as research at all by the narrow understanding of the term in force before World War II. In the humanities, interpretive criticism—which now is considered "traditional" but was once a subversive innovation—and creative writing are two prominent examples.

The most striking evidence of the rising prestige of generalist models of research is reflected in academic publishing, where change has been driven by the marketplace as well as by shifts in intellectual fashions. Until the early seventies, the role of university presses had been to subsidize the kind of scholarly work whose market was too small to interest a commercial publisher. With the relaxation of the Cold War in the seventies, along with a recession, the funds began to dry up that the American government had poured into universities after the Soviet Union launched the Sputnik satellite in 1957. As government financial support for higher education waned, university presses had to think more commercially in making publishing decisions, to market their lists more aggressively, and to copy trade-press advertising techniques.

The effect was to reduce the publishability of scholarly books that speak solely to specialists and to increase that of books that address wider audiences, even if still mainly academic ones. The book addressed to specialists could still be published, but only if its author brought out larger implications of the subject for readers beyond the immediate field. We need only glance at the book advertisements of academic presses to see that academic research is now far more likely to flaunt its broad-gauged general appeal than its specialism. Though esoteric titles can still be found, more common are titles that focus on a specific topic but indicate a more generalized import: *Building New*

Democracies: Economic and Social Reform in Brazil, Chile, and Mexico; Tales Out of School: Gender, Longing, and the Teacher in Fiction and Film.

Consider this advertisement for *Tales Out of School*, by Jo Keroes: "Keroes' major contribution . . . is to (quite deftly) use literary and film criticism as tools for exposing the power and gender politics that shape and reflect modern society" (Southern Illinois University Press). Whereas fifty years ago such scholarship was expected to find a tiny hole in the corner of the field and "cover" it in a scrupulous but limited way, the point now is to make a provocative or major statement about a big subject like race, democracy, or justice. It is not that specialization has vanished, but that its larger payoff (the "So what?" or "Who cares?" question) is flaunted.

To be sure, breathless prose about major statements and provocative breakthroughs is often as empty in the promotion of scholarly writing as it is in other areas of marketing. Then, too, the need to make a major statement in order to get a job, a grant, tenure, or even admission to a graduate program puts premature pressure on younger scholars to come up with the grand synthesis, to cross boundaries, and to shatter the ways in which others have previously thought about the subject. And today this pressure falls on young scholars at the very moment when the academic job market is at its worst. Nevertheless, I would argue that it is not a bad thing that the doctoral candidate who in 1945 might have written a dissertation on "Certain Aspects of Robert Southey's Juvenilia" would in 1990 be likely to write one on "The Construction of Gender in the Discourse of Romanticism." Granted, it is better to write a modest but solidly researched book on Southey's juvenilia than to churn out heavy-breathing nonsense on gender and romanticism. The quality of execution being equal, however, I think most students would rather take a course from a scholar whose intellectual reach may exceed his grasp on an ambitious topic than from one who has chosen a safer but more limited one. And though the charges of mere trendiness against current research are often merited, those who make them forget that the older forms of research—which are now held up as a model of integrity from which we have fallen—were in their own time widely ridiculed for their pedantry, intellectual timidity, and irrelevance. Even when research fails to live up to its author's or publisher's pretensions, the fact that generality and broad impact are now valued seems to me a sign that we expect academic work be more culturally significant than we once did.

It is these changes that have paved the way for the new vernacularism in academic writing, though the books that academic presses promote as paradigm-smashing "major contributions" are not always written in vernacular styles and may indeed be unreadable by nonspecialists. Indeed, the fact that academic writing on broad issues of *general* concern is often couched in specialized *vocabularies* helps explain why academic writing still looks specialized even though its subjects and arguments no longer really are.

Here is where the incorporation of a vernacular voice into academic writing marks a significant change, though the trend has obvious risks. Nobody looks more foolish than an academic straining to get down with the folk or with his or her students. In *The Pooh Perplex,* Frederick Crews parodied an older version of this academic type, whom he called Murphy A. Sweat: "Today I want to tell you guys about a terrific book that you all ought to read for the final exam, if you haven't already. It's very very big in the English tradition, and has lots of really key things in it. It's called *Winnie-the-Pooh,* and it was written by Al Milne, an English 'chap' who took quite a liking to me when I went to see him after the War."[6] Despite the danger of falling into the Murphy Sweat mode, the appearance of a vernacular voice in academic writing seems to me a promising development for education, if you agree that improving education requires closing the gap between teacher talk and student talk.

ROACH MOTELS

Among the things that occasioned the above thoughts was the first and only reference I have ever encountered in an academic publication to "roach motels." In case you haven't noticed one in your supermarket or hardware store, a roach motel is a pesticide-filled receptacle that's used to trap and kill cockroaches. The packaging depicts a large leering insect creeping through the door of a motel room, above which runs the slogan, "Roaches check in, but they don't check out."

The academic reference to roach motels appears in Michael Bérubé's book *Marginal Forces, Cultural Centers: Tolson, Pynchon, and the Politics of the Canon*. In the book Bérubé challenges the opposition between center and margin that has dominated recent discussions of literary canonization. He argues that "access to the cultural center" need not mean being co-opted or corrupted, since such access also presents an "opportunity to reconstruct the cultural center."[7] The point leads Bérubé to take issue with critics who assume that when countercultural writers like Thomas Pynchon are taught in universities, their subversive power is inevitably domesticated and robbed of its critical impact on the culture outside. In the eyes of these critics, Bérubé writes, the academy is a kind of "necropolis" where would-be transgressive art goes to die. It is as if universities were like "roach motels, never letting out what they let in."[8]

Bérubé is not lining up with conservative critics of the humanities who recommend plain speech as an antidote to theoretical jargon. Like Henry Louis Gates, he has things both ways by combining the vernacular with the language of theory and cultural studies: "I wrote in my opening chapter that insofar as American critics ask writers of different ethnicities to assume different burdens of representation, canonization is a different affair for different writers. Am I saying now that canons don't kill people, people kill people? that canonicity is neutral, like technology, and that only its human uses are good or bad? Let me not be misunderstood."[9] Just as Bérubé assumes that a writer may become canonical without necessarily selling out, his prose illustrates that it is possible to write like a professional academic without sounding like a machine or a zombie. One can have "canonicity" and roach motels in the same paragraph.

BECOMING A MAN ON WHOM NOTHING IS LOST

So far as I know, roach motels did not yet exist when I did my graduate work in English and American literature at Stanford from 1959 to 1963. But if they had they certainly would not have fit into my picture of what was possible in academic writing. My graduate training taught me that for my writing to qualify as scholarly and academic, I had to sound markedly different from how I sounded when I conversed with nonacademics or even with my academic colleagues in informal situations. "Sophisticated" was the word most frequently used to denote the tone you were to strive for. Not that any of my professors took me aside and told me to sound sophisticated, much less advised me on how to do so. On the contrary, being sophisticated meant that you already *knew* such things—if you had to be told you would never make it. Graduate school sophistication was like class privilege as described by George Orwell in his essay "Such, Such Were the Joys": the whole point was to *already* have it by inheritance; if you had to struggle and work for it, it was tainted.[10]

In your writing, the main object was to make it seem that you not only knew everything worth knowing about your subject—if you didn't, how did you justify writing about it?—but that you had "of course" thought of everything that could be said about it. (The "of course" trope was satirized by W. B. Scott in a parody of the 1940s, in which a literary critic anguishes over the placement of "of course" in the first sentence of his essay in progress: "James could not, of course, have foreseen the hydrogen bomb." "James could not have foreseen the hydrogen bomb, of course.")[11] This pose of total knowingness had taken a new twist with the advent of the New Critics, who had challenged the older generation of scholars after World War II and who were still relative newcomers when I began graduate school. The rising prestige of the "critic" added a new pressure on the would-be professor, who now had to seem not only deeply learned, like the old-fashioned "scholars," but also brilliantly analytic, with a mind teeming with "insights" into texts and everything else. Before World War II, the image of the research scholar had allowed—or even encouraged—professors to be mentally ponderous and slow, by contrast with the "intellectuals," who were mostly journalists and accordingly dismissed by academics. The rise of criticism as an academic mode legitimated the intellectual in the academy. The academic critic was supposed to be not only learned, but smart and quick on the draw, "one of the people on whom nothing is lost," as Henry James had urged aspiring novelists to try to be.[12]

James's fiction and criticism, whose academic prestige was at its peak when I arrived at graduate school, helped to define the new professional ideal for aspiring academic critics. Being professional meant

sounding omniscient, clever, and, above all, incapable of being surprised. (Paul de Man would subsequently replace James as the model
of imperturbability for many academics.) It was this authoritative tone
that I learned to aim for when I wrote my seminar papers, my doctoral
dissertation, and eventually my first articles and books, the tone of a
shrewd, penetrating intelligence who, of course, was two or three
jumps ahead of everybody else. There was no place for my everyday
personality and voice, which would have threatened the facade I was
trying so hard to construct. The need to keep up this pretense of omniscience helps account for the feeling of being a fraud that still haunts
many academics.

To get a sense of what the academy at that time could do to a prose
style, consider the strange case of Norman Maclean, a professor from
whom I took a course at the University of Chicago in the late fifties
who, after his retirement, turned to writing fiction and published the
best-seller *A River Runs Through It*. It is revealing to compare the ele-
phantine style of Maclean's scholarly writing in the following example
from an article of the early fifties on *King Lear* (1), with the Hemingway-
esque prose Maclean wrote once he retired (2):

> 1. The problem of artistic consummation, being the problem
> of magnitude in the highest degree, is imperilled by its own
> scope, but fortunately there is a part of *King Lear* that by as-
> sent is its most tragic region, the region where suffering
> takes on such dimension that even Shakespeare could find
> no better word than "madness" to contain it. Furthermore,
> since the madness of Lear is almost entirely Shakespeare's
> invention and is crucial in the transformation of the many
> stories of King Lear into the only *Tragedie of King Lear*, it
> brings us face to face with both the tragic art and the tragic
> artist. Now, to speak of a consummate poetic accomplish-
> ment is to imply that the kind of criticism which views all a
> writer's problems as unique has overlooked a part of the
> whole truth. For, to speak of an artistic attainment as pos-
> sessing magnitude in the highest degree is to imply the exis-
> tence of attainments somewhat analogous and in this and

that common respect somewhat inferior; it implies either this or the existence of a critic who has some a priori conception of a poem more wonderful than any yet written, in which case the critic should change to a more wonderful profession and contribute its culminating splendor.[13]

2. In our family, there was no clear line between religion and fly fishing. We lived at the junction of the great trout rivers in western Montana, and our father was a Presbyterian minister and a fly fisherman who tied his own flies and taught others. He told us about Christ's disciples being fisherman, and we were left to assume, as my brother did, that all first-class fishermen on the Sea of Galilee were fly-fishermen, and that John, the favorite, was a dry-fly fisherman.[14]

Though the distance between the critical article and the short story is so great that such comparisons may be misleading, it seems striking that readers would never guess that the passages could have been written by the same person.

As a fledgling academic, I assumed that I had no choice but to write more or less in the turgid fashion of the first Maclean passage, which I saw not as turgid but as serious and substantial. Had I looked more closely, I could have discovered that many of the leading figures in literary studies had already broken with this pretentious style and were developing a more colloquial academic idiom. At the top of the profession were scholars who wrote with lucidity and wit, including such figures as Richard Ellmann, Northrop Frye, Marjorie Nicholson, Ian Watt, Maynard Mack, Rosemund Tuve, and, a little later, Wayne C. Booth. In retrospect, I can see that the line was already starting to blur between academic critics and New York intellectuals like Irving Howe, who had once been dismissed as mere journalists but who had now become academics (Howe was one of my professors at Stanford) and were gaining in respect.

In his 1961 book *The Rhetoric of Fiction,* Booth showed that it was possible to write with theoretical rigor and scholarly depth without sounding pompous:

"Deep Readers of the World, Beware!"

I have no doubt that this reading of "The Aspern Papers" will seem as much an over-interpretation to some of my readers as the Freudian interpretation of *The Turn [of the Screw]* seems to me. But I hope that even so my point will stand: Although mere ease of reading can never be a final test of the quality of a work, to dramatize one troubled vision of another troubled vision, or of troubled waters, can produce a kind of difficulty that is incompatible with some kinds of literary effect.

If I could only finish on that safe and sane note, my problems would be relatively simple. I could simply knock off a few—a very few—points from the master's total and go about my business. But all this while that governess and her Freudian interpreters are waiting in the wings, waiting to be explained or explained away.[15]

Booth's argument that fictional works inevitably engage in rhetorical persuasion, which questioned the then powerful New Critical dogma that "True Art Ignores the Audience," is now justly regarded as a breakthrough moment in the study of prose narrative. Yet Booth's mixture of formal and colloquial styles may have been an equally significant innovation. I am happy to be corrected, but I doubt you will find another member of the Modern Language Association before 1961 who used the expression "knock off" in print. But though I read and admired Booth's book, its implications for academic writing did not register with me at the time. It was only many years and several books later that it dawned on me that I might try to write that way myself.

Not that I or my fellow graduate students were always as solemn as I am probably making us appear. On the contrary, at student parties and at the campus bar, we ridiculed stuffy academic usages well into the night. For months the student group I hung out with listened endlessly to a record by the British comedy troupe *Beyond the Fringe,* that featured a delicious parody of Bertrand Russell and the precious accents of the BBC: "One of the advaunt-ages of living in Great Court Trinity,

I seem to recall, was the aupor-tunity to meet and trap the then young G. E. Moore in a logical fallacy by means of a cunning semantic subter-fuge."[16] Speaking up in a seminar the next day, however, we would strain for the very preciosity we had satirized the night before. The vernacular selves that were rebelling against the pretensions of aca-demic discourse were splitting off from our academic speaking and writing selves, in my case to occupy separate mental compartments for many years.

We did not talk among ourselves about this split, but if we had we probably would have made the excuse that we had no choice, that we were doing what "the profession" required us to do to get ahead. If I allowed my vernacular voice into my writing, I told myself, I would fail to get a degree, a good job, promotion, or tenure, or I would not get published, or if I did get published nobody would respect or cite me. For fellow students who did rebel, there was the option of creative writ-ing, and the Stanford creative writing students often treated us on the critical and scholarly side as dryasdust pedants who would not recog-nize a good poem or novel if it hit us in the face. We got even by treating the creative writing students as inarticulate children, oblivious to the assumptions that guided them. Since the creative and the scholarly pro-grams ran on separate tracks, however, their perspectives did not cor-rect and cross-fertilize each other.

In any case, there seemed no liability in keeping my vernacular voice out of my academic writing. That voice did not seem to have any-thing of interest or relevance to say to the academic world, whereas the professorial voice I was trying to construct had access to an exciting new language that opened up intellectual secrets and conferred power in the world. This was not power in the public world of journalism or commerce, to be sure, but that power seemed so compromising that renouncing it felt like no great loss. Here I was reflecting that other lesson of James and his fellow literary modernists, that journalism and commerce were completely different from the intellectual world and less interesting and authentic. In this respect, my fellow graduate stu-dents and I were on the same page after all with the creative writers—all children of the fifties for whom academe was an escape from the conformist white collar world peopled by the Lonely Crowd, the Organization Man, and the Nation of Sheep, in the titles of the pop sociology books of the period that taught us how to think about our generation. There was even a sense of mission in the idea that by becoming college teachers we could rescue students from this degraded conformist culture by turning them into intellectuals like ourselves.[17]

If there was self-deception and arrogance in this view, as I now think there was, they resided not in the idea that teachers should try to turn their students into intellectuals, but rather in the narrow and limited conception of what an intellectual might be. I and many of my fellow graduate students failed to see that as long as our intellectual selves were cut off from the vernacular selves that we kept out of our writing, we were not likely to reach, much less offer salvation to, most of our undergraduate students or anybody else. Those undergraduates, except for the select few who had come over to our side, lived in that other world that spoke in the language we had put on hold. So the gap between our vernacular and academic voices reproduced itself in the distance between us and most of our students.

Here is an example of the kind of writing that the education I have been describing resulted in in my own case. I quote from the opening pages of my first book, *Poetic Statement and Critical Dogma:*

> The antithesis which has grown up between the propositional and the dramatic seems to me neither necessary nor desirable. Accordingly, the present study has a dual aim: first of all, to demonstrate the unfortunate theoretical and practical consequences of several types of antipropositional theories; and secondly to outline a poetics which finds a place for the propositional and assertive element in poetry and yet also does justice to the contemporary emphases upon organic unity and experiential complexity uniquely achieved in poetry. Such a poetics would enable us to transcend the crippling either/or distinction between the propositional and the dramatic.[18]

Reading the galley proofs of the book, I still remember my thrilling certainty that such writing would knock the critical world on its ear. I felt like Mark Twain's Duke anticipating the effect of his announcement of the Royal Nonesuch: "LADIES AND CHILDREN NOT ADMITTED. 'There,' says he. 'If that line don't fetch them, I don't know Arkansaw!' "[19]

And as academic writing of the early seventies goes, I think, the specimen does have some good qualities: the writer is engaged, he wants to change the way people think about poetry, and he says up front what he thinks. What strikes me now, however, is how remote my tone, syntax, and diction are from anything I could have imagined myself *saying* to anyone in an actual conversation: "The antithesis which has grown up between the propositional and the dramatic seems to me neither necessary nor desirable." I now suspect that I wrote this way because, whatever my fantasies about audiences, deep down, I didn't believe that anyone was likely to read what I was writing.

This is not to say that my vernacular voice was less real or authentic than my academic voice, or that academia alienated me from my true self. How I talk in the Laundromat or the hardware store is no more or less the real me than how I talk in a seminar room; both voices are constructions—products of socialization, conventions, and institutions. What was wrong with my academic voice, I now think, was not that it was somehow less real or more artificial than my vernacular voice, but that these voices were strangers to each other.

Written expository prose is not oral conversation and should not try to be, and there is no reason why academic writing on topics like poetic theory should try to sound like casual chitchat. There is nothing wrong with writing specialized prose for an audience of specialists. But (as I argue in the next chapter) even an audience of specialists will have trouble hearing you if your writing fails to touch down at any point with the conversational register. I proved the point with the nonreception of *Poetic Statement and Critical Dogma,* which sank out of sight after receiving five or six reviews in obscure journals. I had not expected to be offered an endowed chair, but I had at least assumed my book would be noticed by the handful of theorists who find meaning in questions like whether poetry is "propositional" or not. When this didn't happen, I began to rethink the way I had learned to write in graduate school.

Others will have to judge whether my writing today is any better than the sample of thirty years ago that I've quoted. Some may say I have simply become more glib, or that I haven't changed as much as I like to think. And there are those—both academics and nonacademics—who will argue that writing more accessibly and reaching a wider audience means dumbing yourself down and compromising your intellectual standards. Better, they will say, to make a permanent contribution to scholarship that gets six reviews (a lot by some standards!) and is appreciated by fellow specialists than to churn out middlebrow potboilers that make a brief public splash and then disappear forever into the abyss. My own view, however, is that this side of the technical sciences, general accessibility is fully compatible with intellectual integrity. As I see it, the better I get at addressing nonacademics, the better I become as an academic writer.

One further experience seems worth mentioning that prompted me to rethink my graduate school ideas about academic writing: my first invitation to give a public talk, arranged by a former student at the university where he had recently been appointed. Going over my text the night before the talk, for the first time I read a piece of my academic writing with an ear to how it would sound when delivered orally to an audience of strangers. To my horror, I realized that not even a specialist audience would be able to follow the endless, serpentining sentences, the "which" clauses piled atop one another, the turgid phraseology, and the overloaded paragraphs in which the intended main point competed with so many subordinate points that no hearer would ever find it. I stayed up all night rewriting the paper to make it minimally audience-friendly. How far I succeeded I don't know, but I believe that moment triggered a process, one that still continues, of unlearning the picture of academic writing I had previously formed.

In *Getting It Published: A Guide for Scholars and Anyone Else Serious About Serious Books,* the editor William P. Germano traces the unfortunate titles of many academic books to the fact that "the author has never spoken the title aloud before submitting the manuscript": "Speak the title aloud. If you can't say it easily, get rid of it. If you hear yourself saying, 'See, it's a reference to . . .' or 'It's a pun on . . .' get rid of it.

If you have to take a breath in the middle of the title, it's too long. *Sects and Sex Among the Sikhs* is a tongue twister, not a title."[20] This is excellent advice, and it applies as much to the text in academic books as to their titles. (Wayne Booth, by the way, credits the stylistic virtues of the *Rhetoric of Fiction* to his wife, Phyllis Booth, who commented on drafts as Booth read them aloud to her.)

As I think back now to that first public talk, I believe it began a conversation between my academic and my vernacular self, two parts of me that until then had not been introduced. In everything I have written since, I feel that these voices have inched a bit closer to each other. Perhaps someday they will meet and merge, though this may not be a good thing. It may be best to preserve a tension between your academic voice and your vernacular voice, letting each keep the other honest.

PUTTING VOICES INTO CONVERSATION

All this is a way of suggesting why the appearance of a roach motel in an academic book seems promising to me, a small example of how academics can touch base with the language of students and other non-academics by reconnecting with the vernacular voice they repressed or set aside in order to become academics. I want to close this chapter with some further examples of the mix of vernacular and academic registers that is less rare today in academic writing than it was a generation ago.

My first example comes from an article on teaching written by composition and rhetoric specialist Richard E. Miller: "Thus, if we take, for example, the frustrated student who 'goes off' in class—announcing he's only taking the expository writing course because it's required, that he was graded more fairly in high school, that all this writing about culture has nothing to do with what he plans to do with his life—it is safe to say that nothing in the content of what the student has said can be construed as surprising; rather, what grabs everyone's attention is the fact that the student has chosen to make this statement within his teacher's hearing."[21] This passage gets some of its vernacular sound from Miller's ability to ventriloquize the voice of a generic alienated student, the kind who feels that the writing he does in school "has nothing to do with what he plans to do with his life."

A second example of imagined student vernacular written into academic discourse comes from James Nehring, in *"Why Do We Gotta Do This Stuff, Mr. Nehring?" Notes from a Teacher's Day in School:* "Teachers have grown weary of telling kids why they gotta do stuff. Worse yet, I fear we've stopped asking *ourselves*. So we tell the kids with knuckle-headed determination that they gotta do it, so just do it. And when pressed, we say it's on the test or it's just something that an educated person should know. . . . While all this is going on in the kid's mind, the teachers follow a related mental path. You learned this last year, says the teacher. Don't you guys remember anything?"[22] Would the alienated students Nehring ventriloquizes here find this writing attractive? Students are so used to hearing official talk from educators that deviations from that talk may come across as bizarre rather than down-to-earth, if not a teacherly trick or an unconvincing attempt to be one of the kids. Changing the perception that academic and vernacular language do not mix won't happen overnight, but efforts like Nehring's and Miller's help.

Miller, in another ventriloquizing passage, confronts the arguments of current liberatory educators: "With the seductive rhetorics of liberation and resistance in the air, I've learned that it isn't long before the conversation produces charges that I'm selling out, cashing in my ideals, kissing up to the man."[23] Contrast "kissing up to the man" with "rhetorics of liberation and resistance," a parodic reference to "liberatory educators" like the late Paulo Freire in *The Pedagogy of the Oppressed* or Freire's acolyte, Henry Giroux.

Here for comparison is Giroux:

The notion of the liberal arts has to be reconstituted around a knowledge-power relationship in which the question of curriculum is seen as a form of cultural and political production grounded in a radical conception of citizenship and public wisdom.

By linking the liberal arts to the imperatives of a critical democracy, the debate on the meaning and nature of higher education can be situated within a broader context of issues concerned with citizenship, politics, and the dignity of human life.[24]

By remaining on a high plateau of abstraction, Giroux's writing forestalls the kind of blunt response Giroux himself probably would make in a conversation with friends—such as, "Get real!" or "Says who?" Such abstract writing keeps us safely insulated from that part of us that might otherwise express such inconvenient thoughts—which is probably the point.

To take an example with even more direct pedagogical application, in an essay in the collection *Reading and Writing Differently: Deconstruction and the Teaching of Literature,* David Kaufer and Gary Waller quote a recent critical exponent of Michel Foucault, who calls the "current deconstruction of the individual . . . 'profoundly liberating in its effects,' a successful dismantling of 'the system of constraints with which Western civilization has established the norms and limits of humanity.'" Kaufer and Waller comment as follows:

> Yes, one says, as one prepares for class, how true. And yet, once in the classroom, *how* true? Do we simply walk into the classroom, eyes ablaze with a strange light, and announce to the football team's star linebacker or to the girl by whom "cute" is accepted as a compliment that he and she are no longer transcendent subjects but are parts of a collage of dislocated languages, their sense of "self," that he and she are, like the literature text they have just bought in the bookstore, the products of an ideological struggle that must be ruthlessly and endlessly deconstructed?[25]

Though Kaufer and Waller identify with teachers who aim to "dismantle the constraints" by which Western culture produces its subjects, their comment points up how ineffectual such talk is likely to be when it fails to touch base with the talk of the linebacker student and his "cute" classmate. On the other hand, Waller and Kaufer's mixture of styles represents a bridge discourse that makes it possible to imagine communication between the academics and the students.

Again, I am not suggesting that using phrases like "kissing up to the man" or "Says who?" or references to roach motels or linebackers automatically makes academics more authentic or immunizes them against self-deception. It is not a question of finding a voice that is immune from sounding foolish—there is no such voice—but of bringing voices into conversation that are so insulated from each other in the culture and the curriculum that they do not converse inside our heads.

Which brings me back for the last time to roach motels. I like to think that the appearance of roach motels in an academic book is a small but significant indication of the emergence of a vernacular voice in academic writing that can lessen the gap between academic and nonacademic culture and thus make schooling less remote and irrelevant to students. The increased freedom enjoyed by today's academic writers to borrow the idioms and terms of popular culture is one kind of evidence for this change. Does this mean that academic writing in general is getting better? Not necessarily. What it does mean is that academics can now get away with writing readably, that their careers will not inevitably suffer for it. "I had to write that way to get a job" or to get tenure is no longer a legitimate excuse, if it ever was.

There is reason, then, to hope that the closing of the gap between academic and vernacular discourse represents something more than a short-lived trend. Not only have traditions of positivistic specialization weakened, but the merger of academic and vernacular discourse exemplified by academic public intellectuals like Bérubé pervades our culture. With the growing convergence of academic and journalistic writing, it is increasingly possible to produce academic writing that can interest nonacademics. For this development to go further, however, we need to disabuse ourselves of the widespread myth that academia and intelligibility don't mix. To this myth we turn in the next chapter.

7 Scholars and Sound Bites

THE MYTH OF ACADEMIC DIFFICULTY

CALL IT WISHFUL THINKING, but I have argued in this book that it is possible to do justice to the complexity of academic subjects while communicating clearly to nonspecialist audiences. I was reminded that this is a minority view, however, by the reaction of students in a recent graduate class. They were incredulous when I claimed that they did not have to write obscurely in order to make a positive impression on professional audiences. One or two firmly insisted that a certain amount of obfuscation is a prerequisite for professional success. I suspect that when students write ponderously and evasively, often it is not because they couldn't do better but because they are convinced that this is the kind of writing their professors want. And they are doubtless right some of the time.

Students are hardly alone in thinking that academic communication is inherently opaque, and perhaps the better for it too. One of the most pervasive beliefs in our culture—shared by academics and nonacademics alike—is that the concerns of the intellectual world are so difficult that only a small minority can understand them. According to this view, serious academic scholarship, like modern poetry as it was once famously described by T. S. Eliot, "must be *difficult*." Eliot reasoned that because modern civilization comprehends unprecedented "variety and complexity," the modern poet had to become more and more "allusive and indirect, in order to force, to dislocate if necessary, language into his meaning."[1] It is a short step from this premise of the necessarily increased complexity of modern writing to the conclusion that scholarship has to sacrifice readability in order to be the real thing.

Few would want to deny that the world of knowledge and thought is challenging and difficult—if it were not, there would be no need for scholars to double as teachers. And there is no disputing that most work in the more technical sciences is inherently arcane. Here is an abstract submitted by a student for a recent undergraduate (!) symposium held on my campus:

> The AML Tumor Supressor Gene on Chromosome 5, Band Q31: Localization and Evaluation of Novel Candidate Genes
> Interstitial deletions or complete loss of the long arm of chromosome 5, centering at 5q31, are seen in a variety of hematologic malignancies, including acute myeloid leukemia (AML) and myelodysplasia (MDS) . . .

Some would maintain that the inaccessibility of such a passage is not in principle different from the kind of inaccessibility that marks much research in the humanities, and that this is not necessarily a bad thing. In any discipline, the argument goes, a serious engagement with the subject matter demands a form of writing that will be comprehensible only to specialists.

True enough in many cases, perhaps. But even in the case of propositions about "interstitial deletions," opaque as they are to me and others who know nothing of cancer genetics, educated readers can readily comprehend what such research will be used *for*—to treat malignant tumors. Furthermore, as I argued earlier, even the most esoteric science has to be translated into nonspecialist terms in order to make an impact on its field, and researchers with superior command of technical science often struggle if they lack the verbal and rhetorical skills to explain the significance of their research in a grant proposal. The point is even more applicable to most work in the humanities and social sciences, which generally requires less technical information and specialized vocabulary than its counterpart in the hard sciences. Why, then, does research outside the hard sciences seem as opaque to many people as research inside? Is there a gap between perception and reality?

I believe there is, and I want to look at some academic writing habits in this chapter to advance my thesis that we academics make our intellectual culture look more opaque, rarefied, and beyond normal capacities of comprehension than it is or needs to be. I want to suggest that the reputation for obscurity of academic writing, though not completely unearned, rests on misperception, that such obscurity is less frequent—and is more peripheral and local—than we tend to think, especially in the work that makes a significant impact on its field. Contrary to the belief of the graduate students I mentioned, you don't get ahead in this business by hiding or fogging over what you think. What too much academic writing does do, however—and these are the habits that earn that writing its bad reputation—is mask its moments of clarity, bury its best sound bites, and coyly steer away from confronting the all-important "So what?" and "Who cares?" questions.

Underlying our exaggerated image of academic difficulty is the belief—again found both inside and outside academia—that academic communication is fundamentally different from everyday vernacular discourse and the sound bite communication of the popular media. I noted in my introduction that since the emergence of the modern research university and the popular media around the turn of the century, the very concept of what is "academic" has been derived from a presumed contrast with popular culture. If something is accessible to nonacademics it can't be academic, and if it is academic it can't be generally accessible. What defines academic discourse as academic—and forbiddingly "intellectual"—is presumably its being everything that popular media communication is not, above all its inability to be reduced to sound bites.

DARE TO BE REDUCTIVE

The pervasiveness of this belief among academics explains why, short of a charge of plagiarism, "reductive" is about the worst thing that can be said about a piece of academic work. Up to a point I share this antireductive attitude, feeling abused when my own ideas are reductively caricatured by critics, and ashamed, I hope, when I realize I have committed this offense against others. What I object to, however, is knee-jerk antireductivism, the refusal to see that there are legitimate reductions, useful and necessary simplifications that can be distinguished from those that seriously misrepresent and mislead. What troubles me is undiscriminating suspicion of simplification and reduction as such—as if a piece of writing could not be reductive and nonreductive at different moments and for different purposes.

George Steiner exemplifies this knee-jerk antireductiveness for me when he states categorically that "simplification, levelling, watering down, as they now prevail in all but the most privileged education, are criminal."[2] To be fair, Steiner is replying to the misconceived populism that equates intellectually challenging education with elitism and oppression. But Steiner's categorical equation of simplification with bad forms of leveling and watering down is equally misconceived, for simplification is not only crucial in teaching beginning students, but a necessary component of all effective intellectual communication, even when it is addressed to experts in a field. I believe that blanket suspicion of anything that might be called reductive—which often masks a fear of making an assertion lest one be criticized—is more important than jargon in producing obfuscatory academic writing and teaching.

The academic fear of getting caught being reductive is an overlooked aspect of the much-lamented conflict between research publication and teaching. The conflict does become impossible to overcome if all reductive simplifications are assumed to be necessarily vulgar and demeaning. Since beginning students need reductive simplifications before they can move on to the complications of a text, an issue, or a field, the pressure on academics to avoid being reductive, to eschew sound bites, to complicate as much as possible and at all times, clashes with the interests of good teaching. Indeed, as long as knee-jerk antireductivism colors our view of academic research, teaching can only remain a low status activity despite the best-intentioned efforts to honor and reward it. For if the reductiveness necessitated by teaching is seen as inherently incompatible with the researcher's integrity, then it follows that teaching is irrevocably wedded to inferior modes of thought and expression.

It is not surprising, then, that some instructors resist being reductive even when their teaching would gain from it. A graduate-student friend describes a history course he took in which the professor's daily monologues were so incomprehensible that he and his classmates were completely lost. One day, when he could stand it no more, my friend interrupted the stream of obfuscation and asked the professor if he would please stop and clarify his point. At first the professor responded defensively, but finally he grudgingly proceeded to draw a chart on the blackboard that reduced the two hundred years of cultural history he had been covering to a simple dichotomy. In a flash, the shape and point of what the professor had been laboring for weeks to get across became clear to the students. Yet what struck my student friend was how ashamed and embarrassed the professor was as he schematized his material: "I can't believe I'm doing this," he muttered several times. For my friend it was the most illuminating class of the semester, but the professor felt ashamed. He had been reductive.

THE GIST BUSINESS

The chances of improving the quality of college teaching, then, may depend to a large extent on whether we rethink the assumption that "academic" and "popular" occupy opposing ends of the communication spectrum. If American higher education is serious about its claims to be democratic, it must be committed to popularizing the esoteric and the difficult. But if professors assume that reductive communication is incompatible with intellectual complexity, we doom ourselves to be poor translators, which is to say, poor teachers.

I want to go further, however, and argue that it is not only the interests of teaching that are compromised by the opposition of reductive popular discourse to antireductive academic discourse, but the interests of academic research as well. The reluctance of the professor in the above anecdote to provide his class with a simplified map of his topic figures also to limit the impact of his writing. I submit that translating academic ideas into terms accessible to nonacademics produces not only better teaching, but better research. In other words, reductive moments are as important to effective communication *between academics* as they are to effective communication between academics and the nonacademic public.

The point can be illustrated by another story about an incident that took place at a 1996 symposium at the University of Chicago, "The Public Intellectual," much of which focused on this issue of the extent to which academic work can and should be made accessible to nonacademic audiences. At one moment in the proceedings one of the speakers was asked by an audience member why academics do not make clearer "the gist" of their research. The professor's reply was immediate and blunt: "We're not in the gist business." He went on to say that if it's the reductive gist of an academic argument that you want, you can call the university public relations office or take out a subscription to the *Chronicle of Higher Education* or *Lingua Franca*, but don't expect us academics to lower ourselves to reductive popularization.

Yet there was something odd about the professor's comment: in the very act of disavowing his involvement in "the gist business," the professor contradicted his own claim. For in concisely summing up a complicated position, his retort exemplified exactly the behavior that, according to him, academics like himself avoid. It was also instructive that in the discussion that ensued, the professor's reductive statement did not shut out complications, but served as a stimulus for pursuing them. If there was a problem with what the professor said, it was not that it was reductive but that it was wrong.

What was wrong was the professor's assumption of incompatibility between academic complication and "the gist business" of reductive sound bites. Once we accept the opposition, academics are caught in a false choice: either you write like Swift or Orwell or else you contend for the annual Bad Writing Contest sponsored by the journal *Philosophy and Literature*. Again, any effective discourse necessarily has its reductive moments, which do not prevent us from going on to complicate our arguments as much as we please. Reduction and complication are not opposites, but are both legitimate moments in the process of communication. "Let there be light" was the first sound bite.

Academic discourse does not make an impact even on academic audiences, much less on the nonacademic world, without considerable reliance on sound bites and the vernacular. This reliance, moreover, becomes all the more necessary as the problem of information overload increases. In this respect, T. S. Eliot had things only half right: a complex culture does force communication to become more complex, but it also forces it to simplify in order to make the complexity negotiable. That is, ideas cannot circulate in a complex society unless they can be reduced to concise formulations that encapsulate a concept or argument, often in the speech genres of the vernacular. Simplify Whenever You Complexify is the general rule.

Consider the following incomplete list of intellectual sound bites and where the world of ideas would be if we could not take them as a point of departure:

A man cannot step into the same river twice.
I think, therefore I am.
Hell is other people.
The moral equivalent of war
The banality of evil
A poem should not mean/But be.
It is not man who speaks language, but language which
    speaks man.
The mind-body problem
Form follows function.
Blurred genres
History is written by the winners.
The personal is the political.
Bad money drives out good.
There is nothing outside the text.
The master's tools will never dismantle the master's house.
Always historicize!
Social constructionism
Philosophers until now have sought to understand the
    world. The point is to change it.
There is no document of civilization that is not at the same
    time a document of barbarism.
What do women want?

The owl of Minerva takes wing at night.
The other minds problem
The wretched of the earth

In listing these familiar statements and phrases, I am in no way proposing an *Oxford Book of Quotations* view of the intellectual world, whereby Great Thoughts can be lifted out of their complicated contexts without loss. On the contrary, the propositions and concepts listed above can't be adequately understood or discussed without being set in those contexts. But neither can these concepts and propositions be understood and discussed without recourse to the shorthand of such reductive moments. Again, the point is not that complication can be dispensed with, but that moments of reduction are necessary for dealing with complication. Again, reduction and complication are not opposites but moments in a process.

To be sure, if "always historicize" is a kind of sound bite, it is one that only the intellectually initiated are likely to understand. Fredric Jameson's maxim is accessible to other academics and intellectuals outside the field of literary studies, but to circulate among nonacademics it would need further translation. The point, however, is that even initiated audiences understand such academic communication by translating it into terms familiar to outsiders. To understand "always historicize," we translate the maxim into the kind of formulation we would use to explain it to someone who does not: "In dealing with any text or event, always examine the history that made it what it is."

To put my point another way, effective academic writing tends to be bilingual (or "diglossial"), making its point in Academese and then making it again it in the vernacular, a repetition that, interestingly, alters the meaning. Here is an example of such bilingualism from a review of a book on evolutionary biology by a professor of ecology and evolution, Jerry A. Coyne. Coyne is explaining the theory that males are biologically wired to compete for females. Coyne makes his point both in Academese, which I italicize, and in the vernacular, staging a dialogue in the text between the writer's (and the reader's) academic self and his "lay" self: "*It is this internecine male competitiveness that is assumed to have driven not only the evolution of increased male body size* (bigger is better in a physical contest), but also of *hormonally mediated male aggression* (there is no use being the biggest guy on the block if you are a wallflower)."[3] It is this type of bridge discourse that enables nonspecialists and students to cross from their lay discourse to academic discourse and back. Coyne's review appeared in the nonacademic journal *The New Republic,* but there is nothing in the passage that would not and could not appear in a contemporary academic journal or book.

In providing a vernacular equivalent of their Academese, writers like Coyne install a self-checking device that forces them to make sure they are actually saying something. When we recast our point in vernacular terms, we do not simply throw out a sop to the nonspecialist reader, much less dumb ourselves down. Rather we let our point speak itself better than it knows, to come out of the closet in the voice of the skeptical reader. That is why readers, being less invested in a text than the writer is and less inhibited from being reductive about it, are often better than writers at cutting through evasions and getting to the real point. An example is Jane Tompkins's rewriting of a comment of mine in a recent co-written dialogue: "Yes, I agree. You have to build community and conversation into the *structure* of the educational enterprise, or they'll never happen, given that everyone is already maxed out."[4] Tompkins's summary cut through my more ponderous formulations and said what I meant better than I could have said it, not only because I would not have risked a colloquialism like "maxed out," but because I would have been too concerned about hedging my bets to put my point so bluntly.

Some of the best examples of such useful "bottom lining" (as well as some of the worst abuses) occur in book reviews, where, because of space constraints, we tend to cut reviewers some slack about being reductive. Thus in a *New York Times Book Review,* when Graham Robb refers to Alexis de Tocqueville's "idea that in a democracy intimate, personal commitments give way to 'diffuse, impersonal associations,'" Robb translates as follows: "Republican man can openly love his country but not his best friend."[5] Tocqueville himself would not have put it that way and might not even have had the thought, but this is my point

Robb's reductive summary gets at implications of the author's words that may not have occurred to him.

One of the worst results of the structured isolation of teaching is that it closes down the process of hearing our own thoughts played back to us by others and hearing our Academicspeak translated into colloquial terms. Students provide such feedback, but only up to a point. A more collaborative curriculum that gave us more chance to hear our points played back to us by peers who are less protective about them than we are would therefore figure to raise the quality of academic writing. We don't know our own thoughts until we hear them restated and altered by others, a fact that especially holds for academics, who have a special need to hear our insider discourse translated into outsider's terms ("maxed out") and to learn to write such self-translation into our own texts. Again, it is not a question of foregoing insider language in favor of clearer outsider language, but of writing an outsider's perspective into insider texts.

These arguments parallel the thesis developed by Bruce Robbins in *Secular Vocations: Intellectuals, Professionalism, Culture,* which questions the widespread view that professionalism is inherently narcissistic, cutting itself off from accountability to the nonprofessional public, that professionals become insiders by turning their backs on lay outsiders. Robbins answers critics of professionalism like Louis Menand, who argue that "as humanistic study has become increasingly professionalized, its practitioners have become less and less disposed to respond to any intellectual challenges except those presented by the work of their colleagues within the discipline." Though Robbins concedes a grain of truth to Menand's critique of academic disciplines "in the name of *outsiders,*" he points out that such criticism has long been pervasive among disciplinary insiders themselves. Robbins concludes that "Menand is wrong, after all, to rely on the familiar assumption that professional means private, exclusive, esoteric, inaccessible. For the easy, habitual antithesis between the professional and the public excludes just what Menand himself exemplifies: the professional's own will, *as* professional, . . . to take over and mobilize the point of view of 'people outside the profession,' to enter into some sort of dialogue with the extra-professional public." As Robbins goes on to argue, the history of professionalism suggests that professions fail to survive unless they enter into a dialogue with the extra-professional public.

Citing Thomas Haskell's *The Emergence of Professional Social Science* and other histories of professions, Robbins argues that "professions are not hermetically sealed, but porous. . . . Address to outsiders, according to these histories, is indispensable to professional speech."[6] Again, the discourse of the outside public is already inside professional discourse. Robbins's argument supports my claim, I think, that incorporating the voice of the outside public makes professional writing more rather than less effective with other professionals. To translate Robbins's terms into mine, academics advance not by turning their backs on the perspective of those outside their immediate field, but by writing that perspective into their scholarship, creating a dialogue like the one the ecologist Coyne produces above.

The historian Patricia Nelson Limerick sums the point up with her typical color and flair:

> There is no necessary tug-of-war between activities as a public intellectual and activities as a scholar. When you speak to a public audience, you operate under a healthful mandate to escape specialization and think big. In truth, every academic field desperately needs synthesis; every topic lies buried under a flood of specialized studies. Speaking to a nonacademic audience puts you in a Noah role; while everyone else disappears in the flood, you make your selection of arkmates and sail off safely. When you return to Mt. Ararat, or the academic world, you have taken the journey that will give you the perspective to put the details of academic study into a larger picture. Gaining practice in confident but thoughtful generalization in your travels outside the university, you can come up with ideas that will advance your career as an academic.[7]

Precisely: when academics address outsiders they get practice looking at their field from their big-picture perspective, and that perspective enables them to speak more forcefully to fellow insiders. Far from sacrificing their careers when they devote themselves to public intellectual work and lower-division teaching, Limerick suggests, these activities can actually serve academics' self-interest.

BURYING THE POINT

When academic writing is obscure, the reason often lies not in excessive complication, as we are prone to think, but in the relative infrequency of reductive moments, moments when Academese is translated into terms intelligible to nonexperts. Alternatively, even when such reductive moments do appear, they come at the wrong moments in the text, too late to help. (I learned early on that I was more likely to discover the point—if there was one—of an academic conference paper if I skipped the paper itself and came in for the discussion afterwards, where the audience's questions force the presenters to disclose what they are trying to say; even better was to forego the session and attend the cocktail party, where I could bluntly ask, "What was *that* about?") These are among the ways academic writing makes itself look more forbidding and incomprehensible to uninitiated readers than it needs to be.

To illustrate the point, I want to look at some passages from Eve Kosofsky Sedgwick's *Epistemology of the Closet*, a pioneering work in contemporary gay studies. Sedgwick's very title constitutes a kind of caution flag, as if to warn readers not to expect any compromises with reductive vernacular discourse. And much of the writing in the opening pages of the book bears out the warning: "For meanwhile the whole realm of what modern culture refers to as 'sexuality' and *also* calls 'sex'—the array of acts, expectations, narratives, pleasures, identity-formations, and knowledges, in both women and men, that tends to cluster most densely around certain genital sensations but is not adequately defined by them—that realm is virtually impossible to situate on a map delimited by the feminist-defined sex-gender distinction."[8]

This is the kind of prose that discourages casual readers, seemingly bearing out their belief that academic writing is only for the initiated. Indeed, Sedgwick's vocabulary—"identity-formations," "the feminist-defined sex-gender distinction"—is specialized to the point of sounding clinical. Yet if one can get to the *issues* raised in the passage, these turn out to be broad and general: how secure is the standard division of the sexes into male and female? Is this division grounded in biology, or is it socially conditioned? Sedgwick's quasi-clinical language obscures the fact that the questions she raises about the nature of sex and gender are potentially of general interest to nonspecialists.

Even more interesting, some fifty pages into the book the syntactical clouds suddenly part and clarity breaks out. It happens at a moment when Sedgwick turns to summarizing and answering the incredulous questions about gay studies posed by journalists and other lay people as well as academics, who have forgotten or don't know that the writers in question were either probably or certainly gay:

Has there ever been a gay Socrates?
Has there ever been a gay Shakespeare?
Has there ever been a gay Proust?

Sedgwick replies:

Does the Pope wear a dress? If these questions startle, it is not least as tautologies. A short answer, though a very incomplete one, might be that not only have there been a gay Socrates, Shakespeare, and Proust, but their names are Socrates, Shakespeare, and Proust; and beyond that, legion—dozens or hundreds of the most centrally canonic figures in what the monoculturalists are pleased to consider "our" culture, as indeed, always in different forms and senses, in every other.

What's now in place, in contrast, in most scholarship and most curricula is an even briefer response to questions like these: Don't ask. Or, less laconically: You shouldn't know.[9]

"Don't ask. You shouldn't know" is about as vernacular as you can get, echoing the Jewish mothers of popular culture, including (for those old enough to remember) Gertrude Berg on the *Molly Goldberg* show. The passage illustrates how even the most intellectually challenging academic writing communicates by at times translating its arguments into folk maxims recognizable to a lay audience.

The passage shows that the rhetorical ballpark of academic writing is not as far removed as we might think from that of popular editorial writing. Compare Sedgwick's encapsulation of her opponents' view as, "Don't ask. You shouldn't know," with the lead paragraph of an op-ed piece by William Safire on the congressional debate on the impeachment of President Clinton: "In blowing off the House Judiciary Committee's 81 interrogatories, a mockingly evasive Bill Clinton told the Congress of the United States, Take your impeachment process and stick in your ear."[10] Sedgwick goes on to complicate her point more than Safire does, but her complications are framed by the same kind of reduction employed by Safire. What differentiates Safire and Sedgwick is not that only the journalist uses sound bites, but that he puts his best sound bite up front, where it will control how readers process the rest of his text, whereas the academic buries her most effective sound bites fifty pages into a denser prose that prevents some readers from ever reaching them.

I came to this realization when I assigned *Epistemology of the Closet* in a graduate course several years ago and got several complaints from students that the book was unreadable. I pointed these students to the "Don't ask. You shouldn't know" section, asking if they did not at least find *this* material to be as reader-friendly as they could wish. To my surprise, the students seemed not to have noticed the section nor the change in style it represented. At first I thought the students had been so numbed by Sedgwick's impenetrable opening pages that they had stopped reading before they got to the more readable passage. In discussion with these students, however, I saw that something more interesting had happened: by the time they arrived at the clearer section their expectations had been so colored by the impenetrable earlier part that they did not notice when the writing became suddenly accessible. Like many who are frustrated by academic "theory," these students so expected Sedgwick's text to be unintelligible that they failed to notice when it was not. Like most people who encounter an academic text, they figured that if it seems comprehensible they must be making some mistake.

Had Sedgwick positioned her clearer sections more prominently, some of the cruder antagonisms of the culture war might have been averted. Even sympathetic readers of her text are likely to overlook the surprising passage in which Sedgwick credits her deconstructive way of reading to the arch anti-theorist Allan Bloom, whose courses she took as an undergraduate at Cornell: "It was from Bloom, as much as from more explicitly literary and deconstructive theorists or from more leftist ones, that I . . . learned the urgencies and pleasures of reading against the visible grain of any influential text."[11] Even more serious, many readers will tend to miss what is probably Sedgwick's most significant contribution to current public discussions of homosexuality, that the "ritualized debates between nature versus nurture"—is gayness biologically determined or socially conditioned?—are unresolvable due to the inherently unstable and volatile nature of sexuality itself.

To be sure, a conservative journalist like Safire can take for granted a consensus among readers on his assumptions that a writer who makes counterintuitive claims like Sedgwick's cannot. Some will argue that this is simply the nature of things, that poststructuralism and queer theory are too subversive of received common sense to attract many general readers, so that for Sedgwick to "clarify" her argument would be to compromise with the dominant discourse, if not to sell out. Yet if Sedgwick could translate her points into the vernacular without loss of complexity in one part of her text (as I believe she does in the "don't ask" section), then it is hard to see why she could not have done so in other parts as well. At the least, she could have moved some of her vernacular moments up to the front where they could control the reader's reception of the denser arguments.

Fredric Jameson, despite having copped some bad writing awards, provides an interesting counterexample in *The Political Unconscious*, which he front-loads with the memorable "Always historicize!"[12] Jameson makes clear early on that to always historicize well we need Marxism, which he calls "that untranscendable horizon that subsumes such apparently antagonistic or incommensurable critical operations, assigning them an undoubted sectoral validity with itself, and thus at once canceling and preserving them."[13] To be sure, phrases like "untranscendable horizon," "subsumes," "incommensurable" and "sectoral validity" are far from the vernacular of anyone who is not a theory head or a cultural studies specialist (though such phrases are not exclusive to any academic field). Jameson's language is turgid but his point remains clear because his reductive formulations have kept the bottom line in view: "Marxism comprehends all the other -isms."

Jameson's writing, then, differs crucially from truly opaque academic writing by framing itself in reductive formulations, without which *The Political Unconscious* would probably not have become a top academic best seller. Since Jameson tells the reader up front what the big point of his book is, readers can slog through lengthy sections that they may only partially comprehend—like the heavy lifting of the eighty-five page introductory chapter, "On Interpretation," with its formidable analyses of Hegel, Althusser, Greimas, Freud, and numerous other thinkers themselves noted for their difficulty.

Jameson here follows some of the oldest and simplest rhetorical advice: "Tell 'em what you're gonna tell 'em; tell 'em; tell 'em what you told 'em."[14] Though readers may get lost attempting to keep up with the details, they can always find their bearings by keeping in mind the reductive meta-argument presented in the opening pages—always historicize; always see that Marxism "subsumes" other ways to historicize. The point is not that such writing should be skimmed in Cliffs Notes fashion, but only that its notorious difficulties are local, "subsumed," as Jameson might say, by a meta-commentary that is reductively given up front. This is a very different procedure from that of academic texts that fail to provide such meta-commentary, where one gropes for pages trying to discover the author's point and why he or she bothers to make it. There is certainly plenty of this latter kind of academic writing around, but I submit that it does not get into circulation.

WHERE YOU SAY IT

When I served in the early 1980s as the director of a university press, I became aware that academic writers often give little thought to such rhetorical matters as *where* one places one's points in a text. In reviewing and editing manuscripts, I repeatedly came upon central arguments hidden in mid-paragraph or mid-sentence, obscured by surrounding subordinate clauses, or coming too late in the text to be likely to be noticed, much less to control how readers would process the book. (I recognized these features in my own writing, as I had learned to write in graduate school [see the previous chapter], features not easy to change even now.) I also found repeated cases where the argument the author had chosen to make central was less interesting or important than arguments that were subordinate or marginal. Some—by no means all—university press and journal editors let such problems pass without comment. In part this is because academic editors are overworked (and underpaid), but I suspect it is also because some editors, like other people, expect academic writing to be unintelligible to all but a few experts.[15]

And until recently, these expectations had some basis. Zachary Karabell is right when he says in his recent book, *What's College For?*, that "people outside the university rarely care, and even more rarely can understand, what academics are talking about." Yet Karabell goes on to add that "people do care about similar issues" to those raised in academic work.[16] As many academic fields have come to be concerned with contemporary culture (including its relation to the past), and with issues of politics and cultural representation of the kind with which Sedgwick and Jameson deal, more people outside the academy now do care about "what academics are talking about," even if their interest is sometimes hostile. It is as if this new interest had appeared so suddenly that academics have not yet adjusted. We go on writing as if nobody out there cared, and we are surprised and hurt when it turns out they do care and blast us for being opaque or politically correct. The recent "science wars" that were touched off when Alan Sokal's deliberate travesty of postmodern nonsense was solemnly accepted and published by the avant-garde journal *Social Text*[17] represent but one example of the way intellectual disputes that would once have been conducted in the privacy of the seminar room today tend to be fought out in the public spotlight.

Sedgwick (like the editors of *Social Text*) has received numerous bashings from journalistic reviewers, who have generally misunderstood her work. One of the nastiest, meanest, and most uncomprehending recently appeared in *The New Republic*, by Lee Siegel.[18] Siegel's attack belongs to that now familiar genre that offers to give the hurried reader the unvarnished truth about academic work that they would otherwise have to waste time puzzling through on their own. Yet Siegel fails to grasp Sedgwick's most important ideas, particularly her key point about the unstable nature of sexual identifications and classifications. I don't claim that such hostile misunderstandings would not have occurred had Sedgwick brought her accessible pages to the front of her book instead of burying them, or had she made better use of her vernacular skills. At the least, however, she would have made her book harder to misrepresent and trash with impunity. Though avant-garde academics are often right to complain that they have been grossly misrepresented by their critics in the culture war, their training in rhetoric should have taught them the harsh lesson of public communication: whoever declines to use sound bites (or buries them from view) will be at the mercy of the sound bites of others.

The most striking recent example of this rule is the popular misunderstanding of deconstruction, an ironic outcome since the problem of the sound bite—or the relationship between a text and its self-characterization—is one that deconstruction sheds considerable light on. One of the most widely ridiculed deconstructionist theories is that in an important sense texts are "unreadable," as the late Paul de Man frequently argued. Such theories seemingly confirmed the charge of detractors like Dinesh D'Souza, David Lehman, and John M. Ellis that, as D'Souza put it, "Deconstructionists hold that all literature is empty of meaning"—that words can mean anything we want them to mean. I myself thought de Man's thesis self-evidently preposterous when I first encountered it in the mid-seventies and I said so in print.[19]

J. Hillis Miller, however, explains that when de Man writes of "the unreadability of the text," he means "the text's inability to read itself."[20] That is, what de Man argues is that there is a discrepancy between what a text says and what it says it says when it summarizes its own meaning, in a sound bite, for example. Reformulated this way by Miller, de Man's point is not only not silly but brilliant, as well as very useful for basic writing instruction. I have cribbed from it myself in the list of dos and don'ts on "How to Write an Argument" at the end of this book, where I point out that "an effective argumentative essay really consists of two texts, one in which you make your argument and a second one in which you tell readers how and how not to read it." Every writer has had the experience of becoming aware, deep into an essay, that the examples and evidence one has been amassing not only do not clearly support one's thesis, but could be used to support an opposing one, that the evidence we use to prove our point can be used against us, that "evidence," in short, never speaks simply for itself. Thus clarified, the deconstructive idea of the unreadability of the text becomes less obscurantist and far more interesting—and pedagogically important—than it appears.

Deconstructionists argue that this discrepancy between what a text *says* and what it *says* it says is not a mere mistake, accident, or aberration, but a structural feature of communication itself. The inability to achieve a perfect fit between our examples and evidence and what we want them to exemplify, a fit that leaves no residue of unwanted implication, can't be completely eliminated through further revision, for it is rooted in divisions that are sedimented into language—in the fact that the same set of facts can always be used to demonstrate opposing conclusions. When we adduce evidence for a claim, what our evidence is evidence *of* or *for* is always contestable, a point that explains why policy debates often take the form of battles between competing applications of the same agreed on facts. This is not to say we have to give up (or could give up) trying to control our meanings, but only that complete control will elude us.

Unfortunately for the fate of deconstructionism, the clarifying sound bite I just quoted from Miller, which in my case caused the scales to drop from my eyes, is buried in the middle of a long paragraph about something else on page thirty-eight of a book whose main point is about "the ethics of reading." Would the reception of deconstruction have been any more friendly had Miller moved his sentence up to page one and then proceeded to write a whole book about how the sentence's point has been missed: that the point of deconstruction is not that texts are meaningless or literally unreadable, but that texts misread themselves? Perhaps the reception would not have been different, but we don't know because nobody has yet written such a book.

All this is well and good, you will say, but surely my claim is resoundingly refuted by the popularity and professional visibility of "theory," which is simultaneously both academically influential and unreadable. The theory fad clinches the case, does it not, that academic work becomes influential not despite but because of its obscurity, that to get ahead in the academy you must avoid sound bites, vernacular, and clarity and make your writing as difficult as possible, if not completely opaque.

The best retort to this argument is simply to list the many prominent literary and cultural theorists who write accessible, sometimes even entertaining prose: Roland Barthes, Terry Eagleton, Stanley Fish, Henry Louis Gates, Nancy Fraser, Richard Rorty, Bruce Robbins, Jane Tompkins, Wayne Booth, Walter Benn Michaels, Jonathan Culler, Marjorie Garber, Michael Bérubé, James Phelan, W. J. T. Mitchell, Lennard Davis, Jeffrey Williams, Nancy Miller, Sandra Gilbert, Susan Gubar, Robert Scholes—the list goes on and on. Even Homi Bahbha, Jameson's frequent rival for bad writing competitions, writes very readable journalism for the *New Statesman*, whose ideas overlap with those in his academic books.

One illustration of these theorists' reliance on the vernacular would be a list of their article titles drawn from popular songs: "Short People Ain't Got No Right to Live" (Fish), "Me and My Shadow" (Tompkins), "What's Love Got to Do with It?" (Gates); and from popular films: "The Good, the Bad, and the Ugly" (Mitchell).[21] Eagleton has actually put literary theory to song lyrics, as in his parody of vulgar Marxist criticism, "The Ballad of English Literature":

Chaucer was a class traitor
Shakespeare hated the mob
Donne sold out a bit later
Sidney was a nob. . . .

There are only three names
To be plucked from this dismal set
Milton Blake and Shelley
Will smash the ruling class yet

Milton Blake and Shelley
Will smash the ruling class yet.[22]

Yet despite the evidence that theory is often more accessibly written than average academic prose, theory remains synonymous with obscurity. Here is further testimony to the myth of academic difficulty and its power to blind us to what is under our noses.

I do not underestimate the inherent difficulty in bridging the enormous gap between academic and nonacademic communication (or even the very large gap between the discourses of academics in different disciplines). But neither should we exaggerate the distance between the academic and the popular, especially if doing so excuses bad academic habits of communication. What has obscured the areas where academic and nonacademic discourse do intersect is not just the necessarily specialized vocabularies and conventions of the intellectual world, but our assumption that these worlds have nothing to say to each other. This assumption, the myth of academia's insuperable difficulty, keeps us needlessly pessimistic about the chances of bridging the gap between research and teaching, about the potential of academic institutions to reach students, and about the academic potential of students themselves. The myth also misleads those students into thinking that the forms of thought and expression they learned while growing up have to be abandoned if they hope to do well in school.

Again, none of what I have said in this chapter should be mistaken for the claim that all academic scholarship can or should be addressed to nonacademic audiences. The ability to do advanced research and the ability to explain that research to nonprofessionals do not always appear in the same person. There is a division of linguistic labor, in the phrase of philosopher Hilary Putnam,[23] by which the work of research and the work of popularization is divided among different people, as Friedrich Engels served as rewrite man for Karl Marx. Yet even Marx's most difficult texts have their Engels moments—Engels could not have summarized Marx's doctrine if they did not. In short, it is time to rethink the view that the university is not in the gist business.

8 Why Johnny Can't Argue

IN FACT, THIS CHAPTER TITLE HAS IT WRONG. Johnny *can* argue competently when he is in a real conversation that requires him to be persuasive. As I have pointed out, children learn to argue as soon as they are old enough to lobby parents or babysitters to let them stay up late or buy them an ice cream cone, a bike, or a skateboard like the one the kid across the street has. But Johnny—and Susie—do often run into problems when it comes to the kind of argumentation that is recognized and rewarded by academic institutions. School argument seems so remote from arguing with your parents or friends that there seems little carryover in these practices.

Schools should be tapping far more than they do into students' youthful argument cultures, which are not as far removed as they look from public forms of argument. I observed earlier that twelve-year-olds debating the merits of a Michael Jackson concert or a Mariah Carey video are making the same kinds of claims, counterclaims, and value judgments as those made by published book reviewers and media critics; there's even a continuity between the shrugging adolescent who says, "It sucks" or "That's cool," and the scholar or journalist who uses more sophisticated language. Instead of taking advantage of the bridges between youthful argument worlds and those of public discourse, schools generally make it hard for students to recognize their argumentative practices in those of academia. At worst, students get the impression that to do well in school or college they have to check whatever argumentative inclinations they have at the classroom door. I have heard high school teachers say that they've given up teaching argument because their students find it "boring." And in a post–Columbine High School age, anxieties about school violence can lead educators to discourage contentiousness in students. This is short-sighted, however, for arguably the real prescription for violence is to bottle up youthful passions and give them no legitimate outlet. Properly channeled, argument can be a substitute for violence rather than an incitement to it. As Deborah Meier has said, "Fighting with ideas rather than fists or guns or nasty sound bites could be a welcome relief."[1]

To be sure, students' problems with academic argument are often traceable to academic subject matter, which may have little connection with what they care about. But even when we change the subject and invite students to write about what personally interests them, if making an argument is part of the assignment the quality of students' writing doesn't necessarily improve. Once students have to translate their personal interests and experience into the formalized conventions of written Arguespeak, their interests and experience no longer seem their own.

There are ways, however, to make Arguespeak less foreign—and less boring—and the first step is to make clear to students that this language is an extension of everyday conversation. In the real world, we make arguments within some motivating conversation, whether we are chatting about last week's party or writing a letter to the newspaper in response to an editorial. Countless expository essays launch themselves by constructing a version of the "standard view" move, as it might be called: "The standard view of X runs like this. Here, by contrast, is what I think." In making the standard view move, we write a conversational partner into our text in order to set up our response. This summary-and-response pattern represents the deep structure of most written argument. In casual conversation, students unconsciously follow this structure, obeying what the linguistic philosopher Paul

Grice calls "the conversational principle," which enjoins that we make our speech responsive to what our interlocutors have just said.[2] Academic assignments, however, often violate this conversational structure, asking students to come up with a thesis in a vacuum rather than to draw on their tacit conversational knowledge. I am thinking especially of the traditional five-paragraph theme in which students are asked to state a thesis and back it up. The five-paragraph theme does give students useful practice in stating a thesis and supporting it, but it fails to reproduce the conditions of real-world argument, where writers form their thesis in response to other writers or speakers.

WHAT CONVERSATION ARE YOU IN?

I want to suggest in this chapter how a more conversational view of argumentation can demystify academic writing and help high school and college students write better. The first step is to recognize that when student writing is flat and unfocused, the reason often lies in a failure to provide students with a conversation to argue *in*. I come to this conclusion the hard way, after teaching argument badly for many years. During that time, my most frequent critical comment on student papers was, "What's your argument?" or "What's your point?" My students' lack of improvement suggested that the exhortation to get an argument or a point is about as helpful as advising someone to "Get a life." Eventually it dawned on me that what counts as a makable "point" or "argument" is not as simple a matter as it seems. How do you go about finding a point if you haven't already got one? How do you know you've got one when you see it?

I thought back on my own writing struggles—how did I know when something I said qualified to be a main point or argument? I realized that it had as much to do with what other people were saying or thinking as it did with the intrinsic qualities of my text. Without those others out there and the conversations they were having I had no chance to have an argument of my own, even if—especially if—I wanted to change that conversation. Any hope I had of being original depended on others, since without them and their conversation my writing would literally be pointless. Here was a clue to why the student writing I was seeing often lacked a clear point: my students were trying to make a point without having a conversation in which to make it, an impossible feat.

Their difficulty was doubtless increased by the nebulous nature of the conversations of the academic humanities, where the kinds of arguments typically made are often mystifying. The problem, however, also arises in other academic disciplines, whose central conversations are often kept from students on the ground that they don't yet know the fundamentals of the subject, when in fact those conversations are the most fundamental thing of all. But if we can let students in on the secret that intellectual writing and discussion are extensions of their normal conversational practices, much of the mystification can be dissipated and the struggling students have a shot at catching up.

The point I make in this chapter, that students write better when they have conversations to enter, is implicit in much current composition and rhetorical theory, where conversation has become a central concept. The idea that discourse is inherently "dialogical," that we internalize external conversation in virtually everything we say, has been developed in various ways by influential thinkers such as Bakhtin, Rorty, Derrida, McIntyre, and Vygotsky. The idea is implicit in Kenneth Burke's celebrated depiction of intellectual history as an endless parlor conversation into which as individuals we drop in and out. My effort in this chapter will be to reduce "conversationalism" to its essential elements, making it more user-friendly for writing instructors and students than existing writing textbooks have done. The key point is that in order to make your own argument you have to write someone else's voice into your text.

PLANTING A NAYSAYER IN YOUR TEXT

Let's try to apply this principle. Here is a typically flat piece of student prose by an eleventh-grader, Ellen, writing on Chinua Achebe's novel *Things Fall Apart*: "In the novel *Things Fall Apart* by Chinua Achebe, an African man known as Okonkwo struggles with Ibo life and traditions. He can be characterized as a tragic hero and was acknowledged as the man with title and honor. Okonkwo was portrayed as a hero because of the way he defended and what he tried to prove to his village and for his village."[3] Note that Ellen has no problem with the mechanics of grammar, punctuation, and syntax. Nor does she lack a clear thesis; she argues that Okonkwo, the main character of Achebe's novel, is a tragic hero. Why, then, does her writing seem flat and one-dimensional, lacking force and emphasis?

What is missing, I submit, is not an argument but an indication of *why* Ellen thinks her argument needs to be made at all. Her opening fails to survive the "So what?" or "Who cares?" test: Achebe's Okonkwo is a tragic hero. So what? Who cares? Why say it? Who needs to hear it? Who would argue otherwise? I hasten to add that high school students are not the only writers who fail this "So what?" test. Is there anyone who has attended talks at a professional conference who has not wished that certain speakers had asked themselves the "So what?" and "Who cares?" questions?

Ellen's failure to address these questions helps explain why her writing sounds as if it is not addressed *to* anybody, why it doesn't give the impression that Ellen thinks there is anyone out there who needs to know that Okonkwo is a tragic hero. I don't know the assignment Ellen was responding to, but her writing sounds like the kind that tends to be elicited by instructions like "Discuss Okonkwo as a tragic hero," assignments that ask students to do something without knowing why it could be worth doing. The goal of this kind of assignment is usually to check up on whether Ellen has read the novel, knows basic information such as the standard definition of a tragic hero, or can write coherent sentences. Such assignments assume that Ellen needs *first* to master these elementary operations of reading and summarizing a narrative before she is ready to enter a higher-level conversation in which she engages with real issues and readers. Unfortunately, this kind of an assignment not only fails to prepare Ellen for that next step of engaging with real issues and readers; it probably will convince her that academic paper writing has nothing to do with engaging with real issues and readers.

Some will argue that the unimpassioned quality of Ellen's writing is a result of her not really *caring* about abstract literary questions like whether Okonkwo is a tragic hero or not. This could be true, and asking Ellen to write about something closer to her own experience may draw more engaged writing from her, though it also may not. My point, however, is that asking Ellen to write about such questions in a conversational vacuum itself helps ensure that she won't care. She may find it easier to care, however, if we provide her with a sense of the kinds of conversations that can take place about tragic heroes.

Others will argue that what Ellen lacks is a real reader, who could be supplied if she were asked to write the paper to her classmates, or perhaps to a small group within the class. This standard tactic is certainly worth trying, but it isn't likely to make a significant difference in Ellen's writing. For what Ellen needs is not just a real audience, but the understanding that she has to write that audience into her text. This is not something Ellen has to worry about when she engages in face-to-face conversations with her friends, family, and classmates, for in such oral situations the agenda is set by what others present have just said. In written discourse, however, which is implicitly addressed to an audience not present, the agenda (or context) has to be constructed explicitly by the writer.[4] To give point to what she says in writing, Ellen has to construct a conversation in which to say it.

In order to write a conversation into her text, Ellen needs to do something that can be hard for everyone but especially hard for young people: to imagine a person whose beliefs are different from her own. In order to motivate her argument that Okonkwo is a tragic hero, Ellen needs to imagine someone who doesn't already think what she thinks and then write that person into her text. That is, Ellen needs to imagine a person who is sufficiently "other" to her that that person needs to hear what Ellen wants to say. In other words, Ellen needs to think about her thesis in a contrastive or counterfactual way, something that means asking herself, *tragic hero as opposed to what?* To give point to her essay, Ellen needs to plant a hypothetical naysayer into her text, someone who would argue that Okonkwo is *not* a tragic hero but something else.

Now for reasons I suggested earlier, planting a naysayer in your text, a move in which you deliberately make trouble for yourself, is likely to seem counterintuitive if you have been socialized to think of school as a place you get through by *staying out* of trouble. The five-paragraph theme and other typical assignments reinforce this view by influencing students to think of writing (and academic study generally) as a business of stringing together true statements, statements that can't be challenged. Teachers need to help students see why this apparent common sense is not only misleading, but a sure-fire recipe for dull writing and student boredom. Unless we produce some problem, trouble, or instability, we have no excuse for writing at all.

How, then, can Ellen plant a naysayer in her text, and thereby produce a motivating problem? The easiest way is to imagine other plausible readings of the text besides hers. If you've read *Things Fall Apart* you'll recall that it's tempting to regard Okonkwo as an unqualified villain rather than a tragic hero. In fact, teachers who have taught the book tell me that students tend to find Okonkwo so repulsive that it's a challenge to get them to take him seriously. Okonkwo is rigid, overbearing, and unyielding with other tribal members, he behaves brutally to his wife and his mistress, and among the tribal traditions he defends and carries out is the ritual slaying of a child. Reflecting on these plot details and the negative views of her classmates might enable Ellen to construct the naysaying conversational partner whose counterfactual voice of otherness her argument needs to give it point, someone who sees Okonkwo as a simple villain.

If Ellen can think along these lines, she might eventually rewrite her opening in this way: "For many readers of Chinua Achebe's *Things Fall Apart,* the novel's main character Okonkwo may be so clearly repulsive as to seem a simple villain. Yet it is important to recognize that Achebe presents Okonkwo not as a mere villain but a tragic hero. Okonkwo, after all, is honored by his village for defending its traditions, however offensive those traditions may seem to us." By constructing a hypothetical reader who finds Okonkwo "so clearly repulsive as to seem a simple villain," this revision furnishes the naysayer whose "as opposed to what?" perspective would justify Ellen's argument. Someone could still ask, "Who cares if Okonkwo is a tragic hero?" or "So what?" but at least now Ellen's text anticipates and implicitly answers these questions: "Some readers care—those who think Okonkwo is just a straight villain; they care, so my claim is consequential."[5]

Of course if the naysaying, counterfactual reading is not plausible, then Ellen will seem to be creating a straw man. This would happen, for example, if readers could not plausibly see Okonkwo as *anything but* a tragic hero, as might be the case if, say, Achebe had repeatedly described Okonkwo in the text as a tragic hero, or had subtitled the novel *An Ibo Tragedy*. Ellen would either have to find another alternative reading to contrast with hers or change her thesis. Then, too, we can imagine more sophisticated critical conversations Ellen might try to enter—trying to get her essay published or submitting it as a master's thesis—that would require her to write a more complicated set of other voices into her text: "Though in obvious ways an evil man, Okonkwo nevertheless achieves a kind of tragic stature in the colonialist setting of the novel. As a residual African tribesman whose culture is being destroyed by the forces of colonialism and modernization that arrive in the novel's final chapters, Okonkwo is as much the tragic victim as the victimizer of others. On the other hand, though Okonkwo might be a victim to most postcolonial readers, he would certainly be a victimizer to feminists."

Instructing students to write a naysayer into their text is the single most effective device I have come up with in teaching writing. (Supplying lists of standard transitional words and phrases—*but, therefore, thus, on the other hand,* etc.—and requiring students to use them comes in second.) This device works even more effectively when I borrow the "argument templates" designed by my wife, Cathy Birkenstein-Graff, which we will look at in a moment, templates that give students standard formulas like "At this point my reader will probably object that . . ." and "Now I do not mean to suggest that . . ." In my experience, instructing students to write a naysayer into a text as part of the assignment and providing templates for doing so enables them right away to make argument moves they have never made before. This technique is far more effective than explaining in the abstract processes like how to have a point.

But what if students have trouble inventing the naysaying conversational partner they need in order to write argument? Constructing such a reader may be too hypothetical and abstract a process for inexperienced students. It becomes easier if you can refer to a specific person who says something you can respond to. After all, even experienced writers of argument often find their task easier when they come upon an article or book that serves as a foil for what they wish to say. In fact, it's probably by engaging with real people in this way that writers learn to construct hypothetical interlocutors. Furthermore, when the interlocutor is real rather than imagined, writers gain a leg up in answering the "Who cares?" question and warding off charges of creating a straw man, since they can point to at least one person who cares. We tend to write better, in short, when we are in conversation with actual others.

CONVERSATIONALISM TESTED

As you can see, I am steering toward making a case for assigning secondary commentary—criticism—especially in the humanities, where primary texts have ruled the roost. (I make this case at greater length in the next chapter.) My argument was informally field-tested by my former student and collaborator, Andrew Hoberek, when he taught English as a visiting instructor at the University of Puget Sound. In a course on the fiction of Flannery O'Connor, Hoberek assigned a paper in which each student was to choose an O'Connor short story from the reading list and do a close reading of it. Students were given the option of addressing specific questions such as "What is the meaning of the monkey at Red Sammy's BBQ restaurant in 'A Good Man is Hard to Find'?" On reading the papers, Hoberek found that most of the class had difficulty with the assignment, producing unfocused and disorganized essays.

Hoberek decided to follow up with a second assigned essay. As in the first, students were to perform a close reading of an O'Connor story of their own choosing. This time, however, they were to compose their reading in response to one of O'Connor's published critics. As Hoberek put it in a handout, "Choose an article or book chapter on the Flannery O'Connor short story you have chosen, summarize its argument, then disagree with it." To make sure the students' disagreements with their chosen critic led back to rather than away from the literary work itself, Hoberek also stipulated that the students must make specific reference to the story in question.

The two assignments thus constituted a fair, if unscientific, test of how having an actual critical conversation to enter affects student writing. Hoberek found that his students' writing in the second assignment was discernibly better focused and more sharply argued than in the first. Entering a conversation with a critic gave his students a clearer sense of what they wanted to say and why it needed saying. Hoberek also thought that the conversational second assignment lessened the distance between the struggling students and those who had been doing best in the class. Whereas the open-ended invitation to explicate a text had left the strugglers at sea (even when given explicit suggestions like "explain the symbol of the monkey"), being asked to summarize and respond to a critic gave them clearer guidance on how to produce an explication. This result shouldn't surprise us, seeing that these students had little experience discoursing about the deep meaning of monkeys and other literary symbols, but they had plenty of experience conversing with other people. Having a specific critic's claims to respond to helped them write with more authority about symbolism. It also helped them begin to produce a bridge discourse that mingled the critics' analytic language with their own.

To let you judge these claims for yourself, here are two excerpts from Hoberek's student papers. Granting the inevitable degree of subjectivity in judgments on these matters, I think the examples show that the two students did write better when presented with critical conversations for them to enter:

In the first assignment, one student, Zach, opened his essay as follows:

> "You might as well put those up," she told him. "I don't want one."
>
> "I appreciate your honesty," he said. "You don't see any more real honest people unless you go way out in the country" (O'Connor, CW, p. 271).
>
> In this passage from "Good Country People," Manly Pointer has just learned that Mrs. Hopewell has no intention to buy a bible from her. She comes flat out and tells

him that she does not plan to buy one. He appreciates her honesty and touches on his belief that the only real, good honest people live way out in the country.

What Pointer says here could be interpreted in a couple of different ways, depending on how the tone of the statement is taken. . . .

Zach here does hint at a conversation that his paper will try to enter— one between readers who interpret a statement by Pointer in "Good Country People" in "a couple of different ways" that Zach presumably will arbitrate. He leaves unclear, however, how the possibility of several interpretations of Pointer's statement is a problem and what the stakes are if it is. He leaves the reader groping, I think, to get a handle on what Zach thinks the issue is.

Here is how Zach approached the second assignment, where he was asked to put himself explicitly into conversation with a critic:

Jon Lance Bacon, in chapter eleven of his book *Flannery O'Connor and Cold War Culture,* links the issues of modernization in the south and a loss of heterogeneous culture, with that of conformity and mass consumption. . . . At one point in his chapter, Bacon looks at this issue specifically in regards to Coca-Cola. He mentions instances where Coke appears in O'Connor's work to "indicate the reach of American consumer culture within the region (Bacon, p. 120)." . . .

I disagree with this, however. Coca-Cola, while representing "the American way of life" is still by and large a product of the South. . . ."

The second version shows a clear gain in focus and rhetorical purpose. For one thing, it is easier to summarize Zach's argument: Bacon claims that Coca-Cola functions for O'Connor as a symptom of the invasion of Southern culture by American mass consumerism, but this can't be right since O'Connor shows Coca-Cola itself to be a Southern product.

Not only is it clearer in #2 than in #1 to whom and to what claim

Zach is responding, but the stakes are also clearer: it matters if O'Connor shows Coca-Cola coming from outside the South or not since she would be suggesting in the first instance that the South is being destroyed by external social forces, but in the second that it is contributing to its own destruction. Zach still needs to work on sharpening his points and making himself more reader-friendly. For example, his statement that Coke "is still by and large a product of the South" would become more pointed if he added, "—and is not something imposed on the South from outside, as Bacon would claim." But he and his instructor are now in a better position to address such surface-level problems, since Zach's argument now has a firm conversational structure and setting.

In a second example, a student named Danielle opened her first paper as follows:

> In Flannery O'Connor's short story, *Good Country People*,
> Mrs. Hopewell found herself very disturbed by some of the
> literature her daughter Hulga was reading. She noticed
> words that had been underlined in blue pencil in a random
> book, amongst them: "We know it by wishing to know noth-
> ing of nothing" (269). The question of believing in nothing
> came up frequently in the story and each character had their
> own interpretation of belief. However, the outcomes for the
> characters who believed in something were more of a nega-
> tive experience than for those who believed in nothing. In
> other words, the characters who believed in something in
> *Good Country People* were the ones who ultimately were led
> to disappointment, disillusionment, and pain. O'Connor por-
> trayed belief and faith as negative experiences.

Danielle here has the makings of a conversation that would open a space for her claim: since we would normally think of "belief and faith" as positive things, why does O'Connor portray them as "negative experiences"? But since Danielle is not quite able to construct such a conversation, her opening flunks the "So what?" test: so what if O'Connor portrays belief and faith as negative? Why is that important and to whom?

Here is Danielle in the second paper writing with the benefit of a real critic as interlocutor:

> In Chapter 2 of Dorothy McFarland's studies of Flannery
> O'Connor, she says that O'Connor intended that both the
> peacock and Mr. Guizac be identified with Christ in her
> short story "The Displaced Person." McFarland asserts
> that this identification is clear and sees Mrs. McIntyre's
> responses to both the peacock and Guizac as symbolic of
> her attitude toward Christ (indifference and rejection).
> Mr. Guizac is killed in the end like a sacrificial Christ and
> the peacock lives on "symbolizing the glorified Christ" (35).
> Although this view of Guizac and the peacocks is highly
> interesting, I assert that both can be seen outside of a Chris-
> tian context and still give light to "The Displaced Person."
> Both the peacock and Mr. Guizac can be seen beyond the
> Christ symbols, as symbols of change which bring about re-
> actions from Mrs. McIntyre and Mrs. Shortley ultimately dis-
> placing them.

Again, it seems evident that being in conversation with a critic has enabled the student to give clearer focus and consequentiality to her writing: after conceding McFarland's claim that the story's symbolism may refer to Christian beliefs, Danielle argues that it can just as plausibly be read as a comment on social change and displacement. Who cares? Well, at least one critic does.

Someone could still ask, "But who cares about *that*?" So what if some professor can squeeze Christ symbolism out of a story that somebody else can use to squeeze out something else? Would anyone care about such intramural debates who wasn't an academic or trying to get a grade from one? It is certainly true that claims and disputes that academics consider significant often seem trivial and petty to those outside the club. If we really value tolerance and respect for others' views, we can't be reminded too often that what seems manifestly weighty to ourselves and our circle may not amount to a hill of beans to others. "Let there be light" might draw a "So what?" from an atheist. This is precisely why it is always important when reading student work—or one's own—to keep asking "So what?" with a range of different possible audiences in mind.

Zach's and Danielle's examples help answer the objection that being asked to read literary criticism can only distract students from primary works of art. This is a risk, to be sure, but it is one that teachers can anticipate and correct for, as Hoberek did when he required his students to refer closely to their chosen short story while disagreeing with its critic. Responding to a critic does not draw Zach and Danielle's attention from the particulars of the work, but actually helps them focus on those particulars in a more pointed and purposeful way than they did in their first effort.

Granted, Hoberek's students were well-motivated college English majors who could be turned loose in the library to find critical articles they could understand and use. This is not an assignment that all undergraduates and certainly most high school and elementary students can do, though I suspect many would rise to the challenge if they had to. As I argue in the next chapter, even beginning students (and even students in the elementary grades) can engage with expert commentary if that commentary is made simple and accessible enough. Again, students are already engaging in spirited conversations outside school about films, music, sports, and other subjects. If we teachers can configure expert conversations in accessible ways, we can draw students into them.

ARGUMENT TEMPLATES

But before students can effectively enter intellectual conversations, many will need help to produce the conventional formalizations that characterize written argument. When Hoberek's Puget Sound undergraduates took issue with Flannery O'Connor's interpreters, they had to perform sophisticated operations such as gracefully negotiating the transition from quoting or paraphrasing a critic to generating their own formulations. These moves seem disarmingly simple, but they are often hellishly perplexing for inexperienced writers and sometimes even for experienced ones. Yet as educators we often shy away from giving students explicit instruction on such moves, partly in order to avoid overemphasizing surface features of language, partly out of the recognition that students learn better when they discover things on their own rather than have them told to them.

The problem is that we will probably wait forever for some students on their own to produce formulations like "Whereas X argues that . . . , I contend that . . ." or "My reader will probably object. . . ." Most of us learned to imitate such Arguespeak by osmosis through our reading, but many students don't read in that imitative way, in which one identifies with the voice of persuasive authorities whom one wants to be like. For such students, not to provide explicit help in using Arguespeak amounts to concealing secrets from them and then punishing them with low grades when they fail. In other words, withholding crucial formulas from students is at least as disabling as teaching such formulas too mechanically. It is simply condescending for educators to withhold tricks that they themselves have mastered.

In an earlier chapter, I mentioned compositionist David Bartholomae's suggestion (cited approvingly by Mike Rose) that "when stuck, student writers should try the following 'machine': 'While most readers of _____ have said _____, a close and careful reading shows that _____.'" Cathy Birkenstein-Graff, who has taught composition at Loyola and DePaul Universities in Chicago, has actually developed a version of such an argument machine. Birkenstein-Graff found that her struggling students wrote better when she provided them with the following argument template:

Title: _____

The general argument made by author X in her/his work, _____, is
that _____. More specifi-
cally, X argues that _____.
She/He writes, "_____."
In this passage, X is suggesting that _____
_____. In conclusion,

X's belief is that _____.
   In my view, X is wrong/right, because _____.
More specifically, I believe that _____.
For example, _____.
Although X might object that _____,
I maintain that _____.
Therefore, I conclude, that _____.

Birkenstein-Graff's template gives students a sense of what it feels like to live inside the language of written argument, to hear what they would sound like using a voice of intellectual authority that most have never tried.

Birkenstein-Graff anticipates the objection that such templates squelch creativity. In an explanatory handout, she notes that the template in no way dictates or limits students' *thinking*, only the conventional forms for it. She argues that the template actually facilitates creative thinking by helping students negotiate stumbling blocks that often prevent them from doing justice to their best ideas. Once students get the hang of the argumentative moves—quoting and summarizing others' arguments, restating them in the students' own language, framing a response—they are free to deviate from the template as they choose. Birkenstein-Graff recognizes that there are many different forms of argument, that a formula like "Whereas X says, I argue . . ." is only one (though one that is pervasive). She believes, however, that students will gain more from mastering this basic form than from trying to learn many forms all at once and thereby learning none. She and I are currently at work on a book on how to write argument that will make central use of her argument templates.

In a freshman composition course that Jane Tompkins and I co-taught at UIC this year, we devised the following template to help our students make arguments out of their personal experiences:

In *A Life in School: What the Teacher Learned,* Jane Tompkins tells the story of her experience as a student and a teacher, emphasizing [HERE STATE THE THEME YOU

WANT TO DEAL WITH] _____.
   Tompkins believes/describes/asserts [HERE ELABORATE
ON THE THEME] _____.
My own experience as a student was very much the same/
both similar and different/quite different. Whereas
Tompkins _____,
I _____. [NOW
ILLUSTRATE YOUR POINT WITH AN INCIDENT FROM
YOUR OWN LIFE.]

Here is another templatelike device devised by Paul Fortunato, a
graduate teaching assistant at UIC. Asking his students to respond to
a critical essay on the literary work they chose to write about, Fortunato
provides the following:

> There are various ways and combinations of ways to re-
> spond, including:
>
> - *disagree* with some key statement
> - *agree* with something the critic says and then say even
>   more about it than he or she did
> - point to something the critic says that seems *to go con-*
>   *trary* to something else he or she says
> - point to something the critic says and give a *counter ex-*
>   *ample* from the text
> - argue with the critic by showing that he or she is *leav-*
>   *ing out* some key aspect of the story or some key issue
>   or argument
> - blow your critic out of the water by showing that he or
>   she is *totally wrong*
> - praise your critic for making an extremely important
>   point, and *add something* important to that point

A final example of an argument template comes from the National
Academy of Education postdoctoral fellowship program, which contains the following question, designed by Howard Gardner:

> In fifty words or less, complete this sentence: Most scholars
> in the field now believe . . . as a result of my study . . .

Incorporating such templates into standardized tests for high school students might help raise the intellectual level of such tests while making them less confusing:

> In fifty words or less, complete this sentence: The author of
> this [set] passage argues . . . I, however, would argue . . .

There is always the risk that teachers will use such templates in a mechanical and sterile way, just as there is a risk that prescriptions like "write a naysayer into your text," "enter a conversation with a critic," or "summarize a critic and then disagree" will turn students into robots. But I hope this chapter has persuaded you that these are risks that need to be taken, especially if you agree that the alternative is to keep students in the dark, desperately trying to guess what the teacher "wants," a predicament that produces its own kind of robotic response. Ultimately it seems better to give students the frameworks they need than to leave them to figure everything out on their own. It is better for teachers to be up front about what we "want" than to be coy and ultimately obscure. Johnny and Susie are often forceful arguers out of school, and they can be forceful arguers in school if the moves of the game are not kept from them.

9 Outing Criticism

IN THE LAST CHAPTER I presented evidence that students write more cogently about a text when they respond to another commentator than when they respond directly to the text itself. I argued that when students write poorly (on other subjects as well as literature), the reason is often that they are asked to generate an idea or interpretation in a void rather than to enter a conversation. But given the unfamiliarity of the conversations of the intellectual world, most students need help grasping these conversations and writing them into their texts. If this argument is valid, it follows that *criticism* needs to be assigned far more frequently than it usually is in college and high school courses.

To many teachers, however, the idea of assigning criticism sounds like a surefire prescription for classroom disaster. Here are the most common objections I have heard when I have proposed the idea:

1. Give me a break! Many of my students won't even read the primary texts I assign, so how can I expect them to read secondary stuff *about* the texts?
2. It's a struggle as it is to get my students to talk in class; assigning criticism would only deepen the pall of silence.

You college types just don't understand what we have to cope with in high schools.

3. What my students need is firsthand experience of reading texts themselves; reading criticism about the texts would only come between them and this primary experience.

4. Assigning criticism makes sense at the more advanced levels of education, especially with students who hope to go on to graduate school in the humanities; but for the vast majority of students the basics of reading the text closely need to come first.

5. My classes do read criticism for the research paper we require, and they invariably tend to parrot the stuff, ape its worst jargon, or commit plagiarism. When it's up to me I discourage students from consulting secondary material.

6. I've tried assigning criticism, but my kids find it opaque and boring.

It is hard to fault these objections, since assigning critical texts *can* indeed produce all the dismal classroom results they adduce. The lifeless writing that is often elicited by research paper assignments does seem to indicate that the students in question aren't yet mature enough to make creative use of criticism, as opposed to parroting it. I, too, have induced the familiar "pall of silence" by inflicting published criticism on students that was obscure, or remote from their interests, or both. Few college undergraduates and even fewer high school students hope to become professional critics when they grow up, and professional skills are not needed for a keen appreciation of the arts and may even kill it. Why, then, ask students to read criticism, especially when there's so much excellent primary literature around waiting to be read?

CRITICISM IS ALREADY THERE

I grant that assigning criticism *will* probably backfire if a way is not found to bridge the gap between critical discourse and student discourse. Most *published* criticism is addressed to initiated readers rather than students and therefore is not suitable for classroom use, an obstacle I will come back to later in this chapter. Nevertheless, there is a simple reason why we need to find a way around this obstacle: "criticism" is just a fancy word for what any of us do when we respond to any text. Therefore, students are *already* producing a form of criticism as soon as they begin to talk about a text in class or write a paper about it. Now, it just makes no sense to ask students to produce a kind of discourse that they rarely see an example of. It makes no sense to withhold from students the discourse that we expect them to produce— and punish them for not producing well. Mike Rose may have criticism in mind when he observes in *Lives on the Boundary* that college faculty—and the point holds for high school teachers, too—"for the most part, do not provide freshmen with instruction on how to use knowledge creatively—and then penalize them when they cannot do so."[1]

In this sense, there is something misleading about the very phrase "teaching literature." Even if a teacher asks for nothing more than the students' gut reaction to a text, and even if that reaction amounts to nothing more advanced than "Oh, wow" or "It sucks," it has to be formulated in "secondary" critical language. Like Molière's gentleman who suddenly realized he had been speaking prose all his life, we need to recognize that criticism is what we inevitably do when we talk about a work of art. As the critic Chris Baldick rightly points out, "It is a fact too often forgotten that the real content of the school and college subject which goes under the name 'English Literature' is not literature in the primary sense, but *criticism*. Every school student in British education is required to compose not tragic dramas, but essays in criticism."[2] Even in creative writing courses discussions have to be conducted in critical discourse. Criticism, then, contrary to the above objections, is not something "imposed" from the outside on literature and students. It is already there from the start, inevitably "coming between" the text and the students as soon as they have anything to say about the text. So the choice is not between students' speaking or not speaking criticism, but between speaking it well or badly.

It is important, then, to "out" criticism in its inevitable presence in the teaching of literary and other kinds of texts. To get criticism out of the closet and into the class reading list is also to bring the critical conversation into the class, for individual critical acts, as I argued in the last chapter, make sense only when they are entries in a critical conversation. To repeat my earlier argument, students must not only read texts but find things to *say* about them, and in any walk of life finding something to say will be difficult if the conversation about it is kept out of sight.

When we fail to assign criticism (or the comparable secondary discourse in nonliterary disciplines), we send a message to students that we don't think they are up to producing the quality of talk about texts that we expect of real-world commentators. Assigning criticism helps not only students, however, but teachers, who need issues and models of talk to sharpen the intellectual challenge of their courses. Assigning criticism provides an alternative to the two sterile options between which the teaching of texts too often swings: either the teacher *tells* students what the text means and they write it down, or the teacher shuts up and lets the students air their personal responses. Neither approach results in a serious engagement with the text or helps students internalize the rigors of interpretation and analysis.

But surely, you say, learning to feel a vivid personal response to a text should take first priority in introductory courses, deferring a more analytical response to a later stage of education and the student's development. But there is something circular about the assumption of developmental stages in this objection: *of course* beginning students won't be prepared to read criticism if they are not asked to. Nor are students ever likely to progress to a more articulate form of commentary once they get the impression that a vivid personal response is enough. (Students sometimes tell me they like literature courses because anything you say in them is valid.) As for the objection that studying criticism leads students to ape mindless critical jargon, recycle clichés, and develop other bad habits, these are excesses that teachers can correct for when they occur. Students' first efforts to talk and write in disciplined critical ways are indeed likely to be awkward, forced, and imitative, but going through this growing stage is preferable to falling silent or staying arrested in a limited personal voice. It is better to have a stock of clichés—which can be built and improved on—than nothing to say at all.

Teachers in fact tend to reward—as they should—those students whose responses most closely approximate competent critical discourse. The same teachers who warn students to avoid "secondary sources" usually end up giving the best grades to those whose writing most closely resembles those sources. And students especially stand out when they demonstrate they can enter adult critical conversations. So teachers who discourage a student from studying criticism are with-holding from him or her the discourse that they themselves take for granted. Such teachers remind me of millionaires who exhort the poor to quit being so obsessed with material wealth.

GETTING 'EM TO TALK

Some teachers, however, will concede that students need a critical con-versation to enter in order to speak and write well about a text, but they will argue that, in any good course, this conversation is provided by the students' in-class discussion of the text. Why look beyond the class discussion to written criticism? Because such criticism is needed as a model of how to discuss texts in a rigorous way. We teachers often settle for a level of classroom talk that falls short of what students could produce if we asked more of them and provided more models and help. We tolerate a low level of articulation and let students vent opinions and feelings instead of really engaging with—or even listening to—their classmates. Such classroom venting has been encouraged by the vogue of an uncritical "reader-response" approach to literature, in which the very idea of doing justice to the text is viewed as authoritar-ian, and a vivid student response is seen as a sufficient goal even if it is patently narcissistic. A similar slackening results from a permissive misapplication of the theory of "multiple intelligences," whereby a stu-dent who analyzes or argues poorly may be invited to do a dance or carve a sculpture as an alternative, as if these were equivalent tasks.[3]

I have been reinforced in these judgments by my recent reading in the scholarship on student discourse in literature classrooms. To take one example, consider *Authorizing Readers: Resistance and Respect in the Teaching of Literature,* by Michael Smith and Peter Rabinowitz. This book represents a welcome critique of those reader response methods of teaching literature in which getting students to respond vividly overrides concern for how well their responses are grounded in the text. Rabinowitz and Smith want students to respond in their own strong ways to texts, but they also want these responses to be something more than a narcissistic exercise in self-expression. Precisely because of the sharply critical tenor of Rabinowitz and Smith's perspective, however, I was disappointed at the mediocre level of articulation they accept when they quote from student responses.

Here, for example, are an eleventh-grader's comments on a short story, thoughts that Smith praises (with no dissent from Rabinowitz) for the gain they show in "authority," in the kind of "contentious talking back to texts" Smith says he wants:

> Why do they put such a high title, minister's son, I mean so what? Cause he's a normal person like everyone else. He's not any better. I mean, if anything it sounds like he's [the minister's] worse. He sounds like the strict dictator over the entire family. But, this, sounds like one of those families, one of these stories that takes place like, way back when, but still has like, a modern sort of insight into it, I mean it's showing that those, all those you know, God-fearing families aren't all what they're cracked up to be. But, sort of cynical . . . story.[4]

Granted, oral transcriptions of even the most literate speakers tend to be incoherent to the point of nonsense; granted, the student here is going through a process, discovering what she wants to say as she gropes for the words; granted, to fairly evaluate this response we would need to compare it with her previous responses, which are not presented to us; and granted, nobody expects eleventh-graders to sound like Samuel Johnson or Oscar Wilde. Nevertheless, Smith and Rabinowitz's positive treatment of this specimen suggests to me that they do not expect as much from eleventh-graders as I think they are capable of producing.

To be fair, as teachers we often have so much trouble getting our students to speak up at all that we forget about whether they are speaking *well* and settle for a less-articulate level of talk than we should. Anyone who has had the excruciating experience (as I have) of turning a group of initially eager students to Mount Rushmore faces knows this temptation well. When classroom silence becomes deafening, "getting them to talk" tends to become the *goal* of class discussion rather than the starting point it should be for progressing to something more rigorous down the road. Questions about the intellectual quality of student talk go by the boards, since such quality concerns—Is the talk well-focused on an issue or problem? Is it relevant to the text? Is it staying on point? Are the students listening and responding to each other or merely trading assertions and counterassertions?—seem a luxury the teacher can't worry about.

Then, too, in schools where lecturing and memorization drills are still dominant (or are making a comeback under the pressure to "teach to the test"), teachers who want to hold discussions in their classes understandably come to glorify such discussion for its own sake even when its quality is not very good. In schools where the battle between lecture and discussion methods still has the feel of a holy war, it becomes easy to romanticize the hard-won discussion class as an ultimate goal rather than a starting point. Teachers then boast that their students are "active learners" when a more honest assessment would be that the quality of their activity is less than what it could be.

I find a similar limitation in the popular practice of introducing "group work," in which the students are broken into smaller groups. ("Let's *Not* Break Up Into Smaller Groups" is an essay I want to write some day.) Kenneth A. Bruffee, one of the leading theorists of this form of pedagogy, offers a thoughtful and persuasive explanation why putting students to work in small groups on well-defined tasks will enable them to take responsibility for their learning and become socialized more readily into academic discourse communities.[5] In my observation, however, though breaking the class into small groups does tend to get most students more engaged, it does little to raise the quality of discussion and at worst results in the blind leading the blind. Then, too, the very intimacy and comfort that are gained by breaking the class into small groups tends to retard students' training in public-sphere communication, which involves addressing an audience you *don't* know and may never meet face-to-face.

For these reasons, then, I believe in-class discussion as it is often conducted is not sufficient to furnish the sharply focused conversations students need if they are to enter intellectual discussions at a high level. This is not an argument against small discussion classes, though, as I suggest in my last chapter, I believe small class size has been ascribed a quasi-magical power that is overrated. It is an argument for applying a higher standard to class discussions, even introducing an element of formality into them by developing explicit guidelines.

In short, then, if "getting them to talk" is a problem, teachers should respond not by abandoning the demand that students develop an academic voice, but by providing more models and guidance for developing such a voice and integrating it into their student voices. Otherwise we will again penalize students by withholding the kind of critical discourse from them that we expect them to produce.

The problem of "criticism" is not limited to literary studies, since studying any subject entails speaking and writing some form of analytical meta-discourse. Though the critical talk of the humanities may be more mystified and mystifying than those of other disciplines, it is paradigmatic of how mystification operates in other disciplines as well. The problem is especially acute in literary studies, however, because their critical discourse is not only unfamiliar to students, but is not derivable from the primary object of study, as it can be in other fields. That is, the texts studied by historians, sociologists, and psychologists often provide students with the kind of language they need in order to discuss those texts, whereas literature students won't get the critical language for discussing Shakespeare's plays out of the plays themselves. Writers like Gibbon, Weber, and Freud write argumentative prose, whereas Shakespeare's "arguments" have to be inferred as "themes" imbedded in narratives and figurative language.

It is the distance between the theme-talk of literary criticism and the narrative or lyrical language of the literary works it describes that explains why for many students such talk seems like so many rabbits arbitrarily pulled from a hat. After all, the words "theme," "symbol," and "meaning" do not appear *in* most literary texts, nor are they familiar in everyday discourse. Literary critical language thus seems doubly removed—from both the text's language and the students' language. No wonder students doubt that the "major themes" teachers find in literary works are actually "there" in the text, which never mentioned them, after all, and no wonder desperate students run to the Web, as we saw in chapter 2, to see if anyone in cyberspace can tell them what gardens mean.

THE PROBLEM OF THEME-TALK

Students must read criticism, then, if we expect them to speak and write in a disciplined, critical way. But assigning critical texts is only a beginning, and one that will backfire unless a way is found to bridge the gap between critical discourse and student discourse.

One of the best discussions I know of why critical discourse needs to be taught and why it is so difficult to teach is found in Robert Scholes's justly celebrated book *Textual Power*. Scholes argues that learning to read literary texts and speak and write critically about them should be an extension of reading the "cultural text" of the wider world.[6] Scholes usefully demystifies the idea of reading by noting that readers of texts and cultures are engaged in the same type of activity as football quarterbacks who "read" defenses. "Textual power" for him goes beyond the literature class and the conversation of critics to the workplace and the exercise of democratic citizenship.

But how can textual power be taught? For Scholes the problem of the literature classroom is how to help students make the move from stories to themes, or from following the details of a narrative—who does what to whom?—to "thematizing" such details as exemplifications of generalized meanings. As Scholes puts it, how are students supposed to get from a perception about a text like "It's about this soldier in a trench" to an observation like " 'It's about fear'—or shame, or betrayal, or hypocrisy, or human frailty, or whatever? . . . The problem is how we get from the things named in the story—character things, situation things, event things—to the level of generalized themes and values," which tend to be implied rather than directly stated.[7]

In asking how students can progress from stories and characters to "generalized themes and values," Scholes seems to me to have put his finger on the operation that, more than any other, tends to separate initiates from novices. Scholes recognizes that reading criticism can give students the needed vocabulary for making this move from what happens in a text to its "generalized themes and values." He argues, as I have in this book, that students need to be part of a critical conversation in order to read and think well. "At some level, in some way," Scholes writes, "our students must be invited" into the debates of critics; "we must make available in the most efficacious form some of this critical controversy itself."[8]

Scholes also recognizes, however, that the gulf can be so wide between the language of even the most reader-friendly criticism and that of high school and college students that introducing critical discourse only deepens students' alienation and boredom. The more fluently the instructor speaks the language of criticism, the more he or she risks losing the class. As Scholes vividly puts it, "the ultimate hell" of teaching for him is epitomized in "the image of a brilliant instructor explicating a poem before a class of stupefied students."[9] As this comment suggests, the kind of thematic talk about texts that Scholes and I want students to master is precisely the kind that induces stupefaction.

Consider, as a case in point, the daunting quality of Scholes's own comments on a Hemingway sketch from *In Our Time:* "Even war itself has been diminished here to its least heroic aspect: a frightened, defenseless creature pursued by relentless machines that spare his life only because their mechanical violence is randomly effective." Moreover, for Hemingway, "to be in '*Our Time*' is to be in a world where human qualities are regularly crushed and brutalized by social and biological forces too powerful for individuals to resist."[10] Like Scholes, I think high school and college students *can* produce this powerful critical talk about "generalized themes and values," and can extend that talk from literary texts to the wider "cultural text" of their lives and their society. But how can teachers make these things happen?

TEACHING CRITICISM: SOME EXPERIMENTS

Part of the problem, as I suggested earlier, is that published criticism tends not to be appropriate for school and college classrooms. When teachers recoil at the idea of assigning criticism, they are often thinking of opaque or unreadable criticism whose effect in their classes has been or would be deadly. Yet even when criticism is lucid and well written it may be poorly suited to students' needs, and end up only confirming suspicions that such material has nothing to say to anyone who is not an academic specialist. Even presumably accessible literary journalism—that found in *The New York Times Book Review* and other newspaper book review sections—is written for initiated readers who presuppose references and allusions most students will not recognize. We look back with nostalgia on the days when generalist men of letters like Lionel Trilling wrote for general readers, forgetting how few those general readers were and how Trilling himself was often regarded as obscure by his contemporaries, as he would be to most students today.

To make critical discourse safe for school and college classrooms, then, teachers must be selective and must seriously gauge the level of discussion and vocabulary their students are ready for. The undergraduates whose writing on Flannery O'Connor we looked at in the last chapter were at the stage where they could be turned loose in the library to find critics they could understand and respond to, but not all students are ready to do so. In my own teaching, I have collected over the years a small number of published critical essays—or parts of essays—that work well for me, but a good deal of trial and error has gone into this process. In this section I turn to some practical attempts I have been involved in to make criticism user-friendly for classrooms.

One such attempt to create critical conversations that college undergraduates can enter is a textbook edition of Mark Twain's *Adventures of Huckleberry Finn* that I have coedited with James Phelan of Ohio State University. The book, subtitled "A Case Study in Critical Controversy," contains the text of Twain's novel and a selection of critical essays representing some of the debates it has provoked, including the recent one over whether the book should be assigned at all in view of charges that it is racist. A second "Critical Controversies" textbook, on Shakespeare's *The Tempest*, also edited by Phelan and me, was published in 2000. Though these texts are aimed at college students, our edition of *Huck* has been used in high school courses, and Phelan and I hope to do adaptations for secondary and possibly even elementary school students. Another Bedford text organized around controversies is *Falling into Theory*, a collection of critical essays on recent culture war issues edited by David Richter, with a preface by me.[11]

The Graff/Phelan "controversies" edition of *Huck* gives teachers and students a way to put into classroom practice the approach I call teaching the conflicts and that Phelan and I, in our introduction, call "learning by controversy." The book's critical essays are grouped around three major controversies: 1) The controversy over the novel's ending: "Did Mark Twain Sell Jim Down the River?" or does the slapstick comedy of the final chapters, as critics have charged, undermine the serious moral and social critique implied in Huck's emerging rejection of conventional morality and his commitment to freeing Jim? 2) The related controversy over race: "Does *Huckleberry Finn* Combat or Reinforce Racist Attitudes?" 3) The controversy over gender and sexuality: "Are Twain's Sexual Attitudes Progressive, Regressive, or Beside the Point?" To help students enter these critical debates we provide a modest amount of editorial commentary that aims to clarify and simplify the main issues as well as an introductory essay, "Why Study Critical Controversies?" that explains what the editors think students can gain from reading criticism and critical debate alongside literary works. This introduction addresses many of the objections to reading criticism that I have discussed in this chapter.

As of this writing, *Huck* has sold over 30,000 copies and, judging from the feedback Phelan and I have received and a survey done by Bedford Books, is generally regarded as effective by teachers who have used it. Some high school teachers have also reported using it with success. My own view, if I do say so myself, is that it is one of the best texts available for providing critical disputes that students can enter, and models of critical argument. I believe our texts and Richter's *Falling into Theory* are better tools for teaching criticism than, say, the companion Bedford series of "Critical Casebooks," which expose undergraduates to current revisionist literary approaches but fail to represent— and in some cases hardly mention—the traditional approaches that the newer ones are revising. I also like to think that in bringing together critical essays that speak directly to one another, these "controversy" texts provide students with a focus that is missing from traditional casebooks, which present a variety of different interpretations that do not address or refer to one another.[12]

On the other hand, having myself used the Graff/Phelan *Huck* and the Richter *Falling into Theory* in college undergraduate courses, I think we still have work to do to make such texts accessible and usable to most college students, to say nothing of high schoolers. I have found these texts to be very effective with students who already have some grasp of literary critical discourse and the conventions of expository argument. I find them less successful, however, with students who lack such a grasp and are not sure they want one. Phelan and I hope to make our text more user-friendly for such students in a revised edition now in progress.

One example of the unexpected problems I encountered when I taught our *Huckleberry Finn* text (in a class at the University of Chicago) was occasioned by our editorial decision to highlight the problem students often have with the search for "hidden meanings" that drives literature classes. We note in our introduction that Twain himself seems to side with this student skepticism when he opens his novel with the famous "Notice": "Persons attempting to find a motive in this narrative will be prosecuted; persons attempting to find a moral in it will be banished; persons attempting to find a plot in it will be shot." Furthermore, as Phelan and I point out, Twain not only warns us explicitly against "ponderous academic analysis." He sets up other obstacles to such analysis in the work itself, as we say, "by using Huck's voice to narrate the book, by including a range of colloquial dialects, and by sometimes satirizing the pretensions of genteel speech."[13]

Our intention was to flush out the Huck-like objections to intellectual analysis that students might harbor, but to do so in a way that would allow these objections to be answered and overcome. We went on to suggest several answers to these objections ourselves: 1) If Twain had as little interest in serious moral issues as his "Notice" seems to indicate, why then did he choose to write about slavery, and have his hero wrestle intensely with his "conscience" over whether to free Jim? 2) It is not likely that the novel could have achieved its classic status in our culture if it had not engaged some serious moral and social issues. For these reasons, we suggested, Twain could not have intended to be taken seriously in implying that his novel was mere entertainment without serious moral substance. Furthermore, the fact that Twain wants his novel to be fun does not rule out his wanting us to think about important moral and social issues.

These arguments, however, turned out to be more persuasive to

Phelan and me than they were to some of my undergraduates, who were reluctant to dismiss Twain's "Warning" so quickly. If Twain did not really mean what he said, they asked, why did he say it? Twain's pervasively comic tone persuaded them that, however serious its subject matter, the novel was really meant to be read only as entertainment, not as serious moral investigation.

Phelan and I had sought to "empower" a certain anti-intellectualism so that teachers would be able to answer and overcome it, but we evidently empowered this attitude all too well. I came away feeling that we needed to explore the question of reading for entertainment and reading for deep meaning more thoroughly. Critics since Van Wyck Brooks have suggested that Twain himself was radically split over whether to aim at being a serious artist or a popular entertainer, and Twain's text is indeed ambivalent over whether it is to be taken as entertainment or art or both, an ambivalence that helps explain the lapse into slapstick humor at the end.[14] I raised this possibility of ambivalence with my students, but I ended up wishing Phelan and I had written the issue more extensively into our text, as we hope to in a revised edition.

GROWING YOUR OWN CRITICISM

This experience teaching our edition of *Huckleberry Finn* did not weaken my conviction that published criticism is a vastly underused resource in humanities courses, but it suggested that teachers often need to edit that criticism or even rewrite it (as well as cut it down to readable proportions). And when published texts fail, we need to "grow our own" critical texts in class handouts. To be sure, this can be a lot of effort at the outset, but in the long run it should save work since it should produce better results and since homemade handouts can be recycled and borrowed by fellow teachers.

In a project I mentioned earlier involving teaching Shakespeare's *Tempest* to college and high school students, Thomas McCann of Community High School in West Chicago composed the following exchange, to which he asked students to respond in writing. McCann imagined two artists, Agnes and Beaumont, who have been commissioned to compose an animated cartoon version of *The Tempest* "so

that children in elementary and secondary schools can understand it."
McCann asked his students to weigh the arguments of the two cartoonists against the evidence of the play itself and give their views on which
of them seems most true to Shakespeare's original, as well as think
about what being true to an original might mean:

Agnes: In my . . . drawings, I wanted to show Caliban as a foul,
animal-like creature. He is dirty, and he wears few clothes. He is un-
shaven, with tufts of hair spotting his entire frame. He would be
hunched over, instead of standing erect as a civilized human being
would.

Beaumont: I don't see that at all in the play. Caliban is simply
wearing what is appropriate for the island on which he was born.
His clothing and his manner of living suited him fine until Prospero came along to judge him. You can't say he is uncivilized. He
is merely different. He had language and customs that were civil
enough for his environment. Prospero ridicules Caliban because
Prospero judges Caliban's manners and apparel to be inferior to his
own. How can one say that one person's culture is superior to
another's?

Agnes: Well, there certainly is evidence in the text that Caliban
is a beast. Prospero addresses him as "Thou poisonous slave, got by
the Devil himself . . ." (I, ii, 391). Miranda talks about him being
"Abhorred slave, Which any print of goodness wilt not take . . ."
(I, ii, 431–32). When Stefano and Trinculo happen upon him, they
refer to him as "A strange fish" and "a monster" (II, ii, 28, 67).

Beaumont: Of course they would think of Caliban as a beast,
since they are Europeans who feel uncomfortable with anything that
is different from them. In their opinion Caliban is a beast, but Caliban sees himself as a King, someone who has rightful dominion
over the whole island. Caliban points out to Prospero that "This
island's mine by Sycorax my mother, Which thou takest from
me . . ." (I, ii, 406).

Agnes: You've got to be kidding! Prospero was the Duke of Mi-
lan. He would be the epitome of civility. He came to the island and
tried to improve Caliban's condition by teaching him language and

showing him some appropriate manners. Prospero represents the legitimate triumph of art and civilization over raw nature.

Beaumont: Does anything give us the right to use horses to pull plows and mules to carry burdens? Were they consulted?

Agnes: Of course not! They are beasts. By virtue of human beings' superior intelligence they have a right to rule the animals.

Beaumont: You are saying, then, that anyone who has a superior intelligence has a right to rule over someone with less intelligence and turn that person into a slave?

Agnes: You're twisting things now. I'm talking about the behavior of humans toward animals, not humans toward humans.

Beaumont: You must judge Caliban to be a human. He can speak and reason and use tools. He can do anything a human being can do. Do you see him as an animal because he looks different?

The issues McCann's dialogue raises are those that most of us would like to see literature students engage with: where does Shakespeare stand in relation to the characters in his play? How do readers go about deciding? The issues further open out into philosophical, moral, and anthropological problems that go beyond literature—the problem of cultural relativism, for example: is Caliban to be judged by an absolute standard of values, or are his customs and manners appropriate to his own culture? Are our contemporary views on such issues relevant to reading Shakespeare?

Not surprisingly, this exercise did not turn eleventh-graders or college students into masters of intellectual discourse overnight. Some students still found the issues elusive even when reduced to such simplified and schematic terms. Some had a hard time seeing the connection between the debate between the cartoonists and the play they had read, encountering the difficulty I have mentioned of moving from the dramatic (and in this case archaic) language of the play itself to the theme-talk of the disputants. Some seemed puzzled at the assumption of the exercise that meaningful debate about literary texts—or values— is possible: isn't the beauty of literature, some students asked, that it can mean anything you want it to mean? Aren't values inherently personal and subjective?

At the least, however, working with McCann's home-grown dialogue gave the teachers involved in the project a better sense of where our problems and challenges lay and where we might go from here. We came away confirmed in our conviction that working with critical texts can enable students to produce a higher quality of critical thinking and writing than they normally do. Students *can* enter the critical conversations of our culture, but not until we start making those conversations available to them.

10 The Application Guessing Game

With Andrew Hoberek

NOTHING MORE GLARINGLY ILLUSTRATES the academic world's formidable ability to induce cluelessness than the university application process. More dramatically than anywhere else, the application process illustrates the failure of the academic club to socialize hopeful entrants into its customs, beliefs, and behaviors. This failure shows up at every link of the academic food chain, from high school students applying to college to college undergraduates applying to graduate school to graduate students applying for academic jobs and even to professors applying for grants.

This chapter is based on our experience working together from 1995 to 1998 as director and assistant director of the then new Master of Arts Program in the Humanities (MAPH) at the University of Chicago. A major part of our annual cycle consisted of sifting through and choosing among hundreds of graduate applications. The more we sifted, the more we realized we were getting a quick and disheartening education in what talented recent college graduates think is in their interest to say in order to gain the opportunity to do graduate work in the humanities. Most disheartening was the realization that the problems with the applications often stemmed not from deficiencies in the applicants, but from someone else's failure to make clear to them what was wanted.

Our experience suggested that graduate school applicants are getting either bad advice or no advice at all. Since only a tiny fraction of undergraduates hope to go on to graduate school, and an even tinier fraction actually do, this might seem a limited problem that can be rectified by better advising. Better advising would indeed help, but the problems exposed by the graduate application process go much deeper, exposing fundamental deficiencies in undergraduate education. The applications we saw suggest that the intellectual habits encouraged by undergraduate study (and in turn by secondary schooling) are preparing students poorly not just for graduate school, but for most walks of life.

What motivates this curious withholding of information? The reasons are complicated, but clearly they have something to do with long-standing tensions between undergraduate and graduate study, a product of the feeling that undergraduates need to be protected from the professionalism of graduate research. This attitude reflects the hostility toward institutions that since the 1950s has been a feature of American intellectual life, shared by artists, conservative aesthetes, radical critics of professionalism, and other otherwise disparate groups. Academic humanists have been eager to disavow their affiliation with institutions, and this guilt or shame at being institutionalized issues in a reluctance to contaminate others with the institutional taint. (At its most extreme, this attitude leads some instructors to try to avoid wielding their authority in the classroom, a move that paradoxically throws students deeper into the dark about how one gets and uses power.) This entrenched anti-institutionalism discourages us from seeing graduate education as the professional training it inevitably is. Loath to "impose" our institutional practices even on those who want to follow in our footsteps, we end up unintentionally turning those practices into mysterious guild secrets.

The graduate application process thus turns out to be a surprisingly good vantage point for examining the "Don't Ask, Don't Tell" character of academic noncommunication. The process is also a good place from which to measure the especially damaging impact on students of bad communicative practices in an age of financial crisis for research universities. In the days when financial support was generous and college teaching jobs were plentiful, gaining admittance to a Ph.D. program was relatively easy even for applicants who possessed the shakiest conception of academic research.

Our two careers, though separated by thirty years, illustrate the point: both of us were admitted to top doctoral programs (Stanford in 1959 and Chicago in 1989, respectively) with strong financial support, even though as applicants we had only the foggiest notion of what was meant by terms like "research," "the profession," and "academic field." In the past decade, however, this situation has changed entirely and probably permanently: were we to apply today, the hazy knowledge of the profession that we displayed would almost certainly hurt our chances, if not disqualify us altogether. Here, as elsewhere, in today's climate of shrinking budgets and much stiffer competition for far fewer Ph.D. slots, the costs of being clueless in academe have escalated.

"I LOVE LITERATURE"

Chicago's MAPH is a case in point: many of its students pay $30,000 in tuition in the hope that the MA program will get them into the Ph.D. program for which they originally applied. That is, these applicants land in MAPH because they could not be funded at the Ph.D. level, as many of them would certainly have been only a decade ago. These students naturally wonder what the difference is between themselves and those who were accepted to the Ph.D. program. And so far as we can judge, there is often no discernible difference except that the successful applicants had a better sense of what to say in their applications (Andrew personally attests to reading numerous applications better than the one that got him into Chicago's Ph.D. program in English in the late eighties). Many of the program's students, in other words, go deeply into debt to find out from MAPH what their college education failed to tell them.

We are not talking about esoteric secrets here, much less about a bag of cheap tricks for advancing in a careerist academic game. We are talking about rhetorical principles that could readily be imparted to any grad school applicant. But as things stand, bright and sophisticated graduate applicants are unwittingly making exactly the moves that are certain to undermine their chances.

For example, in the statement of purpose every applicant is asked to write, the vast majority say they want to go on for a doctorate because they "love literature"—or art history, philosophy, classical archaeology, history, or what you will. Here is a typical statement, made up by us but instantly recognizable, we bet, by experienced application readers: "Ever since age three I've been passionately in love with the sensuous sounds of words. So when Mother Goose was read to me in my crib, I somehow knew I was destined for a lifelong love affair with literature." Now contrary to recent accusations, it is not true that today's academic humanists are so besotted with theory, political correctness, and arid research that pure love of literature no longer matters, or even counts as a disqualification. It is not that love of literature is no longer considered a good thing, but that in a graduate application this love is taken for granted and therefore does not score any points: love of one's subject is a necessary qualification for graduate study, but it is not sufficient to get you in. After all, the other five hundred or so applicants also presumably love literature, impressionist painting, or whatever they wish to study—there are precious few other reasons for getting a Ph.D. these days. Even those who would argue that love of literature should be the primary requirement for joining the academic club would be loath to commit themselves to the care of a doctor whose only qualification was that she really loved the human body. In Ph.D. application workshops we developed for MAPH students, we suggested that the point they needed to get across was not that they love their subject, but that they are ready to join an intellectual conversation about what they love. They need to translate their passion for their subject into an indication that they know how to discuss it publicly with other knowledgeable people, rather than simply enhancing their private enjoyment of art, philosophy, or classics. This means showing that they have some plausible picture of the academic field or subfield they envision themselves joining.

Here is one of the many possible ways we suggested our advisees could improve on "I love literature" and Mother Goose: "My wish to continue graduate study at the Ph.D. level has been sparked by an interest in our recent version of the ancient debate over the social functions of the arts. More specifically, . . ." To us this revised version doesn't sound arid, dry, or smacking of shallow careerism. It does manage to give an indication of how the applicant imagines channeling a personal passion for the humanities into the sorts of conversations in which scholars and critics engage.

But surely, it will be objected, most undergraduates will not know enough about such academic conversations to initiate groundbreaking new paradigm shifts in their statements of purpose. Are we not making unrealistic demands on undergraduates, even those smart and committed enough to be serious competitors for graduate school admission? In fact, such demands *are* unrealistic if college undergraduates are not encouraged to think of their work as part of a larger cultural and critical conversation, as generally they are not.

We will come back to this point in a moment, but for now suffice it to say that in our experience undergraduates are often more than capable of producing the kind of meta-commentary we urge, which involves not much more than the basic rhetorical principle that what you say should have something to do with what people around you are saying. Such a strategy is effective because it suggests that the applicant is already starting to enter the conversation, if not yet a finished professional. As is often the case in and out of academe, success depends on bootstrapping: showing that you've already begun to do what you want to learn how to do.

Then, too, as I have suggested in the last two chapters, asking students to frame arguments within a conversation actually makes writing easier, since it replaces what often seems a vague mandate to "discuss" a topic with straightforward guidelines that give students something to push off from, thereby addressing the perennial complaint, "But I don't know what you want in this paper." By the time students are ready to apply to graduate school, the instructions should become something like, "Figure out the received wisdom about your text or topic and show how you refute or go beyond it." The cocktail party (as Kenneth Burke once noted in analogizing it to the intellectual life) provides a familiar analogy: people who walk up to a conversation, listen to what is going on to find out what the interlocutors are already talking about, then make a contribution to this pre-existing conversation generally have more success than those who interrupt whomever is speaking and launch into an unrelated discourse about whatever happens to be on their minds.

TRAINING PUBLIC INTELLECTUALS

But how do we know that our improved version above is more likely to impress graduate application committees than the original? And, at a time when so many who do go on for a Ph.D. fail to find teaching positions, is prepping students to impress such committees wise and ethically defensible? As it happens, these were exactly the questions that Chicago's MAPH was devised to address. MAPH is one of the growing number of new master's programs that aims to encourage career alternatives for graduate students in the humanities besides the traditional doctoral/college-teaching track. The aim of MAPH is to produce not only better academics but better citizens, people who can enter the conversations not just of the academy but of the wider public sphere. Approximately half the fifty to sixty students who enroll in its one-year program do so in the hope that MAPH will help them get into a doctoral program and eventually become college teachers. The other half, however (as well as a significant portion of the former group whose priorities change during their year in the program), take the MAPH degree with a range of other potential occupations in mind, including high school teaching, museum and gallery curatorship, journalism, editing, and business. To enhance this option, the university developed internships for MAPH graduates in local firms such as the Monsanto and Nuveen Corporations, and MAPH's academic advisers work closely with the University's office of Career and Placement. MAPH aims to produce neither corporate functionaries nor missionaries bringing the light of academic reason to the rest of the world, but to reimagine effective academics and nonacademics alike as public intellectuals, able to talk to audiences beyond their immediate circle.[1]

Aiming as the program does to serve both academic and nonacademic career aspirants, MAPH necessarily operates on the faith that writing and research in the academic humanities can speak to the needs of corporations and other nonacademic institutions as well as of the academy. It assumes, that is, that not only do the corporate and the academic worlds have important things to say to each other, but that the same thinking, research, and writing skills can be adapted for use in both worlds. As it evolved, the program became a year-long writing seminar on addressing readers who do not necessarily share one's special terminology, pet assumptions, or political views. The questions we asked students constantly to address in everything they wrote are those that have been stressed in this book: "So what?" and "Who cares?"

We knew that these assumptions about academic communication would seem a stretch to many academics and nonacademics alike, for the conventional wisdom is that the academic research conversation is so highly specialized that to enter it you must turn your back on the larger public sphere. For a long time this was indeed the case (and still is in some disciplines). The gamble that animated MAPH, however, was that the culture of academic research had undergone a profound change since the 1960s, and that training MA students to address a wide range of publics, to ask "So what?" and "Who cares?" *as such questions might be asked by those publics,* would now open doors to both academic and nonacademic careers. So our tactic was not to discourage students from specializing so much as to help them explain their specializations to nonspecialists. We assumed that today's academics, like most everyone in our complicated society, are already specialists; the key question is, can they talk to nonspecialists as well as other specialists? We assumed that these are reconcilable aims, that specialization and generalization are not opposites but complementary aspects of the same process.

To put it another way, we assumed that learning to summarize and enter the conversations around us is excellent rhetorical training whether you aspire to become a professor of late Gothic architecture, a corporate CEO, a labor organizer, a freelance journalist, a talk-show host, or (as we note above) a frequenter of cocktail parties. In fact, "Joining the Conversation" became the unofficial mantra of MAPH, as it has been of this book. In many ways, our principles were no more than an extension of the rhetorical training provided by first-year composition programs—scope out what your intended audience figures to think and construct your own arguments in relation to that.

After our three years of working together (and six years of MAPH's existence as of 2002), we believe the program's record has vindicated our thinking. At the time of our departures from the University of Chicago (Hoberek in 1998, Graff two years later), the program had compiled a well-documented record of success in helping its graduates obtain both nonacademic jobs and admission to Ph.D. programs and professional schools. At last count, ninety percent of MAPH students who apply to doctoral programs are accepted with financial support. This success stems in part from the cultural prestige of a University of Chicago degree, but some Chicago graduates are turned down by doctoral programs and then succeed after training in MAPH. A personal statement by a MAPH student who followed our principles has been published as a model essay in an "insiders guide" to "getting in and succeeding" in graduate school.[2]

To be sure, the fact that screening committees and their members do not necessarily apply the same criteria (and the fact that departments rarely discuss their criteria) probably increases the randomness of their decisions. Some give more weight to GRE scores, grades, recommendations, or coursework than do others. Nevertheless, in our experience it is the writing done by the candidate that tends to make the difference. Nor is this surprising, for as diminished funds and larger applicant pools increase the pressure on departments to make accurate predictions of which prospective doctoral candidates will succeed, more importance falls on the candidates' writing, where the qualities of mind that make for success can be most readily assessed. Working academics don't take courses or standardized tests, but they do write.

Since the statement of purpose and writing sample are the parts of the application over which the candidates have the most control, lack of guidance on these is especially costly. Take the following hypothetical personal statement openings: the first conveys its information in a vacuum, whereas the second frames the same information in a larger discussion:

Before:
    In a college seminar paper, I discussed the prevalence of gendered battle imagery in *Hamlet*. . . .

Improved:

In a college seminar paper on battle imagery in *Hamlet,* I discussed the debates inside and outside feminist circles on the question of how specifically gender colors language and how far imagery can be defined as "male," "female," etc. . . .

The first version shows the applicant has the savvy to apply a current method, feminist interpretation. Unlike the "I love literature" statement cited earlier, which could have been written as readily in the 1920s as in the 1990s, this comment shows that the student is aware of discussions going on in the humanities today. The improved version does this and more, however, suggesting that the applicant is able not only to *apply* a current methodology and produce a reading of a text, but to stand back from that methodology and reading, unpack the assumptions behind them, and relate them to broader debates—indicating why ("So what?") and for whom ("Who cares?") the candidate wrote the paper in the first place.

Both versions reflect the recent politicizing trend in academic literary interpretation, but the second seems less likely to be dismissed as formulaically politically correct. By flagging the debates about gender and imagery in which she is participating, the candidate shows she recognizes differences of opinion about these questions and sees them as controversial rather than given. Such advice does not ask applicants to abandon or hide political convictions (which may or may not be a successful tactic), but rather to explain them to readers who might not agree with them (it happens). In our view, urging graduate school applicants (and graduate students) to acknowledge disagreement can only benefit them later in the job market, where representing one's field to outsiders becomes more rather than less important, since most hiring committees are not composed of specialists in the advertised field.

Here in part is the statement chosen for the *Grad School Handbook* from the Ph.D. application of a student we advised (the names have been altered):

My specific areas of interest have come into focus this year at Washington University where I am exploring the interdisciplinary contexts of literature by taking classes in religious studies as well as social thought. Working with my mentor, Professor X, has stimulated my interest in questions of textuality and contextuality. Does the text exist prior to interpretation? What are the uses of religious rhetoric in critical discourse?

I am interested in applying these broader questions to the historical literary context which most fascinates me—the nineteenth century. My interest in this subject was sparked by a graduate class on "Realism in the Novel," taught by the novelist John Black. I could see myself doing work on the role of the author in the novel and an exploration of how the multiplicity of voices which characterizes novelistic discourse both includes and excludes the voice of the author. Pursuing this in a large scale project such as a dissertation would mean engaging the current debate over whether the author has agency and individual subjectivity or is merely a conduit of intersubjective codes. . . .[3]

Note here how the applicant demonstrates the ability to put ideas raised in different courses into conversation, a skill that becomes crucial in a graduate and professorial career and that, again, is not advanced by the undergraduate textual explication exercise.

THE POINTLESS UNDERGRADUATE ESSAY

The principle of entering the conversation holds also for the graduate application writing sample. In our rough estimate, fully 90 percent of the sample essays that accompany humanities Ph.D. applications are close readings of a single text. With very few exceptions—and these jump out at you because they are so rare—these essays plunge immediately into a reading of a text or artwork with no explanation of why the writer thought the reading needed to be undertaken in the first place. It's easy to see how this happens: the essays were written for a college course in which the reason for writing the paper ("So what?") was already given in the course topic or specific writing assignment, and thus did not need to be mentioned in the paper itself. Unfortunately, such essays do not travel well, since the screening committee members who read them did not take the course, and may not agree with—or even recognize—premises that went without saying in someone else's classroom. Indeed, once such essays move outside the course they virtually become pointless. For since their point is presupposed by the course, it fails to appear in the paper, which gives no indication why or if the writer cares about the stakes of his or her reading or argument. Even worse, such papers may reinforce their writers' assumption that what they do in humanities courses has no purpose beyond earning credit towards graduation or getting into graduate school.

If the writing samples submitted with graduate applications are meaningful evidence, the decontextualized exercises that undergraduates are asked to write in many courses are poor training not just for getting into graduate school, but for explaining oneself and persuading others in any career or situation. The shame of this situation is that applicants who submit writing samples that are studiously pointless would never think to communicate this way in real life. It took them years of education to learn to speak with no context to no one. Even as college students are informally learning on the weekends to converse with a wider range of people, it seems their courses ask them to do just the opposite. Such mystification can only encourage undergraduates to assume that when they come to a college or a university they have to set their everyday rhetorical and conversational competence aside.

Our advice to MAPH students was not to give up textual close reading, which is still a central, indispensable skill for any humanist, but to frame their reading with a meta-commentary that relates it to conversations in the field or the wider culture:

Before
   As I will argue in this paper, Fitzgerald's Jay Gatsby is an arch example of the commodified self produced by twentieth-century urban America.

Improved
   It is tempting to assume that Fitzgerald's Gatsby must be "great" because he seems to transcend the conformity that dominates the twentieth-century America around him. I will

argue in this paper, however, that Gatsby finally is shown not to be a rebel against the commodified self of twentieth-century urban America but an arch example of it.

Whereas the before version states its claim as uncontroversial—and therefore uninteresting—the improved version inscribes and engages with a hypothetical naysayer. To write this latter kind of opening, it is less important to know Fitzgerald criticism (though it obviously helps) than to anticipate the counterarguments that give you a reason for writing and lend interest and bite to your claims.

In encouraging MAPH students to enter the critical conversation, we were letting them in on the process by which the most influential critics generate their ideas. For example, the queer reading of Henry James's "The Beast in the Jungle" at the heart of Eve Sedgwick's formidable *Epistemology of the Closet* is, at bottom, no more than an elaborate disagreement with the guiding assumption of most previous readings of the story: that the protagonist John Marcher's premonition that a fearful beast will one day spring upon him arises from his failure to recognize that he "should have desired [his female friend] May Bartram."[4] Sedgwick's reading clearly passes the "So what?" test, since if accepted it would significantly change our view of James's story, and perhaps of our culture's sexual ideology.

Indeed, "So what?" is a question that academe's most successful rhetoricians often write explicitly into their work. In his recent book *Professional Correctness,* for instance, Stanley Fish refutes the assumption of some cultural studies theorists that a discipline's legitimacy is subverted or "transgressed" once it is shown that the unity of its object of study (e.g., literature, human nature, cultural tradition) is not grounded in God or nature but is "socially constructed." According to several academic economists quoted by Fish,

> "The ramifications of disciplinary practices . . . are often contradictory and complex rather than coherent, the contending visions of theory and practice disparate rather than merging into . . . unity."

To all of which *I* say, "So what?" The fact that a self-

> advertised unity is really a grab-bag of disparate elements
> held together by chicken-wire, or by shifting political and
> economic alliances, or by a desire to control the production
> and dissemination of knowledge, does not make the unity
> disappear; it merely shows what the unity is made of, not
> that it isn't one.[5]

Fish, to be sure, is a master of this kind of incisive argumentation, and his self-confidence is not matched by many professors, much less by college undergraduates. Nevertheless, the strategy Fish uses would not be beyond undergraduates' reach if educators were to be more forthright (and at times formulaic) about it: find someone out there you can disagree with, restate his or her point, and then put in your own oar.

In both the statement of purpose and the writing sample, then, successful graduate applicants (and subsequent professionals) tend to relate their work to larger professional and public sphere conversations that they wish to enter and influence. Again, as our examples of MAPH's before and improved formulations suggest, the principles here are not esoteric or even exclusively academic, but would serve anyone well in almost any situation. To the objection that what we are promoting sounds like the precocious seduction of undergraduates into the world of high academic theory, we reply that in fact our program more closely resembles the truisms of traditional rhetorical instruction. Many of MAPH's strategies for graduate education were adapted more or less bold-facedly from first-year composition pedagogy. In a climate that increasingly cries out for generalists, composition and rhetoric instructors who have notoriously occupied the bottom rung of the academic ladder should get the respect and emulation they deserve.

To take up a final objection, it may be said that the kind of advice we are offering would at best only help doctoral applicants compete better against each other for the same limited pot of rewards. What does the competition for scarce resources in doctoral programs have to do with democratizing education as a whole? It would do nothing to increase the pot, which is where the real work is needed. Furthermore, if all applicants were to get the kind of advice we have proposed here, the value of that advice would automatically diminish.

We grant that helping a few graduate applicants compete for diminished resources does nothing to address the larger problem of how to increase those resources and make good the promise of democratic access to higher education. But our failure to make our academic practices more accessible does have a bearing on higher education's current financial crisis. In the boom years that followed World War II, higher education hardly needed to justify itself in order to attract generous financial support. That is obviously no longer the case: even when economic recovery is trumpeted, little of the rising tide makes its way to the backwaters of humanities education and research. Higher education must make a case for itself if it hopes to maintain its share of social and economic support, but it is hard to make a case to others when our rationale for what we do is unclear to ourselves. Explaining what we do and why we do it has become crucial to the future of higher education. In this respect, the most beneficial result of asking our students "So what?" and "Who cares?" would be that academics ask these questions more frequently of ourselves.

POSTSCRIPT: A MODEST PROPOSAL FOR COLLEGE APPLICATION

At the start of this chapter, Andrew Hoberek and I stated that academia's failure "to socialize hopeful entrants into its customs, beliefs, and behaviors . . . shows up at every link of the academic food chain," including the process of "high school students applying to college." But the graduate school application process with which we have been concerned in this chapter differs in several significant ways from the college application process. Most obviously, the college applicant's nonacademic interests and personal qualities—well-roundedness, the varied talents and interests he or she will bring to the community—come into play to a greater extent than in graduate school applications, where the screening process aims at identifying future professionals in a field of study. This is why college applications are generally read and judged by the staff of the admissions office, whereas graduate applications decisions are usually made by departmental faculty.

These differences make college application decisions harder to predict and rationalize than graduate ones. In college application, the relationship is less direct between the intellectual interests and accomplishments of applicants and their chances of being accepted. In fact, college applicants can be rejected if judged to be one-sidedly cerebral. This problem was brought to our attention by a thoughtful response we received to a version of this chapter that appeared in *College English*.[6] Tim Cantrick, head of college counseling at St. Luke's School in New Canaan, Connecticut, wrote that the advice Hoberek and I give to applicants—show that you can "enter the academic conversation"—is not only likely to be difficult for high school students to follow, but may backfire. Referring to the essay part of the application, Cantrick wrote, "Only infrequently, I'm afraid, do we have students sufficiently well-read to see the connection between their essay topic and a point of contention debated among *academics* on college campuses. Even if we did, the application essay in that context might go unappreciated by admissions officers, themselves uninformed about colloquy of that sort." Cantrick's further observations seem worth quoting at length:

> Which is, of course, why you suggested that our students—high school students generally—might enter the intellectual "conversation" at a more modest level, that is, connecting their application essay's theme with a contemporary issue of larger significance. This shouldn't be difficult, as you point out, for any reasonably intelligent, alert eighteen-year-old who regularly reads a national daily or weekly news publication or watches CNN or otherwise gathers reliable information about our world. I agree, and will encourage our students to incorporate such connections in their essays—at the front or back end. [Cantrick enclosed a form he developed to help his advisees "enter the academic conversation" in their application essays.]

Still, Cantrick wonders, "given the traditional features of the undergraduate application-essay, might it be risky for our senior applicants to introduce into their essays the new and non-traditional characteristic suggested in your article?"

Cantrick explains:

Your article envisions the ideal essay as one where the applicant foregrounds intellectuality in a particular way. To be
sure, undergraduate admissions officers want to admit
bright students who think and speak in the right ways for
academic success in college, but they tend to determine that
aspect of the applicant's fitness from courses taken and
grades on the transcript, and of course letters of recommen-
dation. . . . [They] look to the essay, however, for another type
of insight. Instead of learning more about the applicant's
academic persona, they want to meet the applicant's psychological self. They want to hear a vivid, individual voice.
Standard advice from how-to books and admissions officers
themselves universally holds that the best way to accomplish this purpose is to speak in concrete particulars, especially in the form of stories, character sketches, and detailed
descriptions. . . .

In other words, the undergraduate application-essay, in its
most accomplished and effective form as currently practiced,
shows rather than tells, which places it much lower on the
scale of generality than the kind of essay that explicitly discusses ideas.

In short, Cantrick observes, there appears to be "a genre-conflict" between the undergraduate admissions essay, which is "traditionally thick
with personality," and the graduate-level essay, where abstract ideas
come into play.

Cantrick seems to us right to be concerned about a double-bind
facing his advisees: if they follow Hoberek and Graff's advice and show
in their essays they can "enter the conversation," they may be dismissed
as too brainy. Mr. Cantrick goes on to suggest still further ambiguities
about what is wanted from college applicants:

Under the current regime readings are capricious, and, in
the absence of a standard, responses can only be arbitrary.
Humor that pleases one admissions officer may displease an-

other. Where one will be sympathetic to a particular story, the next will be annoyed. Some will hear tones of voice that others can't. Intellectual content that stimulates this reader might just as easily strike that reader as pretentious. In yet one more article in the popular press about the admissions process, *Time Magazine* (October 23, 2000) reported on this very point, presenting without any sense of irony the absurdly hedged advice of the admissions officers interviewed for the article: For example: "While there's no one formula for soul baring [in the application essay], there are many wrong ones." The typical teenager, whose struggle to recognize and develop the finer points of his soul's identity is not nearly complete by the end of high school, gains absolutely nothing from such "advice," except an excruciating sense of dread.

Mr. Cantrick's observations caused me to recall the applications from high school students I had read when I served on college admissions committees. I remember noticing that applicants almost *never* gave as a reason for wanting to attend University X that they had developed an interest in an intellectual issue or problem that had arisen in any disciplines. The exceptions were scientifically oriented students who described high school science projects that sounded as if they would be in the ballpark of what science professors regard as hard science. I began to suspect that any applicant who could name an issue debated in the humanities or social sciences—e.g., is truth objective or socially relative? is human nature alterable?—would immediately be accepted, if only because such an applicant would stand out sharply from the pack. Admittedly, it never happened, so my hunch remains untested. With these thoughts and Mr. Cantrick's acute comments in mind, I end this chapter with a proposal: make the college admissions essay an academic paper analogous to the writing sample submitted by graduate applicants, though judged by less-advanced criteria. The essay might be one the applicant has written for any high school course or subject, as colleges requested before the emergence of professional admissions offices.

It's true that such academic writing samples would be subject to the sorts of problems that Hoberek and I discussed above in graduate admissions essays. Even so, requiring such essays would have two major advantages over the present system. First, since both applicants and admissions readers will know that the main point of the application essay is to demonstrate academic intellectual qualities, much of the ambiguity and consequent terror that now plagues the essay figures to abate. Second, since high school teachers will know that an academic essay is required in the college application process, they will have an inducement to make serious academic writing assignments and teach their subjects at the highest intellectual level. Of course, if this proposal were adopted, unheard of consequences would follow: high schools that now amount to little more than social centers attached to test-taking factories would have to devote themselves to furthering the intellectual life. Whether America could handle such a thing remains to be seen, but it is worth finding out.

PART IV: TEACHING THE CLUB

11 Hidden Intellectualism

IN THIS BOOK SO FAR, I have been looking at factors that make academic intellectual culture opaque or alienating to many students: seemingly counterintuitive problems and argumentative practices that are rarely explained; curricular mixed messages that further muddy those practices; phobias about adversarial debate and intellectual analysis; obfuscating habits of academic writing; the tendency to withhold the critical conversations that students are expected to enter. In this chapter, I shift the emphasis by examining some ways in which academic and student cultures are closer to each other than they seem and how teachers can take advantage of this convergence.

I start with an account of an arresting memoir "of a Pentecostal Boyhood" that appeared in 1993 in the *Voice Literary Supplement*. Michael Warner describes his improbable journey from his upbringing in a Christian Pentecostal family and graduation from Oral Roberts University to his current identity as a "queer atheist intellectual." It is hard to imagine a more complete break between a past and present life than the one Warner recounts. "From the religious vantage of my childhood and adolescence," Warner writes, "I am one of Satan's agents. From my current vantage, that former self was exotically superstitious." How, he wonders, could he have "got here from there"?

Yet ultimately Warner finds a "buried continuity" in his journey from Pat Robertson to Michel Foucault. "Curiously enough," he writes, though "fundamentalism is almost universally regarded as the stronghold and dungeon-keep of American anti-intellectualism, religious culture gave me a passionate intellectual life of which universities are only a pale ivory shadow." For the Pentecostal faithful, Warner says, "the subdenomination you belong to is bound for heaven; the one down the road is bound for hell. You need arguments to show why."

Furthermore, Warner goes on, for Pentecostals "your arguments have to be *readings;* ways of showing how the church down the road misreads a key text." Throughout his childhood and adolescence, Warner writes, "I remember being surrounded by textual arguments in which the stakes were not just life and death but eternal life and death." He recalls an unusually clever Bible study leader who questioned the doctrine of God's omniscience by demonstrating that the Old Testament "clearly showed God acting in stories that . . . made no sense unless God doesn't know the future." Recalling the intense family debates about this man's Biblical interpretations that took place afterwards in the car ride home and at the dinner table, Warner concludes: "Being a literary critic is nice, I have to say, but for lip-whitening, vein-popping thrills it doesn't compete. Not even in the headier regions of Theory can we approximate that saturation of life by argument."[1]

Warner does not say whether his fundamentalist religious preoccupations helped him with his schoolwork or clashed with it. Nevertheless, his account has intriguing implications for education, suggesting how the "saturation of life by argument" can occur in practices often dismissed as anti-intellectual. His essay invites us to think about student intellectual abilities that go overlooked by schools because they come in unlikely forms. To be sure, since religious fundamentalists rarely become intellectuals of any kind, much less queer theorists, we might conjecture that Warner's intellectualism must have come from something else in his background. Yet I suspect there are many buried or hidden forms of intellectualism that do not get channeled into academic work but might if educators were more alert about drawing on them.

Taking a page from Warner, I want to suggest that educators need to pay more attention to the extent to which adolescent lives are often already "steeped in argument." My own working premise as a teacher is that inside every street-smart student—that is, potentially every student—is a latent intellectual trying to break out, and that it's my job to tease out that latent person and help it articulate itself in a more public form. Not that this "hidden intellectual" self is already there and waiting to be discovered. Students who cross over into the intellectual club are inventing a new identity as much as unearthing one that existed before.

STREET SMARTS AND PUBLIC ARGUMENT

It is not a new idea that students harbor intellectual resources—"street smarts"—that go untapped by formal schooling. What is less widely noticed is that these intellectual resources are overlooked because they are tied to ostensibly anti-intellectual interests. We associate the life of the mind too exclusively with subjects and texts that we precategorize as weighty in themselves. We assume that it is possible to wax intellectual about Plato, Shakespeare, the French revolution, and nuclear fission, but not about cars, clothing fashions, dating, sports, TV, or Bible Belt religion. But no necessary relationship has ever been established between any text or subject and the educational depth and weight of the discussion it can provoke. Real intellectuals turn any subject into grist for their mill through the thoughtful questions they bring to it, whereas dullards will find a way to drain the richest subject of interest. That is why, say, a George Orwell writing on the cultural meanings of ephemeral penny postcards is infinitely more substantial than the lucubrations of many scholars on Shakespeare or globalization.[2]

An excellent recent commentary on the tendency to overlook the intellectualism latent in supposedly philistine pursuits is Thomas McLaughlin's *Street Smarts and Critical Theory: Listening to the Vernacular*. McLaughlin argues persuasively that "critical theory," contrary to both its adherents and opponents, is not the monopoly of academic intellectuals but pervades the thinking of nonacademics. "Not all the sharp minds get to go to college," McLaughlin writes, "and not all the theorists are in the academy."[3] McLaughlin maintains that the street smarts of ordinary citizens harbor "vernacular" forms of theory (he borrows the term "vernacular theory" from critics of African American culture like Houston Baker and Henry Louis Gates), from which academics can learn.

For McLaughlin, vernacular theory can

happen in lunch break gripes about the boss and the bureaucracy, in women's caustic jokes about the power and foolish-

ness of men, in fanzines where ordinary fans review and discuss new music, in discussion groups on the
Internet, in television calls to C-SPAN and talk radio, in
letters to the editor, in living room complaints about fifty-
seven channels and nothing on, in interoffice memos, in
speeches to civic or business groups, in action-oriented news-
letters within movements for social change, in pamphlets
and broadsides, in articles and books, in kids' games about
school and home, in rap music, in coffee shop bull sessions
after a movie.[4]

In short, theory "is an integral and crucial element in everyday culture."[5]

I return at the end of this chapter to the ways by which teachers
can tap into students' hidden intellectualism. First, though, I want to
say something about my personal discovery of intellectualism in unlikely early interests of my own.

CONFESSIONS OF A CLOSET NERD

Warner's account of the buried continuity between his Pentecostal past
and his academic intellectual present made me reconsider how I think
about my own adolescence, which I have elsewhere described in print
as thoroughly anti-intellectual. In my previous book I wrote about my
youthful inability to read with pleasure or comprehension and my alienation from the intellectual ways of talking that school and college rewarded.[6] Presenting myself as a typical child of the anti-intellectual fifties, I contrasted my utter lack of interest in literature and history with
my passionate absorption in sports. Warner's essay makes me realize,
however, that the story—both mine and that of the fifties—is more
complicated and contradictory than I had indicated. I see now that
sports provided me with something comparable to the saturation of life
by argument that Pentecostal religion gave Warner, that my preference
for sports over schoolwork was not anti-intellectualism so much as intellectualism by other means.

Not that I was completely wrong in characterizing the fifties I grew
up in as anti-intellectual. It was indeed a period in which intellect was

undervalued or openly scorned, as Richard Hofstadter would document in his classic book, *Anti-Intellectualism in American Life*.[7] The decade began with the symbolic humiliation of The Egghead by The Man of Action in the landslide victory of General Eisenhower over Adlai Stevenson in the presidential election of 1952. It ended with the emergence of the quintessential anti-egghead, Elvis Presley. My teachers, the closest thing to intellectuals in sight, seemed clearly inferior in worldly prowess and physical attractiveness to sports stars, film heroes, and popular singers. With their obscurely high-minded concerns, teachers were such unreal figures that you did a double take when you ran into one in the grocery store or the Laundromat, amazed that they had a life outside their classrooms. I was startled when I discovered that my seventh-grade English teacher not only played softball at the local park, but threw a ball like a regular guy.

The noun "intellectual" was not in my vocabulary or that of any of my friends. I had classmates who excelled at schoolwork and would later have been called nerds, but these without exception were science or mathematics whizzes, technical geniuses rather than masters of argument or cultural analysis. In the adult world there were the "cultured," whom I associated with the feminized "socialites" at the cotillions and balls who were pictured in sepia photos in the Sunday papers every week. For girls, being articulate and brainy about schoolwork was a sign of being conceited or "stuck up," whereas for boys it marked one as a sissy.

My parents were literate people whose household talk provided me with good models. This was the era, however, as sociologists would point out in books like David Riesman's *The Lonely Crowd,* in which influence over adolescents was passing from parents, grandparents, and school authorities to the "peer group," which at that time meant the exploding postwar youth culture being created by television, the automobile, advertising, and consumerism. When in college I read *The Lonely Crowd,* with its account of the "other-directed" character type that aspires not to be a heroic individual but to fit in and be like everybody else, my first thought was, "That's me!"[8]

My attitudes were shaped by the class tensions of a rapidly changing postwar society. The Uptown neighborhood on Chicago's North

Side where we lived till we joined the suburban exodus in 1955 (my eighteenth year) had become a melting pot after the war. Our block was solidly middle class, but one block away—doubtless concentrated there by the real estate companies—were African Americans, Native Americans, and "hillbilly" whites who had recently fled postwar joblessness in the South and Appalachia. Whereas middle class boys were supposed to be "clean cut" (we would now say "preppy"), working class boys dressed and acted like what adult authorities called "juvenile delinquents" and what I and my friends, with a romanticizing inflection, called "hoods."

Negotiating this class boundary was a tricky matter. On the one hand, it was necessary to maintain the boundary between clean cut boys like me and the working class hoods, meaning that it was a good thing to be openly smart in a bookish sort of way. In my case being Jewish already carried a presumption of being smart that I did not entirely disavow. On the other hand, I was desperate for the approval of the hoods, whom I encountered daily on the playing field and in the neighborhood, and for this purpose it was not at all good to be booksmart. The hoods would turn on you if they sensed you were putting on airs over them: "Who you lookin' at, smart ass?" as a leather-jacketed youth once said to me as he relieved me of my pocket change along with my self-respect. I grew up torn, then, between the need to prove I was smart and the fear of a beating if I proved it too well; between the need not to jeopardize my respectable future and the need to impress the hoods.

As I lived it, the conflict came down to a choice between being physically tough and being verbal. For a boy in my neighborhood and elementary school, only being "tough" earned you complete legitimacy. I still recall endless, complicated debates in this period with my closest pals, Teddy Gertz and Phil Kaufman, over who was "the toughest guy in the school." If you were less than negligible as a fighter, as I was, you settled for the next best thing, which was to be inarticulate, carefully hiding telltale marks of refinement such as correct grammar and pronunciation. My models were Marlon Brando's motorcycle outlaw in *The Wild One* ("Ah don' make no deals with no cowps") and his stevedore in *On the Waterfront* (the now-canonical "You don' unnastan',

Cholly, I coulda been a contenduh"), and for a stretch of several weeks I went about imitating Brando's slurred speech. I spent the entire evening of my first high school date doing my Brando, giving up the act only when it became obvious that my date was not impressed.

MY HIDDEN INTELLECTUALISM

In one sense, then, it would be hard to imagine an adolescence more thoroughly anti-intellectual than mine. Yet in retrospect, I see that the story is more complicated, that I and the 1950s themselves were not simply hostile toward intellectualism, but divided and ambivalent. Hofstadter himself observed that the very hostility toward intellectuals in the fifties had been a backhanded acknowledgment of their "overwhelming importance." Intellectuals in this period were despised, Hofstadter wrote, "because of an improvement, not a decline, in [their] fortunes."[9] When Marilyn Monroe married the playwright Arthur Miller in 1956 after divorcing the retired baseball star Joe DiMaggio, the symbolic triumph of Mind over Jock suggested the way the wind was blowing. Even Elvis, according to his biographer, Peter Guralnick, turns out to have supported Adlai over Ike in the presidential election of 1956. "I don't dig the intellectual bit," he told reporters. "But I'm telling you, man, he knows the most."[10]

Though I too thought I did not "dig the intellectual bit," I see now that I was unwittingly in training for it. The germs had actually been planted in the seemingly philistine debates about which boys were the toughest. I must have dimly sensed at the time that in the interminable analysis of sports teams, movies, and toughness that Teddy, Phil, and I engaged in—analysis the real toughs themselves would never have stooped to—I was already betraying an allegiance to the egghead world. I was practicing being an intellectual before I knew that was what I wanted to be.

It was in these discussions with friends about toughness and about sports and games, I think, that I began to learn the rudiments of the intellectual life that Warner got by debating theology with his parents and Bible teachers: how to make an argument, weigh different kinds of evidence, move between particulars and generalizations, summarize the views of others, and enter a conversation about ideas. It was in reading and arguing about sports and toughness that I learned what it felt like to propose a generalization, restate and respond to a counterargument, and perform other intellectualizing operations, including composing the kind of sentences I am writing now. (My friends Teddy and Phil seem to have used this early intellectual training the same way I did: Gertz has become a lawyer and Kaufman a filmmaker, several of whose films—*The Wanderers, The Right Stuff*—I read as allegories of toughness and intellectualism.)

Early on I had become hooked on sports magazines, becoming a regular reader of *Sport* magazine in the late forties and *Sports Illustrated* when it started publication in 1954. I was also an avid reader of the annual magazine guides to professional baseball, football, and basketball, and the autobiographies of sports stars, notably Joe DiMaggio's *Lucky to Be a Yankee* and Bob Feller's *Strikeout Story*. Here was another set of cultures "steeped in argument": was Bob Cousy better than George Mikan? (Possibly.) Was Ted Williams better than Joe DiMaggio or Stan Musial? (Yes.) Would the White Sox finally beat the Yankees this year? (No.) Could one be a Chicago Cubs fan and also root for the White Sox? (Yes.) This last issue came to a head for me in 1951, when after suffering with the Cubs since 1946 (I was not yet following the sport when they won the pennant in 1945), I switched allegiance to the White Sox, who won fourteen straight games in May and held first place till fading late in the season. When I declared my change of loyalty to the men at the north-side package store where I hung out, they were contemptuous and scornful. Being forced to defend myself daily during the summer of '51 taught me to give persuasive reasons for a controversial choice.

Today you cannot pick up the sports page or listen to sports talk radio without being plunged into controversies over race, gender, drugs, and economics, making sports (as some fans bitterly complain) seem more an extension of the world of political conflict than an escape from it. By contrast, it was only rarely in the sports culture of the fifties that one was forced to confront realities like racial injustice, as when Jackie Robinson broke baseball's color line in 1947. Yet I believe the forms of analysis and persuasion that I picked up in ephemeral sports debates were there to be transferred later to more intellectually respectable concerns. And as humble as our debates over tough boys may have been, they prodded me to reflect on larger issues such as the meaning of masculinity and its symbols—were a "duck's ass" haircut, pegged pants, and a leather jacket necessary accouterments of a tough boy? Could a boy be tough and date "nice girls"? In arguing about these matters with friends I was learning rudimentary semiotics, perhaps even getting a feeling for those hidden meanings in texts and events that academia would later reward me for articulating.

Sports and games is only one of the domains whose potential for literacy training (and not only for males) is seriously underestimated by educators, who see that domain as competing with academic development rather than a route to it. Consider as a case in point a recent memoir by the English professor Mark Edmundson on a high school teacher who "changed his life" by transforming him from jock to intellectual. Edmundson writes that until encountering this teacher's philosophy course, he "had never read all the way through a book that was written for adults that was not concerned exclusively with football."[11] Edmundson contrasts his reading of football books with the passion for Nietzsche and Thoreau that his teacher ignited. But it does not occur to Edmundson that had football books not given him an early sense of what it feels like to engage deeply with a text, he might not have been able later to get much out of Nietzsche and Thoreau. I am convinced that without the formative experience provided by comic books and books like Bob Feller's *Strikeout Story*, I would not have been able to take on more heavyweight fare later on. I will always be convinced that whether children read *something* that absorbs them is more important than *what* it happens to be.

Edmundson's failure to consider that football reading might have been a prerequisite for Nietzsche in his case illustrates again how strong the assumption is that jock culture and academic culture are mutually exclusive. I certainly would have been incredulous myself if anyone had suggested that there might be a connection between the habits of mind I was forming in playground disputes about tough kids and sports and the intellectual work of school. School, after all, defined itself as everything that supposedly debased American popular culture was not, so sports and games could only be an escape from schooling and intellect or an antidote for them.

Only much later did it dawn on me that the sports world was more compelling than school to me because it was *more intellectual than school,* not less. Sports, as I have noted, was full of challenging arguments, debates, problems for analysis, and intricate statistics that you could care about, as school conspicuously was not. Furthermore, when you entered sports debates, you became part of a community, and one that was not limited to your family and friends but was national and public. Whereas schoolwork isolated you from others, the pennant race or Ted Williams's .400 batting average was something you could talk about with people you had previously never met. Sports introduced you not only to a culture steeped in argument, but to a public argument culture that transcended the personal. I can't blame my schools for failing to make intellectual culture resemble the World Series or the Super Bowl, but I do fault them for failing to learn anything from the sports and entertainment worlds about how to organize and represent intellectual culture, how to exploit its gamelike element and turn it into arresting public spectacle that would have competed more successfully for my youthful attention.

For here is another thing that never dawned on me, that the real intellectual world, the one that existed in the big world beyond school, is organized very much like the competitive world of team sports, with rival texts, rival interpretations and evaluations of texts, rival theories of why they should be read and taught, and elaborate team competitions in which "fans" of writers, intellectual systems, methodologies, and -isms contend against each other. In assuming that they had to distance themselves from anything as enjoyable and absorbing as sports, my schools missed the opportunity to capitalize on an element of drama and conflict that the intellectual world shares with sports. Consequently I failed to see the parallels between the sports and academic worlds that could have helped me cross more readily from one argument culture to the other. School culture was devoid of intellectual debate, but it contained plenty of *competition,* which became more invidious as one moved up the ladder (and has become even more so today with the advent of high-stakes testing). In this competition, points were scored not by making arguments, but by a show of information or vast reading, or by the one-upmanship of putdowns and cleverness.

School competition, in short, reproduced the less attractive features of sports culture without those that create close bonds and community.

History, for example, was represented to me not as a set of exciting debates between interpretations of the past, but as a series of contextless facts that I crammed into my head the night before the test and then forgot as soon as possible afterwards. Literature was a series of set passages to be memorized, including the prologue to *The Canterbury Tales* and Mark Antony's funeral oration in *Julius Caesar*. I am pleased that I can still recite some of these passages fifty years later, but this memory work would have been more meaningful had there been some larger context of issues and problems to give it point.

In retrospect, I see that my schooling reflected an uneasy postwar compromise between traditional and progressive theories, theories that might have been explained to students but of course were not. On the one hand, the curriculum reflected the vestiges of a nineteenth-century theory that education should be "mental discipline," which meant that making school as dull and grindingly hard as possible was good for the development of character.[12] To paraphrase a comment by Terry Eagleton on the study of English, making a given subject "unpleasant enough to qualify as a proper academic pursuit is one of the few problems" educational institutions have ever effectively solved.[13] But, after the war this archaic belief in the virtue of hard and dreary schooling was being challenged by progressive theories of "life adjustment" and vocationalism. One result of this mixture was a tracking system in which middle class boys like me took a "liberal arts" program, while working class students took machine shop, mechanical drawing, and other vocational subjects. Naturally, nobody overtly labeled students as middle or working class—something that might have forced us to think about social class—students seemed simply to sort ourselves out that way. Even my liberal arts track, however, was a curious mix of traditional courses with semivocational and life-adjustment ones. So in elementary school along with English and Math I took Home Economics, Typing, and Driver Education. But though the theories behind the curriculum clashed, they united in discouraging real intellectual engagement.

School officially stood for intellect, however, giving intellect a bad name and making sports the saving alternative. And insofar as we still define academic intellectual culture by its supposed contrast with popular culture, our schools continue to miss the opportunity to bridge the gap between the argument cultures of adults and the ones students grow up in arguing about sports, parental authority, dating, dress fashions, soap operas, teen entertainment idols, weight, and personal appearance.

WHY STREET SMARTS ARE NOT ENOUGH

I have argued in this chapter that what looks like anti-intellectualism in student culture is often an alternative intellectualism that grows up alongside schooling but is usually seen as irrelevant to it. In speaking of "alternative intellectualism," I do not mean to suggest that student argument cultures represent a repressed rebellion against intellectual culture. On the contrary, in arguing about toughness and sports as an adolescent, I was not rebelling against traditional academic practices (though I may have thought I was), but was unwittingly learning them. If my schooling repressed anything in me, it was not rebellion against the adult world but adulthood itself.

How, then, can teachers tap into the hidden intellectualism that lurks in ostensibly anti-intellectual or nonacademic discussions? Adolescents who argue with passion about rock bands do not necessarily see the point of arguing about a Shakespeare sonnet, a social or psychological theory, or the mind-body problem. For that matter, they do not necessarily see the point of arguing about rock bands in the intellectualized ways and vocabularies in which academics and cultural journalists discuss popular culture or anything else. In this, however, such students implicitly recognize what has been a central point of this book, that becoming educated has more to do with thinking and talking about subjects or texts in analytical ways than with the subjects or texts you study.

If this argument is correct, then schools and colleges are missing an opportunity when they do not encourage students to take their nonacademic interests as objects of academic study. It is self-defeating to decline to introduce any text or subject that figures to engage students who will otherwise tune out academic work entirely. If a student cannot get interested in Mill's *On Liberty* but will read *Sports Illustrated* or the hip hop magazine *Source* with absorption, this is a strong argument for assigning the magazines over the classic. It is a good bet that a student who gets hooked on reading and writing by doing a term paper on *Source* will eventually get to *On Liberty*, and even if he or she does not the magazine reading figures to make the student somewhat more literate and reflective. So it makes pedagogical sense to develop classroom units on sports, cars, fashions, rap music, and other such topics. Give me the student anytime who writes a sharply argued, sociologically acute analysis of an issue of *Source* over the student who writes a lifeless explication of *Hamlet* or Socrates' *Apology*.

But if this argument suggests why it is a good idea to assign readings and topics that are close to students' existing interests, it also suggests the limits of this tactic. For students who get excited about the chance to write about their passion for cars will often write as poorly and unreflectively on that topic as on Shakespeare or Plato. The problem here is that there is no necessary relation between the degree of interest a student shows in a text or subject and the quality of thought or expression such a student manifests in writing or talking about it. The challenge, as college professor Ned Laff has put it, "is not simply to exploit students' nonacademic interests, but to get them to see those interests through academic eyes."

To say that students need to see their interests "through academic eyes" is to say that street smarts are not enough. Here is a problem with Thomas McLaughlin's otherwise welcome demystification of academic theory in *Street Smarts and Critical Theory*, which I mentioned earlier. McLaughlin is right that "theory" and intellectualism are not the monopoly of the educated, and that schools need to "honor the theoretical skills and practices that students bring to the classroom." McLaughlin becomes less persuasive, however, when he attributes special insight to undergraduates into the semiotics of contemporary culture. The typical undergraduate for McLaughlin is an instinctive postmodern theorist, having grown up in a society that values image over reality and information over goods, one that has developed "a popular culture of intricate semiotic sophistication and technical virtuosity, that deploys spectacular signs, that encourages the creation of personal identity within those sign systems—that is, they have lived the postmodern, and they are adept at reading it's artifacts." According to McLaughlin, living in a postmodern "culture of the sign" has taught American students to decode and theorize that culture. "Just ask a freshman class to analyze an advertisement in terms of the messages that are communicated by the clothes, the hairstyles, the cars, the interiors of homes, etc. They can do so with astonishing expertise."[14] A variant of this argument is the familiar observation that today's adolescents are often way ahead of their elders in the literacy of visual images and computers.

Though true up to a point, such arguments are misleading. Today's adolescents may indeed have "astonishing expertise" in interpreting the meanings of clothes, hairstyles, cars, and other forms of contemporary culture, but it doesn't follow that they can *describe* these meanings articulately—as articulately as McLaughlin does, for example, when he writes of our living in a postmodern "culture of the sign." Nor are all college students able to compose (or even understand) sentences like McLaughlin's about "a culture that values image over reality, that has replaced production with information, that has developed a popular culture of intricate semiotic sophistication and technical virtuosity."[15] In attributing semiotic insight to students, McLaughlin is saying, in effect, "Look how smart my students are when I rewrite what they say."

McLaughlin is right that in some sense today's students "know" postmodern culture in a way that educators should respect and take advantage of. But this experiential knowledge needs terms like "postmodern culture" in order to enable students to enter the public conversation about such issues. Only when students learn to talk the talk of culture will they be able to operationalize the "astonishing expertise" with which McLaughlin credits them. McLaughlin concedes the point, but only in passing and without enough concern for the problem: "We can give [students] a more sophisticated vocabulary for talking about these issues," he writes—issues like "the power of cultural products in personal lives and identity formation"—"but the issues are already part of their interpretive repertoire."[16] Yes and no. Yes, such issues are "already" part of students' "interpretive repertoire," but they are likely to be there in a limited, inchoate way until students become fluent with words like "issues," "cultural," "identity," and "interpretive."

What should worry us, then, is not courses in which students study *The X-Files* instead of Plato, but courses in which students study *The X-Files* or Plato with no obligation to argue rigorously and analytically about *either* subject, to see either "through academic eyes." This is why so much is at stake personally for students in deciding whether or not to commit to that way of seeing and thinking, and why so many fiercely resist a makeover that may alienate them from friends and family. Intellectualism is always fraught with deep social class meanings, as Julie Lindquist points out (in a response to an earlier published version of this chapter) when she observes that it is no simple task to broaden the domain of who and what counts as "intellectual." This, she adds, is "not only because those who work as intellectuals are invested in keeping [the definition] narrow, . . . but also because people outside the academy often don't want to see themselves (or don't want others to see them) as intellectuals, however much theorizing they may do on the street, at the ballgame, or at the corner bar."[17] Lindquist agrees with me that these class meanings attaching to intellectualism and its argumentative styles need to be flushed out into the open and discussed with students, but she rightly warns that even when this is done students may still decline to join the intellectual club.

Lindquist also points out (as does Steve Benton, another respondent to the earlier version of this chapter[18]) that mastering argument alone doesn't necessarily make us free, that our culture is far from being a level playing field or neutral marketplace of ideas in which the best reasoned arguments always win and all groups get a seat at the debating table. I agree. In fact, for me one of the best reasons for organizing the curriculum around controversial issues is that, though doing so would not itself level the social playing field, it would give greater visibility to these important questions about the degree of democratic participation in our culture, questions that now tend to stay safely marginalized within the liberated zone of radical educators.

So here as elsewhere in this book, I put special emphasis on public argumentation as the form in which street smarts need to learn to express themselves to become effective in the wider world. Since argumentation can be contentious, and contentiousness is often viewed by schools as a form of troublemaking or "acting out," students themselves often fail to recognize the academic potential of their argumentative talents. If some groups are culturally more comfortable with public forms of argumentation than others, all have a stake in learning to use argument to express and defend their interests.

TEACHING FOR HIDDEN INTELLECTUALISM

Making students' nonacademic interests an object of academic study is useful, then, for getting students' attention, but this tactic won't in itself necessarily move them closer to an academically rigorous treatment of those interests. On the other hand, inviting students to write about cars, sports, or clothing fashions does not have to be a pedagogical cop-out as long as students are required to see these interests "through academic eyes." I end this chapter with accounts of two college teachers who, after reading the earlier published version of this chapter, provided me with information about how they have tapped their students' "hidden intellectualism" by encouraging them to see their own interests in an academic way. The first is from Ned Laff, a professor of English at DePaul University in Chicago and a counselor of high school students. Laff describes working with a high school student named Andy, "who was continually in academic difficulty and showed little interest in his studies." Andy's main interest in life, he confessed in conferences with Laff, was "to ride my motorcycle fast." Andy told Laff he felt he was "just hanging on, waiting for high school to end so that I can get on with things."[19]

Laff writes that "Andy was simply unable to see how any course he took had any relevance to what he wanted to do—ride his motorcycle fast." Andy's parents and his school's academic counselors were at a loss how to deal with him. They pointed out to him that his interest in riding his motorcycle was no answer to questions like, "What are you going to be doing when you're thirty?" and "How are you going to support yourself?" But Andy was not persuaded by such arguments to take academic work seriously.

Laff took a different tack. When Andy declared that his only interest was in riding his motorcycle fast, Laff surprised him by asking "How fast do you want to ride?" "Are you thinking of a career as a racer, a mechanic, or something else related to cycling?" Laff wanted to legitimate Andy's interest and then challenge him to explain it. He was less interested in pushing Andy toward a career in motorcycling—though he would have seen such an expression of interest as an advance— than with seeing if he could use Andy's single avowed interest to draw him into academic work. Laff asked Andy further questions: "Who rides or works with motorcycles for a living? What do they have to know? How would somebody find out?"

Andy agreed to research these questions by going to the library. After further discussions with Laff, he drafted a letter to the editor of a motorcycle magazine in response to an article on steering technology that had caught his interest. Writing the letter prompted Andy to translate his usual way of saying things—e.g., "This model bike is a little squirrelly in the turns"—into the more precise vocabulary used by design engineers and reporters. In subsequent conversations with Laff, Andy began to open up about the culture of motorcycling—its social clubs, events, symbolic clothing, and behavioral styles. At Laff's suggestion, Andy rented films like *The Wild One*, the 1953 cult film featuring Marlon Brando as the leader of a Hell's Angels–like biker band that terrorizes a small California town, and the later *Easy Rider*, in which biker culture merges with the sixties counterculture. This led to Andy's writing email posts to Laff in which he discussed similarities and differences in the films' treatment of biker culture, where he saw himself in relation to the films, and places where he thought the films had or had not got the biker ethos right. Laff then referred Andy to some academic articles by a social scientist colleague who studied biker culture. By the end of their discussions, Laff felt that Andy was developing into a disciplined writer on the mechanics of cycling and an articulate commentator on the sociology of biker culture. As Laff wrote to me,

> What I think I helped Andy realize is that standard rhetorical strategies (or standard strategies of composition)—e.g., stipulating definitions, description, comparison and contrast—and sharpening vocabulary are more than classroom

exercises. I wanted him to understand that sharpening these skills also has to do with sharpening how we think about ourselves and our educational and personal goals in relation to the world we live in. Andy had begun to discover the power that lay in thinking and writing about motorcycles as well as in riding them.

The second account comes from Professor John Brereton, a composition specialist in the English department at the University of Massachusetts at Boston. Brereton writes:

One way I access the hidden intellectualism in my students is through the ubiquitous research paper in First Year Composition. The research paper has been rightly derided for many failings, as an empty exercise, a temptation to plagiarism, and an artificial task that takes time away from genuinely engaged writing. The students' usual questions—"How many books do we need?" "Footnotes or endnotes?"—show that they tend to think of the research paper in this superficial way.[20]

I try to reenliven the research paper in my comp classes by making it a real exercise in research, and in using research to make a case, to argue, and I do this by encouraging students to write the paper on something they know and are interested in. I build up to the "research" aspect stealthily. The first few days of class we go around introducing ourselves. First day, they tell "where I live"; second day, "where I work"; third day—and here's the trick—"what I know a lot about." I introduce these topics in a way that starts informally—we're just doing introductions, sitting around in a circle—but inches gradually toward precision of analysis. "Where I live" has complexities at my commuter school, where you don't just say Boston, you say Field's Corner or Mattapan or Back Bay. . . . "Where I work" is also complicated in ways that demand precision: "Pizzeria Uno." Which one? Full time? What do you do? "The Gap in the Arsenal Mall." What do you do? Good place to work? Almost everybody in my classes works, about 1/3 full time.

But the secret is "What I know a lot about." Students know a lot about things that schools tend not to recognize as legitimate topics for reflection: babysitting, dance, singing, comic books, cars, being a security guard, rock-climbing, hairstyles, the culture of record store workers as depicted in the film *High Fidelity*, baseball, how to play it or its history or how the Red Sox have been doing. After going around, everyone has committed to a certain expertise, sometimes hard earned (sports statistics memorized for years), sometimes worn surprisingly lightly (raising twins). Homework: think of a controversy, issue, problem, or unanswered question in the area you know a lot about; think also about other people's views of that area and how they might differ from yours or each other's (this provides practice making the key rhetorical moves of saying, "some people think . . . others think . . . I think"); draft a one-page statement and come prepared to talk from it for five minutes in one of the next classes on your expertise, the issue or problem you are raising about it, and the differing views of it. I copy and circulate the best statements as models, but I still haven't told the class that these statements will be the bases of their research papers.

By now I have a body of "experts" in the class, people who know a good bit more than I do about some pretty worthwhile and interesting things: American movies of the past ten years; tuning up a car; emergency medicine; following a potential shoplifter without letting on; bartending at a semi-fancy restaurant; lifeguarding; teaching catechism at a Catholic Sunday school; whether the Celtics need to build for offense or defense; the Bible—many students really know Scripture, chapter and verse, but are often hesitant about revealing it. This becomes my data base, my prime ref-

erence sources, through the rest of the semester. I'm building up the notion that that the class is the audience for the
speaking and the writing and that the students' knowledge
is valuable and worth sharing.

Later in the term, when it comes time for the research paper, I limit it to subjects the students claimed to really know
something about. But here is where the academic rigor of
analysis and argument comes in, where students have to
think about their knowledge and interests in disciplined academic ways in order to do well. Example: a student who
worked in a local greyhound track and knew a lot about betting on the dogs. Early on he had brought in a question
from the field: do "systems" of betting work? His assignment now was to give me a list of ways he could get some
answers to his question. One was interviews; he knew three
system players. One was tout sheets, which all claimed success and therefore forced him to sort out claims and make
evaluative judgments. Another source was the mathematical
knowledge in statistics books, and still another was what
turned out to be a rich periodical and newspaper literature
about betting. The paper turned out very well, mostly based
on interviews. He knew the sources, the setting, and the audience. It was a natural for him to probe the knowledge he
had in order to probe further.

The trick is to get the student to see that there's an issue
imbedded in their knowledge and information that's suscep-
tible to academic intervention, and that might at some point
hook into something that comes up in another course. Here
I sometimes have to discourage purely technical topics that
don't open out into any larger issue—how to cook good spa-
ghetti, for example, or do a better perm. But with a little
prodding I find it's not too hard to edge students toward
such larger issues—how nutritionists, say, debate the relative merits of different foods or ways of preparing them, or
what cultural and ethnic meanings foods and hairstyles take
on, and why.

Brereton thinks that the research papers he receives clearly demonstrate that college students (and high school students, too, with whom
he has worked) have plenty of knowledge, much of it acquired through
great personal investment. "They know," he writes, "and they care,
too—the issues are live ones for them. When schools and colleges tap
these sources of knowledge and passion, they encourage students to
feel a real personal stake in their education, something you can't fake."

12 A Word for Words and a Vote for Quotes

IN A RECENT CANADIAN RADIO SERIES on "The Education Debates,"
interviewer David Cayley makes reference to "the great divide" between child-centered and curriculum-centered models of education.
He suggests that the work of some current educators "straddles" this
divide and thereby makes "a hash" of it.[1] Although Cayley is speaking specifically of Theodore Sizer's writings and their application in
Sizer's national school network, the Coalition of Essential Schools, I
think his comment accurately describes a trend represented by a number of prominent educational reformers, whose work also straddles
and makes a hash of the great divide between progressive, student-
centered and traditional, curriculum-centered models of education.

Such a trend is overdue, for there has long been something deeply
disabling about a split that sets the claims of the pupil against the
claims of the subject matter, as if teaching students and teaching
intellectual content were mutually exclusive. John Dewey himself resisted this either/or dualism, warning his followers (sometimes in vain)
against notions of progressive education that were anti-intellectual and
witless.[2] Dewey thought it was possible and necessary to make education both more sensitive to students' needs and more intellectually de-
manding and rigorous. Yet the persistent conflicts between progressive

and traditional educators have made such a reconciliation difficult to achieve.

In the final three chapters, I look at several teachers whose classroom practices provide models of how to overcome the increasingly stale dualism of "traditional" vs. "progressive" methods. They all accomplish this reconciliation by developing imaginative ways of bridging the gap between academic and student discourse. Taken together, their work represents an antidote for cluelessness in academe.

WORD POWER

In *To the Hoop,* sports columnist Ira Berkow's account of his adventures as an aging playground basketball player, Berkow digresses from basketball at one point to describe how his father, after many unsuccessful attempts to get the adolescent Berkow to read books, gave him a copy of *30 Days to a More Powerful Vocabulary.* Though Berkow at first regarded the book without interest, on picking it up a few days later he "suddenly became absorbed in the world of words." The book, he goes on,

> changed my life. I felt like Alice tumbling into Wonderland.
> The words were exotic and hypnotic: *antediluvian, pedantic,*
> *meretricious, enervated, opprobrium, Brobdingnagian.*
>
> And they weren't just great objects to roll around in your
> mouth. They were weapons. My father had always told me
> that words were power, and now I began to wonder about
> this, the ability to use words to fashion one's thoughts.
> Thought could be power too. [1. 138][3]

Berkow's account reminded me of my own revelatory sense of power at age eighteen when my father made me start looking up unfamiliar words.

You do not have to be very close to the education scene, however, to know that the kind of increase-your-word-power approach that made such an impact on Berkow and me can cause cutting-edge educators to wince, sometimes with good reason. Asking students to memorize definitions epitomizes that "pouring-in" or "banking" view of education that progressive educators from John Dewey to Paulo Freire have powerfully inveighed against. Such a view sees learning as a matter of depositing lecture information into the student brain to be eventually cashed like bank notes at exam and grading time. The problem is that learning that's absorbed without the learner's active participation rarely sinks in. This is especially true for students who grow up in today's increasingly unpredictable world, in which it probably seems less useful than it did when Berkow and I were adolescents to learn information that has no meaning at the time it is presented to you. All this, however, is an argument not for scrapping "banking" modes of instruction, but for rethinking how they are used.

WORD O' THE DAY IN TULSA

In my introduction I quoted Jim Benton, a teacher of at-risk high school students in Oklahoma and now in Texas, on the need for teachers to "acknowledge the foreignness" of academic discourse. Benton says that for "the at-risk students I teach, but, to some degree all students," it is "the teacher who wields all power, because the teacher knows all the proper ways to think and speak." This is why, Benton believes, the usual "methods of building vocabulary and learning academic discourse reinforce the very limitations they are seeking to overcome." The students may pick up some academic discourse in the classroom, but they never to come to regard it as theirs.

Benton did not want to give up teaching academic discourse, but he needed a way of teaching it that would not simply reinforce the students' sense of their distance from that discourse. He decided that the key was to balance the power difference between academic and student discourse. If he was going to ask his students to learn to speak academic, it was only fair that he learn their dialect, which he termed "Realspeak" (an acknowledgment that the students' language is often closer to the language most Americans use than is academic discourse). Once their teacher committed to learning student Realspeak, students became authorities, a bridge was built between academic and student language, and students could feel that academic discourse was as much theirs as their teacher's. Furthermore, giving students' language parity with the teacher's language created occasions for examining in class the advantages and disadvantages of these languages and the unspoken prejudices and fears surrounding them.

The "Word o' the Day" assignment that Benton developed for improving his students' vocabularies seems to me an intriguing example of how new life can be breathed into what some may dismiss as an outmoded tactic. (Word of the Day exercises may be making a comeback, however; they are currently used widely in many Chicago public schools.) As Benton puts it, "Word o' the Day . . . not only teaches vocabulary," but "introduces the tools of academic discourse in a nonthreatening, even empowering way, welcoming students to the discourse as partners with their own area of experience and expertise."

Here is how Word o' the Day works in Benton's language arts classes. Each day throughout the semester, during the last ten minutes of every class, the teacher and students gather around a chalkboard and add one new vocabulary word to each of two growing lists. One list consists of Realspeak words nominated by the students, "derived entirely from the language students speak and hear every day"; the other consists of academic words, "derived from upcoming readings, radio and television broadcasts, SAT/ACT word lists, and words which exemplify . . . the language of English teachers. . . ." The students are "the source of all Realspeak words, and they must remain the authority for their correct definition and usage," but the teacher makes the final choice of which words to add, occasionally making judgment calls when questions of taste arise. Every Friday, the teacher reviews the vocabulary lists at the beginning of class, answers questions, and distributes a quiz that asks students to match Realspeak words to the nearest equivalent in Academicspeak (e.g., "cheesy" = "inferior") or its antonym ("shysty" = "trustworthy"), or to complete a sentence with the contextually appropriate word from one of the lists.

Perhaps the most interesting feature of Word o' the Day is

> an ongoing contest between students and teacher(s) to
> use the words in conversation. If a student can use an aca-
> demese word so casually and correctly in conversation that
> the teacher can hear it but not notice it (and call attention to
> it), the student scores a point for the student. If the teacher

can use a Realspeak word in the same way, he/she scores a
point. . . . The idea of this ongoing contest is that students
will be encouraged not only to learn the words but to own
them.

The competition is valuable, Benton adds, because "it generates significant appreciation and recognition," and, a not insignificant by-
product, it "forces us all to listen very carefully to each other."

Benton was delighted when, after only four Words o' the Day,
"Brian, a laconic basketball player" who had been "slumped back in
his chair," seemingly bored by a lecture on writing principles, suddenly
spoke up and "with perfect smoothness and aplomb," said, "Aw, Mr.
Benton, do we have to listen to another one of your homilies today?"
"Homily" had been on the Academicspeak list.

The ultimate test of Word o' the Day's success, however, came
when students were able to produce and use the academic equivalent
of a Realspeak word and vice versa. At my request, Benton has recon-
structed some sentences generated by his students using words from
both the academese and Realspeak lists:

> Everybody knows a *buster* is somebody you don't like, but ex-
> actly why you don't like them is *ambiguous*. It's like you
> have to know the *context* to know what somebody means,
> if they're *narking* on you or something else.
> A *shysty buster* is *redundant*.
> A *hottie* can be a guy or girl. It's *androgynous*.
> *Irony* is when you say one thing and mean the opposite,
> like, "This class is *the shits* when you actually like it. Or
> when you say that's *bad* in Realspeak and mean it's really
> *phat*, that's *irony*. But you can't tell the difference unless
> you're there. Without the *context*, it's totally *ambiguous*.
> Academese that's *down with it* would be an example of an
> *oxymoron*. Another would be *ornate* Realspeak.
> Here's an *aphorism* for you: *Homie* don't play that game.
> Academese has all these *euphemisms*, saying stuff all nice
> and shit.

Though Benton doesn't know how deeply the game has affected the students' language behavior, his work seems to me to take a promising step toward overcoming the gulf between student and academic discourse.

QUOTATION IN PITTSBURGH AND CHICAGO

Benton's "Word o' the Day" game recognizes that students need not only to learn new words, but to learn how to use them in literate conversations. In this section, I discuss two college teachers who focus on the practice of *quoting* to expand their students' intellectual vocabularies in ways that help them enter literate conversations. When students quote published writers in their own texts, student discourse rubs up against academic intellectual discourse and the languages can permeate each other. Quotation thereby becomes a bridge that lets students imitate academic language while infusing their own voices and inflection into it at the same time.

The first teacher is compositionist Joseph Harris, who describes working with student writers in his book *A Teaching Subject.* The account that especially interests me comes in a chapter on "voice" in the teaching of writing, in which Harris rehearses the debates over the extent to which students should be asked to speak and write in their own voices or to acquire the voice of the academic disciplines. As I noted in chapter 1, Harris warns against exaggerating this opposition, since assigning students and academics to completely separate "discourse communities" rules out any reconciliation between their ways of speaking.

Harris suggests that moments when student writers quote from published writing possess special interest, since it is at those moments that student and academic discourse can converge. As Harris puts it, "one way of getting at the voice or stance of a writer is to look closely at how she quotes and uses the words of others." He adds that we can look

at the problem of quotation as one of trying to keep an upper hand over the languages and materials you're working with, of trying *not* to slip into a form of ventriloquism in which you can no longer tell the words of others—readers, writers, teachers, editors, authorities—from your own. This is often particularly a problem for beginning college students, who are faced with the paradoxical task of both forging their own voices and writing in a way their teachers find interesting and familiar.[4]

The paradox to which Harris here refers throws light on a source of student confusion I mentioned earlier: on the one hand, students are often exhorted to "be yourself" and not simply parrot (or, as Harris puts it, mechanically "ventriloquize") the views of authorities, the most flagrant instance of which is plagiarism; on the other hand, students are often graded down for sounding all too much like themselves and not enough like those who know the conventions of public communication. Their ways of formulating issues and claims are often very distant from those of qualified psychologists, critics, historians, and anthropologists. To compound the problem, students receive mixed messages about the issue, as some teachers urge them to forget trying to sound like academics while others penalize them for failing to do so. Quotation is thus a touchstone moment, for when students quote and then comment on quotations they bring their own language into proximity with the language of authority. At such moments teachers can gauge the distance between the languages and locate bridge discourses in which students replicate an academic voice while "forging their own voice." Students' quotation practices can also help teachers identify students' fears and phobias about academic writing.

Getting some students to quote at all can be a major step forward. I was recently shown a sheaf of papers from a class of eleventh-graders who were asked to respond to a critical essay on *Huckleberry Finn*. I was struck that in the twenty-five essays, not a single one quoted the critic the student was responding to. Perhaps they did not want to bother cracking the text again, but I suspect a deeper reason why they shied away from quoting was that they found the critical language so intimidating that they needed to keep it at a distance. Also, the conventions of imbedding a quotation in a text, a superficial matter but one that can be troublesome even for experienced writers, may have scared them off: does one use a block quotation or not, and why? Do the commas and periods go inside or outside the quotation marks? With what words does one introduce a quotation, and so forth?

On the other hand, students who have got past these elementary problems will often quote copiously but in a mechanical way, quoting without comment as if the quotation could be left to speak for itself. They do not know that quotations need to be *used* to make the writer's own point rather than simply slapped down into the paper to prove that the writer has consulted authorities or agrees with the quoted source. As Harris writes, "One of the things I often tell students is that you want to *do* something with a passage you quote, to talk back to it somehow—that you don't want simply to let someone else speak in your place" (52). Harris presents an example from a paper by a student named Heather, written for a class taught by Harris's colleague Rashmi Bhatnagar. Heather's assignment was to choose a passage in Mike Rose's book *Lives on the Boundary* and relate it to "an event in their lives that had somehow shaped who they now were as readers and writers." Heather's paper dealt with her attitude toward writing as reflected in her experience working on her high school paper. "As might be guessed," Harris reports, Heather and most of the other students in the class "found it easier to tell their stories than to relate them to their reading of Rose" (47). Harris sees Heather's mechanical way of quoting Rose as a telltale sign of her difficulty in bridging the gap between her voice and Rose's academic voice. She can quote Rose correctly enough, but she does not know how to appropriate his statements in order to make her own point. As Harris puts it, "Heather does what many beginning writers do: She hunts around in *Lives* until she can isolate a passage that comes close to what she already wants to say, and quotes that. . . . Her use of Rose is thus of the weakest possible sort, since it doesn't add to or change her story but merely repeats it. The quotation tells us little either about her experience or his book" (49).

Harris then quotes from a later draft Heather wrote after working with her instructor, Rashmi, who urged her to try to integrate her discussion of Rose into her argument instead of "dragging him in at the end of the party, when everything is almost over" (49). As she had done in the earlier draft, Heather describes her shame at seeing her writing publicly criticized, but this time she uses a quotation from Rose to dif-ferentiate herself from him as well as reinforce her own point. Heather is describing Rose's account of how his elementary school students circulated their work without feeling the kind of shame Heather felt:

> Rose said, "The real kick came when I walked through the cafeteria a few days later after our lesson and saw two of my kids showing their poster essay to a third child who was not in our group." God, I would be terrified if my work was on the cafeteria wall. I would be trying to listen to every conver-sation to hear what all my readers thought about my work. That is one thing these kids have over this college student, they can handle other people reading their work. To sum up this paper, the obstacle that I had to overcome was the rela-tionship between my reader and me. And I did (51).

Harris points out that, though Heather's second draft is less polished than her first, it shows an advance in defining the "larger point Heather wants to make about the intensity of her feelings about her writing and the problems this causes for her when it is read." The advance, more-over, is marked by Heather's more purposive way of quoting Rose. As Harris writes, "What I most like here is how Heather has changed the use she makes of Rose. Now she draws on him not merely to support but to complicate what she has to say. Rather than simply suggest, as she did in her first draft, that she and Rose have had similar experiences with writing, Heather now imagines herself as part of a scene he has described and shows how it would be different for her." Heather has thus moved "from the ventriloquizing of her first draft to a more critical use of the quotation," in which, as Harris observes, she "hints that the relations between readers and their writers might sometimes be far more complex and anxious than Rose suggests" (51–52). In other words, Heather has now used Rose not just to echo her own point but to differ-entiate herself from him. The next step for Heather, I think, would be not just to "hint" at her difference from Rose, but to write that differ-ence more explicitly into her text. Nevertheless, quoting from more ma-ture writers like Rose is clearly helping Heather's own writing mature.

My second example is drawn from the classroom practice of Cathy Birkenstein-Graff, who has developed an exercise in "imitative quoting" in her freshman composition courses at DePaul and Loyola of Chicago Universities. Birkenstein-Graff's exercise builds on a point made by Wayne Booth, Gregory Colomb, and Joseph Williams in *The Craft of Research*. As they put it,

> quotations rarely speak for themselves; most have to be "unpacked." . . .
>
> Whenever you support a claim with numbers, charts, pictures, or quotations—whatever looks like primary data—do not assume that what you see is what your readers will get. Spell out what you want them to see as the *point* of your evidence, its *significance*. For a quotation, a good principle is to use a few of its key words just before or after it.[5]

For Booth, Colomb, and Williams, the proposition that "quotations rarely speak for themselves" exemplifies the larger principle that "evidence" never speaks for itself. As they put it, "Your evidence may be accurate, precise, sufficient, representative, and authoritative, but if readers cannot *see* your evidence *as* evidence"—that is, as evidence for *your* particular point rather than some other point that it might support—"you might as well offer no evidence at all."[6] Since what evidence means—like what a quotation means—is always contestable, the writer must frame it a certain way in order to present it *as* evidence for his or her point rather than for someone else's competing point.

Birkenstein-Graff's premise is that in helping her students make quotations speak for their own point, she is helping them bring their language into dialogue with academic language. She has devised a quotation exercise that she explains in the following handout:

> Most people make a common sense mistake about quotation. They assume that what they have to do is make a claim and then put a relevant quotation next to that claim. What often gets forgotten in the process is the need to *connect* the claim and the quotation. In other words, writers often mis-

takenly assume that quotations speak for themselves. As a result they fail to explain how their quotations support or prove the larger point or interpretation they are making.

That is, whenever you quote, you have to go on and show why the quotation supports *your* particular argument rather than another argument you or somebody else might make. You have to do something with the quotation to make it *yours*, not the author's or somebody else who might use it for some other purpose.

The handout continues:

> The single most common mistake writers make is to "drop" a quotation into a paragraph or "dangle" it at the end. In other words, novices simply type in their quotation and then go on to a new idea. Effective quoting, however, involves unpacking the quotation's meaning and explaining it clearly to your readers. Even more, it involves connecting the key terms you've established in your essay with those within the quotation itself.

Birkenstein-Graff suggests a procedure students can use in order to make quotations "theirs": "framing" or "nesting" the quotation in a paraphrase that borrows some of its "key words" and phrases:

1. *Always put a FRAME or NEST around your quotations.*
   a. *Echo* the quotation's key terms (or their synonyms) in your surrounding discussion.
   b. Try following each quotation with an explanatory sentence like, "In other words," or "In this passage, Orwell suggests that . . ."
   c. Avoid beginning or ending a paragraph with a quotation.

Birkenstein-Graff's premise here is that when students quote other writers in their texts, student discourse mingles with academic discourse, allowing the languages to permeate each other. Quoting and glossing quotations thus operates as a bridge that enables students both to imitate the foreign language of academia while giving that language their own spin or even reacting against it. I have found Birkenstein-Graff's exercise useful in working with students who are struggling to write about intellectual texts. I advise them to go back and quote more extensively from their reading and then try to play off the quotations in order to move their own writing closer to the public register.

Here for example are two passages by Réné, an older returning master's degree student at the University of Chicago who was having great difficulty in getting an issue or problem into focus in her writing. She seemed to be straining to sound academic but the results were simply fuzzy. Here is the opening of one of her early papers for my course:

> Smith and Rabinowitz' collaborative text, *Authorizing Readers: Resistance and Respect in the Teaching of Literature,* merges theory and practice (as a reflection of the co-authors' respective backgrounds) in order to create an effective method of producing engaged student-readers. A professor since the late 1960s, Peter Rabinowitz writes from a narrative literary theorist point of view . . .

Following Birkenstein-Graff, I suggested to Réné that she quote more frequently and play off her quotations, letting the quoted writers define issues for her and bringing her voice closer to theirs. Here is Réné writing in response to a classmate, who had criticized the week's assigned text, Robert Scholes's *Textual Power,* for urging the dismantling of what Scholes calls the "secular scripture" of the literary canon.

> Evidence that Scholes does not want to abandon the Great Books of the literary canon is illustrated in his assertion that it is important to study authors like Ernest Hemingway, "who is justified by fame, accessibility, and by the uses to which his work can be put." Instead, Scholes claims that what should be abandoned, is the worshipping of "great authors." It is for this reason that he argues that standard anthologies should be thrown away. Not because the authors

in the anthologies are famous, but rather "because they do not give us a large enough sample of any single writer." Instead he opts to "choose perhaps three collections of short stories by writers whose work will offer good contrasts of styles and values." Therefore it can be said that Scholes does not want to throw away the Great Books, but rather the tendency of teachers to treat them as scripture.

Though this passage still bears traces of Réné's struggle with the academic idiom, it shows how imbedding and playing off a quotation brings her closer to that idiom while helping her write more clearly.

In the first passage, Réné provides no clear summary of the assigned critical text, whereas in the second she lets her quotations to do some of the work for her in summarizing Scholes while making her own argumentative point. She also gains focus by letting her classmate's proposition—Scholes wants to junk the great books—generate her counterresponse throughout the whole passage. The final sentence, which nicely "caps" the paragraph, seems to me especially effective, a far more pointed sentence, in fact, than any Réné had written for me up to then. The words and the formulation are entirely Réné's, but she needed to borrow Scholes's keyword, "scripture," to get where she got. I cite Réné's work as one example of how working with quotations can help students become "bilingual," making the difficult crossover into academic intellectual discourse while remaining in touch with their own voices.

I want to conclude with one other "quotational" tactic I myself have started using in my teaching. It began when I noticed that many students hardly ever made use of the vast inventory of formulas that are generally used to describe *mental* actions, formulas like

> he *argues* (or *contends, maintains,* etc.)
> she *assumes*
> they *challenge* (or *question*) the view that
> I *infer* that
> Whereas they *claim* . . . , I *reply* that
> etc.

In place of such formulas, my students tended to use a formulation like "talks about." For example, instead of writing "Richard Rodriguez questions bilingual education," my students would write "Rodriguez talks about bilingual education." I presented them with a list of standard argument formulas similar to the one above, with instructions that they use at least some of them in their papers from now on. Though the results were sometimes superficial—a student might say "I argue that" but fail to argue more cogently than before—I had the sense that many students were helped and grateful to have their vocabulary enlarged.

In the next chapter I deal with another pedagogical tactic for bridging the gulf between academic and student discourse: building a course around this very conflict.

13 Wrestling with the Devil

IT IS NOT SURPRISING if students feel ambivalent about talking the talk of the academic world, since this ambivalence is pervasive in the larger society in which academics' funny way of talking is a common joke. Nor is it surprising if teachers themselves so internalize this ambivalence that they hesitate to ask students to master academic discourse, or they fail to master it themselves. Like other divisive issues in academia, the unresolved debates over academic discourse tend to reach students in the form of curricular mixed messages rather than straightforward discussions of the problem.

The issue of academic discourse has divided the field of writing instruction, where advocates of teaching persuasive argument clash with those who favor such "expressive" forms as personal narrative, autobiography, and creative writing. Whereas the first group wants students to acquire an academic voice, the second wants to encourage them to find their own personal voices. As compositionist Donald C. Jones observes, since the early 1970s, composition theorists have had "a love/hate relationship with academic discourse."[1]

Jones provides a useful summary of the history and present state of the debate over academic discourse. On the one hand, Jones writes, leaders of the "writing process" movement of the 1970s such as Ken Macrorie urged student writers to move toward the personal and away from the dead scholarly paper. Critics like James Vopat reacted against this view, noting that when he followed Macrorie's pedagogy his students wrote "well and excitedly about their personal experiences, but they were at a loss when asked to write about ideas." (95). As Jones sums the situation up, "We have argued that academic writing should not be taught at all or that it should be the only discourse taught in first-year writing courses. Ken Macrorie and other writing process theorists have rejected any instruction of 'a dehydrated academic tongue.' Yet David Bartholomae and other social constructionists have insisted that teaching students 'to speak our [academic] discourse' should be the central mission of college composition" (95).

The debate has been replayed throughout the '80s and '90s, with "expressivism" defended most notably by Peter Elbow and academic discourse by David Bartholomae and Patricia Bizzell. The debate today seems stalemated, as opposing partisans preach to already converted audiences in separate conference sessions, or to captive student audiences in noncommunicating classrooms. At least one public debate has occurred between Elbow and Bartholomae, at the 1989 College Conference on Composition and Communication meeting in Boston.[2] But such attempts to air and resolve the differences have been sporadic and rare.

On the one hand, the argumentative essay continues to come under attack for supposedly thwarting creativity. Lynn Z. Bloom, for example, complains that students in literature courses become mere "ventriloquists in the language of critical jargon, submerging their own voices in the process."[3] The problem as Bloom sees it is that "argumentative models of every sort, whether New Critical, Deconstructionist, or any other intellectual framework, have isolated the primary creative works from the very students eager to enjoy them. . . . Instead, student writers are required to adopt the critical models of their mentors and to write adversarial literary criticism, becoming junior Literary Darwinists closing in for the kill. What sparks of creativity can survive in this critical jungle?" To counteract this presumably deadening syndrome in which students are asked to conform to "argumentative models," Bloom says she asks her students "to try writing in one or more of the literary modes we're studying in the course."[4]

On the other hand, defenders of argumentative models, echoing Vopat's objections in the seventies, retort that replacing argument with literary modes in the fashion Bloom recommends cheats students. Patricia Bizzell, for example, in *Academic Discourse and Critical Consciousness*, argues that "the abstracting, formalizing power of academic work enables us to understand our experience in ways not made available by common sense or folk wisdom. We ought not to pretend to give people access to this power by admitting them to college, and then prevent them from really attaining it by not admitting them into the academic discourse community."[5] From Bizzell's viewpoint (which I share), teachers who fail to teach academic discourse are withholding a form of power that they themselves take for granted.

Bizzell continues: "We cannot demystify academic discourse for students, cannot teach them to analyze it, until they already understand something about it from trying to use it in imitation of experienced practitioners, such as their professors. In other words, mastery of academic discourse must begin with socialization to the community's ways, in the same way that one enters any cultural group."[6] My sentiments exactly. But though I side with Bizzell, Bartholomae, Mike Rose, and other leaders of the academic discourse party in this debate, I think Bloom's expressivist argument has to be respected, if only because its suspicious view of academic writing is so pervasive among students. Furthermore, the quarrel itself between argumentative and creative writing models seems false and unnecessary. Were there more sustained debate between partisans of these models, the fact might emerge that the opposition between persuasive and creative/personal modes of writing is needlessly overdrawn.

This in fact is precisely the point made by Jones. As he argues, the debate over academic discourse need not be framed as a binary opposition in which we must choose one side and reject the other. Indeed, there is something misleading about the choice "between lifeless academic prose and vivid personal writing," as well as the flip side of that choice that opposes "uncritical personal essays and insightful academic writing" (110). Effective argumentation, Jones observes, is often personal and creative, just as good personal and creative writing often makes a polemical point. Jones is adept at finding moments when this conciliatory point is acknowledged by the defenders of both personal and academic discourse (110). At the same time, Jones recognizes that though the conflict between argumentative and creative models is unnecessary, it does reflect a real division of attitude in our culture and student body. It is all well and good for teachers to assure students that academic discourse need not be dry and dull, but students' experience often tells them otherwise. For this reason, a wise classroom tactic is to pose the question of academic discourse as a topic for debate and treat it as an open one.

This is the approach Jones takes in his first-year composition course at the University of Hartford, which his essay goes on to describe. Drawing on my work on "teaching the conflicts," Jones organizes his course around the debate over academic discourse, assigning short essays and excerpts by Elbow, Bartholomae, and other exponents of the opposing positions. By reading the arguments and examining the assumptions on the different sides of the debate, Jones's students grapple with most of the fundamental rhetorical issues taught in standard writing courses, such as voice, evidence, and audience as well as power, hierarchy, and exclusion. Jones goes beyond most standard writing courses, however, by allowing the students' ambivalent views of academic writing to frame the discussion of how to write.

Like Jim Benton, whose creative adaptation of the "Word o' the Day" exercise I described in my last chapter, Jones has found a way to introduce academic discourse to students without suggesting that their own language always needs to be discarded. Though Jones's ultimate purpose is to help students master academic discourse, he does not take the superiority of that discourse for granted, but welcomes student criticisms of it and turns his course into a testing ground of the disputed issues. Students who feel alienated from academic discourse are thus invited to air their reservations instead of having to suppress them.

Jones opened his course by asking his students how they felt about academic discourse. Not surprisingly, many said they had never encountered the phrase, another symptom of how academic culture leaves its procedures mysteriously unnamed. The students quickly intuited what the phrase referred to, however, and their opinions soon flowed freely. Asked to define academic discourse, the class's answers ranged from "the stuffy BS students use to impress their profs" (98) at one end of the spectrum, to the necessarily rigorous language of the disciplines at the other. But whether they were for it or against it, the students initially tended to agree that academic discourse is the antithesis of personal expression.

Several students, for example, told Jones that when they write academic papers they feel as if they "disappear" as people, as if they were "mouthing the words of others, allowing sources to speak through them unquestioned, unexamined." They go through the motions because they have no choice—"they do it, [but] they hate it"—and they doubt that academic discourse can be produced that is not (in a phrase Jones quotes from compositionist Nancy Sommers) "remote, distant, and imponderable" (102).

In this way, as Jones had hoped they would, the early class discussions flushed out feelings about academic discourse that until then had had no legitimate outlet in the students' academic work: "Some students critiqued academic discourse as similar to 'joining a club and leaving others outside' and 'being in a fashion show where you use words to flaunt yourself.' Others, however, defended 'a more efficient, more accurate language' and 'a challenge to students which should provoke their thinking. . . .' It is difficult for me to capture on paper the tones of the anger and excitement in the students' voices when presented with the opportunity to confront this conflict openly in a classroom" (96).

The challenge, as Jones saw it, was to get the students to see that their conflicted views of academic discourse were not simply idiosyncratic responses, but an echo of the debates over the same issues among their professors and people in the wider culture. Jones wanted his students to see that their disagreements and mixed feelings reflected the clash of philosophical, cultural, and rhetorical principles to which they were being exposed not only in his composition course but in the college curriculum as a whole. In this way, teaching the conflicts over academic and personal discourse became a way of unpacking and clarifying the confusions of what I call the Mixed Message Curriculum.

In providing his students with a picture of the debates over academic discourse, however, Jones hoped they would come to entertain the possibility of a reconciliation. He wanted them to discover that writers do not always have to choose between argumentative and personal writing, but can combine these modes, or alternate between one and the other depending on the rhetorical situation. At a certain point in the class he assigned an essay by Peter Elbow that makes a case for having things both ways, for combining, in Jones's words, "personal writing which describes/renders" with "academic discourses, which explain/analyze" (102).

As the class proceeded, Jones had his students examine examples of their own academic writing done in other courses, in order to test the general claims to which they were being exposed by the debate. Discussion of this writing from the students' other classes enabled the students to examine the discrepancies in the writing advice they were receiving in different disciplines, or even in the same discipline. These comparisons proved especially useful in getting on the table the mixed messages and clashing advice they were getting about whether they are supposed simply to offer information or to present their own argument.

One of Jones's students, for example, described an education professor who encouraged his class to make personal applications of their research, in contrast to her sociology professor, who "wanted only research and no opinion included" (98). The students also compared "a personal response to a musical performance, an application of a sociological concept to a current situation, and a first-year science lab report." These comparisons, according to Jones, enabled his students to "realize that they often composed different forms of academic discourse," that is, that they were already "aware—on some level—of significant discursive variations" (100), and therefore that mastering academic discourse was as much a matter of controlling languages that they already partly knew as it was of learning a completely new language.

Referring to some personal essays the students had written earlier in the semester, Jones asked them how different they now thought such writing was from the writing they had been looking at from other courses. At first they still tended to emphasize the differences, contrasting the dry, objective tone of their lab reports and the more relaxed and conversational tone of their personal essays. As the discussion progressed, however, students began to notice areas of common ground that had been masked by different disciplinary conventions. One student pointed out that whether one is writing a lab report or a personal essay, a writer does whatever is needed "to make us believe what the writer wants us to believe" (101). The distance was lessening in the students' minds between their pictures of academic discourse and of their everyday language.

When the class returned to the compositionists' debate on academic discourse, Jones returned to the question of whether the opposing positions could be reconciled. If the students could see that the opposition between personal and academic writing was exaggerated, they would "learn to function better along the continuum between these theoretical extremes" (101). Once they no longer exaggerated the difference between academic discourse and their own, Jones assumed that his students would "create a smoother transition from the students' first 'personal' essays and their final more 'academic' research writing" (101–2).

This step proved to be important, for Jones found that, however much he stressed the "continuum" between academic and personal expression, students often reverted back to a compartmentalized understanding of academic writing as a genre in which their personal beliefs and ways of expressing themselves could play no role. Some students still characterized "their own production of academic prose as 'spitting out textbook phrases' and blindly copying ideas from other sources" (103), and they complained that they had been taught to take notes and make outlines, but not "how to take the information of others and interpret it as their own," or that they were "trying to sound like an expert on a subject which is actually very foreign to me" (103).

What intrigued Jones now, however, was that though these students "were still resisting academic discourse," they were "now making personal and often passionate assertions about that resistance and their desire to resolve it" (103). In short, by wrestling with the debates of scholars and their own conflicted beliefs over academic discourse, Jones's "students actually were practicing, to the surprise of several, the composition of academic discourse. They were asserting their own opinions" while "using reasons and evidence drawn from more than their personal experiences." Jones introduced Mikhail Bakhtin's influential theory that "internally persuasive discourse," discourse that feels right to us as we speak or write it, is achieved when we mix or "dialogize" our own discourse with that of others, producing a result that is "half ours, half someone else's."

As one of Jones's students put it, the best academic writers know "how to take the information of others and interpret it as their own" (103). Like the vocabulary games and quotation exercises I described in the last chapter, Jones's approach addressed the key problem of the transfer from student discourse to academic discourse. His assignments had created situations in which students could feel they were not parroting the alien language of their teachers but were making the teachers' language their own. Once this point is reached the question of who *owns* the language one is using becomes irrelevant and drops away. Jones observes that, in citing academic theorists like Bakhtin to express their feeling of not owning the academic discourse they produced, his students, paradoxically, were actually starting to feel ownership in what they wrote, producing that discourse which, in Bakhtin's words, was half "[theirs] and half somebody else's" (103). In using Bakhtin to express their alienation from academic discourse, the students were on their way to overcoming that alienation. "Although many of these students still claimed they did not know how to transfer their more direct engagement in personal narratives to academic writing," the very ways they articulated this claim showed that they were making the transfer better than they thought (103). In short, Jones's students were discovering that the reservations they still had about academic discourse could be expressed more powerfully if they couched those reservations *in* academic discourse. "By exploring, articulating, and discussing their beliefs about academic discourses, the students actually were practicing, to the surprise of several, the composition of academic writing" (107).

In a concluding unit, the class wrote essays about academic discourse in which several students reconsidered their earlier resistance to it. Several realized that they were now able to place their personal beliefs "within a larger context of others' opinions" (107), a process that enabled them to be personal and social at the same time. Even more interesting, when Jones asked the class "if their final essays represented an academic or a personal discourse," many students could not categorize their essays as either one or the other. "Their previously binary conceptions of the 'personal' and the 'academic' had become less polarized," as they realized that "academic discourse could include a writer's direct involvement even when cloaked by a lab report's passive voice constructions" (107). As one student wrote, whereas she had come into the course thinking that "academic writing was achieved by separating myself from the piece . . . [by not] interjecting my thoughts," she had discovered that "the only way to write an academic paper is first to internalize the topic," by learning what others have said, then forming your own ideas, "and this is when writing for school (the academic writing I had detested so) will become personal" (108).

What seems especially ingenious to me in Jones's way of teaching academic discourse is how it draws its energy and motivation from the very animosities that students so often feel toward this discourse. Because he does not assume that such animosities are shameful or pretend that they do not exist, Jones can encourage students to bring their negative feelings into the open. His students then discover that they are far from alone in harboring these negative feelings, that many academics and other adults share them, that their doubts about academic discourse are mirrored in the debates of their teachers themselves. Instead of trying to convert his students to his own positive view of academic discourse, Jones invites them to struggle with these debates in the faith that they will find that their reservations about academic discourse will be more powerful if they learn to use that discourse to state them.

Like the ways of teaching intellectual discourse developed by Benton and Birkenstein-Graff, Jones's tactic of bringing students into the debates over academic and personal discourse reconciles traditional and progressive educational principles. Jones's objective is in many ways a traditional one: to bring students' writing and speaking closer to accepted standards of cogent exposition and argumentation. But in pursuing this traditional objective, Jones carries out the progressive imperative to respect and work with students' previously formed language habits. Such an approach recognizes that though there are many tensions between the discourses of intellectual argument and everyday speech, the two are not ultimately incompatible, since they have a common root in social conversation. To paraphrase a remark of Jones's student, whether we are academics, journalists, or garage mechanics, we all have a stake in making people believe what we want them to believe.

TEACHING THE DEBATE ABOUT "BECOMING AN INTELLECTUAL"

Whatever subject I am teaching, I find myself increasingly asking the kinds of questions Jones asks his students about academic discourse and their relation to it. Such questions invariably open out into broader questions about intellectualism and its languages—What is an intellectual? What are the pros and cons of becoming one yourself? How would becoming an intellectual change the way you talk? These questions are central ones in units I have helped high school teachers to design for their classes. One of these collaborators, Hillel Crandus, who teaches English at Downer's Grove South High School in the Chicago suburbs, has developed a unit in his eleventh-grade literature classes on "Becoming an Intellectual." Crandus and his students debate questions like the following: do you describe yourself as an intellectual? What would you gain or lose if you translated your street smarts into more academic language? Is being an intellectual a good or bad thing? Should "intellectual" be synonymous with "nerd" or "dweeb" or with being cool? Is intellectualism opposed to street smarts, or can the one be a latent form of the other? What are the students' nonacademic interests and pursuits, and do these harbor hidden intellectualism?

Crandus finds that high school and college students are intrigued by these questions and differ in interesting ways over them. For some the suggestion that they are or might want to become intellectuals seems patently ridiculous and bizarre, while for others it seems a plausible outcome of their education. Similar disagreements arise over the question of the degree to which intellectualism may already be latent in their nonacademic interests. As Crandus probes such questions in class discussion, his students' ambivalence about them gets flushed out into the open, terms and definitions for discussing the questions are sharpened, and standard equations such as intellectual equals nerd, snob, pompous ass, and so forth get challenged and debated.

Crandus's unit also takes advantage of the fact that questions about hidden intellectualism are centrally posed by many of the most frequently taught high school literature texts, including Mark Twain's *Adventures of Huckleberry Finn,* Richard Wright's *Black Boy,* and J. D. Salinger's *Catcher in the Rye.* (Once you start looking for this theme, it becomes hard to find a work of American literature that does not raise questions about intellectualism.) Furthermore, these texts often dramatize debates about intellectualism by focusing reflexively on language— as in the contrasts between Huck's and Jim's dialects and the stilted language of conventionally educated society, or between Holden Caulfield's colloquial idiom and the language of the "phonies" who surround him.

Crandus builds on the fact that these texts are widely taught as initiation stories, addressing the ways adolescents become—or in Holden's and Huck Finn's case, refuse to become—initiated into the adult world. Crandus assumes, however, that "initiation," the term that motivates the unit, should not be treated as a teacher's word that students themselves are not expected to use. Unless students learn the empowering critical terminology that governs the unit, the initiation will be incomplete. His premise is that students *can* use such terms if they are encouraged to do so and provided with models, especially if the cultural power conferred by intellectual discourse is made clear. Here Crandus had to recognize that his view of language sets him against Huck and Holden themselves (and presumably against Twain and Salinger), whose vernacular dramatizes their rejection of the hypocritical and inauthentic ways of conventional society and the official forms of public communication. As I noted in an earlier chapter, in the famous "Notice" that opens Twain's novel by threatening prosecution for anyone who attempts "to find a moral" in the story,[7] the author virtually warns us not to look for the sort of "hidden meaning" that most English instruction focuses on. Richard Wright, on the other hand, coming from a black working class perspective, recognizes that oppressed people need the power of the dominant language in order to criticize their condition effectively and advance in the public world. Contrasting Wright with Twain and Salinger enabled Crandus to bring his students into a debate over the pros and cons of learning literate intellectual discourse.

Instead of trying to persuade his eleventh-graders that becoming an intellectual is a good thing, Crandus saw he would be more likely to reach that end by sparking a classroom debate on the pros and cons of intellectualism and its forms of talk, letting the students wrestle with their disagreements and ambivalences on the issue. Thus in teaching Salinger's novel, Crandus started by pointing his students to the contrast between Holden's personal vernacular language and the intellectual language Holden and Salinger associate with school. In the email correspondence Crandus and I maintained during the unit, he wrote as follows:

> I called the class's attention to a scene near the start of *Catcher in the Rye* in which one of Holden Caulfield's teachers reads one of Holden's school history papers back to him: "The Egyptians were an ancient race of Caucasians residing in one of the northern sections of Africa. The latter, as we all know, is the largest continent in the Eastern Hemisphere. . . ."[8] Holden is embarrassed to hear the teacher read this paper, which is written in the school language that is Holden's idea of Intellectualspeak, the language associated with "phonies" throughout the novel.
>
> We then spent a bit of time comparing the prose Holden uses in his history paper, noting how the flat, padded prose indicates Holden's alienation and disengagement from aca-

demic work, with the prose Holden writes the book itself in: "Game, my ass. Some game." or "I was standing way the hell up on top of Thomsen Hill, right next to this crazy cannon that was in the Revolutionary War and all. . . ."[9]

Most of Crandus's students agreed that Holden's colloquial voice is meant to be seen as more authentic and thoughtful than the ostensibly more intellectual voice in which he writes the school paper. In the ensuing class discussion, they also began to see how the contrast between official school language and personal language represented choices they themselves might face between identities and views of life.

Crandus then posed the question of intellectualism: if Holden's personal talk is more intellectually substantial than his version of school discourse, who needs school discourse at all?

> Happily for my purposes [Crandus wrote], Salinger too seems to have this issue in mind. Later in the book, Holden runs into one of his old teachers, Mr. Antolini, who gives him the following advice about language: "Educated and scholarly men, if they're brilliant and creative to begin with—which, unfortunately, is rarely the case—tend to leave infinitely more valuable records behind them than men do who are merely brilliant and creative. They tend to express themselves more clearly, and they usually have a passion for following their thoughts through to the end."[10]

Is Salinger here affirming a more positive view of intellectual discourse, which is more likely than informal talk to leave permanent "records behind," or is Mr. Antolini's advice meant to be read as yet another example of adult phoniness?

Crandus put these questions to his students, using the contrasting styles in the novel to move them to reflect on their own language. What is gained and lost by expressing oneself in Holden's personal register? In the register of Holden's history paper? In the register of the "educated and scholarly men" described by Mr. Antolini? Is it possible to translate terms from one of these registers to another? Can they be blended and combined? Could students talk like Mr. Antolini without giving up their Holden-like ways of talking?

Among the other texts Crandus assigns in his "Becoming an Intellectual" unit is an excerpt from my book chapter, "Disliking Books at an Early Age," in which I describe how my youthful alienation from books eventually abated when I encountered critical debates about books in college.[11] Crandus asked his class to summarize my account and express their own feelings about intellectually analyzing and debating what they read. Many of the students were candid in expressing their scorn for such analysis. As one put it (I quoted him and others in Crandus's class in chapter 2 above), "The only thing that overanalyzing leads to is boredom. . . . I like to just read a book, and not so much to analyze it."

But another student, T. E., who also expressed doubts about the value of intellectual analysis, offered a remarkably profound critique of both my narrative and argument. "Does critical analysis really stir up interest in literature?" he wrote. "Perhaps it did for Graff, but will it do so for others who are more truly alienated?" After all, T. E. asks,

> How did Graff even get to the point of even searching for a solution? I question his sincerity in his "admittance" of disliking books at an early age. . . . Not to insult Graff, but maybe his inspiration comes from the fact that he might actually have been a "closet nerd." . . . Please. If Graff's ideal solution is to be "exposed to critical analysis of literature," then every gum chewing high school kid who has ever been caught criticizing something by saying "it sucks" could be an English major.

In my email response to T. E., I had to admit he was right: in retrospect, I had indeed been a closet nerd. I went on to suggest, however, that, despite his disclaimers, T. E.'s penetrating and trenchantly phrased comments suggest that he might be one, too. I added that it did not seem so wildly implausible to me to think that gum-chewing kids who say "it sucks" may become English majors and critics; arguably every sophisticated theory is grounded in a gut reaction of that kind.

What was most striking to me, however, was that in the very process of attacking in-depth analysis, T. E. produced one of the best in-depth analyses of my work I have seen (and my work has been raked over by many professors and journalists). Like Donald Jones's freshmen at the University of Hartford who learned to produce better academic discourse in the process of expressing their reservations about academic discourse, T. E. assumes the voice of an intellectual even as he questions the value of intellectualism. Crandus and I have agreed that he will give a copy of the published version of the present chapter to a future class and see how they respond to my exchange with T. E.

In effect, Crandus's "Becoming an Intellectual" unit asks students to inventory whatever hidden intellectualism they find in themselves, consider what they want to do with it, and determine what kind of voice they want to give it. Again, his aim is not to convert his students into nerds and eggheads, at least not directly, but rather to get them to reflect on their contradictory feelings about intellectualism and its talk. Crandus's premise is that wrestling with the devil in this way is more likely than instructors' exhortations to induce students to discover the hidden intellectual in themselves and to learn the vocabulary they need in order to express it well. "Becoming an Intellectual" continues to be a pedagogical work in progress.

14 Deborah Meier's Progressive Traditionalism

THE TEACHING APPROACH that I have been outlining in this book straddles the divide between traditional and progressive philosophies of education. If I had to nominate one educator whose work best exemplifies this "progressive traditionalism," my choice would be Deborah Meier, whose 1993 book *The Power of Their Ideas: Lessons for America from a Small School in Harlem* could be its manifesto. Meier's work as a writer, teacher, and school administrator provides a rich model of how schooling can be demystified.

Though Meier is politically on the Left, her educational thinking resists being categorized as Left or Right. On the one hand, Meier stands squarely in the progressive Deweyan tradition, arguing that "democratic community" is "the nonnegotiable purpose of good schooling,"[1] that schooling should enable all students to enter the culture's "political conversation across divisions of race, class, religion, and ideology" (7). Meier also embraces the central tenet of progressive education, that in order to move students to a higher intellectual level teachers have to begin from where the learner is and build from there. Meier has no use for conservative nostalgia, answering the charge that American students' performance has precipitously declined by reminding us that "until World War II the average American did not graduate from high school" (69), much less attain the high standards of literacy that are now fondly imagined to have been achieved at some earlier time.[2]

On the other hand, Meier is at one with traditional educators in stressing that schools and teachers need to provide strong models of intellectual authority. She rejects the view of some progressives that students can't become active learners unless teachers deny or soften their authority, getting themselves out of the students' way. Refusing to see classroom authority as a zero-sum game in which students can be "empowered" only if teachers relinquish control, Meier's central point is one that traditionalists should warm to: that schools must become intellectually challenging institutions instead of shopping malls, staging grounds for radical politics, or dispensers of feel-good therapy.

Meier recognizes that no model of educational reform can gain general acceptance unless it embraces both progressives and traditionalists, as well as others who are at odds on fundamental issues. As Meier puts it, changing schools "must be done by people who don't all like the same movies, vote for the same politicians, or raise their own kids in the same way" (38). Paradoxically, because Meier's vision of education welcomes and incorporates disagreement, it has greater power to produce consensus than do rival visions. Meier understands that making intellectual issues central in a curriculum means giving disagreements a prominent, positive role, partly because there is so much disagreement about such issues, but also because disagreement is clarifying. Though such a vision may sound divisive, its underlying premise is one that everyone committed to democracy on the Right, Left, and Center should be able to accept: that improving the quality of education depends on making the intellectual culture of schools more coherent, clear, and challenging. Meier gives educational primacy to those common skills of analysis, argument, and public conversation on which all the contending educational agendas depend for their articulation. She understands that which groups in our society get access to these intellectual skills has everything to do with politics and power, but for her these skills themselves are not the monopoly of any social class or political faction.

Meier understands that learning problems start with the fact that, to many students, the very concept of "education" is nebulous and is never explained. "Young people," she says, "have always had only the foggiest notion of what schools are all about once the 3 R's stage is completed. Even the 3 R's mostly have stood for skill at schooling, only loosely connected, if at all, to anything you do elsewhere" (162). Meier understands, in other words, that effective education involves clarifying the mysterious world of school knowledge and ideas and its connection with "anything you do elsewhere." She sees that in order for such clarification to occur, the world of school knowledge and ideas needs to be organized as a coherent and intelligible culture whose practices make sense.

YOUTH CULTURE VS. SCHOOL CULTURE

In *The Power of Their Ideas,* Meier describes how she (as principal) and her associates transformed the Central Park East Secondary School in Harlem (CPESS) into such a coherent intellectual environment, one that has proved remarkably effective in educating "disadvantaged" students (a label, as she notes, that her students reject). CPESS, which began in 1985, grew out of the Central Park East elementary school that Meier and her associates had founded 1974. Her vision of CPESS arose from her search for an alternative to the shopping mall high school, what Meier calls "the big, mindless high school" where the fact that "the capacity to educate is missing . . . seems almost beside the point" (31–32). Meier's account suggests that at CPESS, intellectual issues and debates have the central role occupied by sports and socializing in many high schools (though one infers that at CPESS sports and socializing themselves are grist for intellectual discussion). By 1993, when her book appeared, CPESS was serving 450 seventh-through-twelfth graders. In a city in which the average graduation rate was 50 percent, 90 percent of CPESS's students graduated from high school and another 90 percent "went directly on to college and stayed there" (16). In the mid-nineties Meier left New York for Boston, where she is now principal of the Mission Hill school in Roxbury. Meier says "the exact same principles apply" to all these schools.[3]

Meier's starting point is a key insight into the disabling separation of adolescence and adulthood in postwar America, one that echoes the writing of Paul Goodman in books of the '60s like *Growing Up Absurd* and *Compulsory Miseducation*.[4] As Meier puts it in a radio interview, "the average adolescent in this country has almost no relationship with anybody who is much different [from] themselves. I mean, they live in an enormously small world, and can't imagine belonging to the many other worlds around them. . . . there are no grown-ups in their little community." Meier observes that this isolation of adolescents from the grown-up world vastly increased in post–World War II consumer culture, which produced

> the first generation of adolescents in the history of the world that were expected to be irresponsible. Young people, who historically would have been expected to go to work, were cut off from adults, with more money for self-indulgent purposes than they are likely ever to have in their lives, and very little incentive then for growing up. Nor were there many models of why it was wonderful to be grown-up. So that we really have institutionalized the idea that just before you become a grown-up you're part of the most alienated and irresponsible subculture anyone could imagine creating.

To house this subculture, Meier continues, "we created this institution of the American high school, which also isolated kids from adults."[5]

Others have pointed to this isolation of the young from the adult world as a factor in school shootings of the 1990s like that at Littleton, Colorado, in which two high school students killed thirteen classmates and themselves. William Damon, director of the Stanford University Center on Adolescence, observed that "there has never in the history of the civilized world been a cohort of kids that is so little affected by adult guidance and so attuned to a peer world."[6] Adults, Meier suggests, actually feel envy and resentment for the insularity and irresponsibility that our culture has granted adolescents, a backlash reflected in the post-Littleton trend toward "zero tolerance" policies.

For Meier, the trouble with such crackdowns is their failure to address the problem at its source, the estrangement of young people from adult culture, an estrangement schools must address in order to have a chance to be effective. At Central Park East School, she writes, "that's one of the central characteristics that's different, that the grown-ups and the kids belong to the same school. They don't just happen to bump into each other in classes and then go to their separate worlds. They really are part of the same community. I think that's a critical part of why the school's powerful" (39). Here Meier both follows and revises Dewey's argument in early books such as *The School and Society* and *The Child and the Curriculum*, books that became the blueprint for the Laboratory School at the University of Chicago and numerous other progressive schools.

Dewey had argued that to overcome the sterility and irrelevance of traditional education, the democratic school had to find a way to integrate the child into the adult world of labor and production. Dewey assumed that children harbored a natural curiosity about adult productive systems and vocations such as farming, transportation, and manufacturing. He reasoned that if "occupations are made the articulating centers of school life," students' interest in adult social practices will transform them from "passive and inert recipiency" to active interest.[7] Dewey's vision had nothing to do with vocationalism; the appeal of the occupational world for him lay in its expression of the heroic project of modernity, the progressive struggle of humanity "to master and use nature so as to make it tributary to the enrichment of human life."[8] What Dewey did not foresee, however, was that the appeal to children of this heroic project would be undermined by the rise of youth culture and consumerism, which alienate the young from the adult world of work and civic participation. Meier recognizes that the structural isolation of youth culture from school culture has greatly deepened since Dewey's time, and that a new organization of teaching and learning is necessary if this isolation is to be counteracted.

Meier argues that the school needs to become a kind of intellectual "counterculture" to counteract the anti-intellectualism of youth culture and the "mindless" shopping mall school. As Meier puts it, to counteract the usual school culture in which "students move about bereft of relationships with anyone but their exact age and grade peers," the school needs to become "a thick, complex and powerful counterculture to balance the one that has been developed for adolescents only," a culture that can act as a "counterforce representing serious adult ideas and concerns to which these novices might now and then apprentice themselves" (113). To become such a counterculture, the curriculum must be more than a series of good courses taught by caring individuals; it has to become a coherent, continuous intellectual community that makes intelligible sense to students. Good teaching is a given, but Meier stresses that to make a difference the key lies in how we *organize teaching and learning* (71). For good organization and teamwork can make teachers better by enabling students to see the relationship between one course, subject, and idea and another. Teachers working together make the world of ideas less mysterious than teachers working in isolation and often at cross-purposes.

It is here that Meier's ability to mesh progressive and traditional educational thinking gives her argument a power lacking in either alternative alone. Meier's stress on organization and community provides an alternative to the bad choice between traditional and progressive educational models, or between strong teachers' authority on the one hand and turning courses over to the students on the other. Meier argues that "teaching as telling" has its limits, that students have to play an active role in their learning (143). But Meier also suggests that, far from being silenced by intellectually aggressive teachers, students need such teachers to achieve intellectual authority themselves. Unlike Jane Tompkins, for example, who argues that students' "feelings and opinions won't surface, unless the teacher gets out of the way on a regular basis,"[9] Meier assumes that for those feelings and opinions to surface—or even to come into existence—students need to see the intellectual game clearly modeled by strong adults. As Meier puts it, the premise at CPESS has been that "adults had important things to teach children, not just a mission to get out of their way" (21).

Meier writes of seeing "children being driven into dumbness by a failure to challenge their curiosity, to build on their natural drive toward competence." Meier adds that nonwhite teachers and parents in particular are rightly frustrated at progressive teachers' "seeming avoidance of 'direct' instruction, as though if we waited long enough children would discover everything on their own." Meier observes that it's "no wonder many African American teachers and parents" see progressive education as a "cop-out, a way of avoiding, not confronting, the chal-

lenge" of actually teaching kids something (21). Meier here acknowledges a debt to Lisa Delpit (whose *Other People's Children* appeared the
same year as Meier's book), who argues that the reluctance of teachers
to be explicit about what is wanted has the effect of withholding secrets
from the minority students who most need them.

THE IMPORTANCE OF BEING ORGANIZED

Meier's stress on organization, which follows from her assumption of
the clublike nature of intellectual socialization, represents a welcome
corrective to the individualistic, great-teacher ideology that has long
pervaded popular educational thinking. That thinking, as William
Ayers points out, is dominated by the romantic idea of the "hero-
teacher, the lone individual" who triumphs through sheer determination and grit over "the backward parents, the hopeless colleagues, and
the sewer of society to redeem the good juvenile delinquent."[10] Ayers
notes that this heroic teacher is idealized in films like *Stand and Deliver,
Dangerous Minds,* and *Dead Poets Society,* which reinforce the belief that
improving schooling is chiefly a matter of inspiring more dedication
and passion in individual teachers, an outcome not likely to happen or
to be sustained for long if it does. Meier, by contrast, recognizes that
improving education means changing the culture of the schools, a feat
that certainly requires inspired individual teaching (as does any educational model), but that also requires the school to become an organized
intellectual community with clear goals and practices.

The success of Central Park East seems traceable to its creation of
such a community based on several programmatic features, ones that
again blur the distinction between the progressive and the traditional.
CPESS replaced fifty-five-minute class periods and disconnected subjects with two-hour classes that combined disciplines. It "provided time
during those two hours for presentations, seminars, group work, and
independent study" (32); instead of short-answer tests, the school instituted demonstration projects. Following a model developed by Sizer's
Coalition of Essential Schools, CPESS instituted portfolio-based graduation exercises, on the order of "a series of doctoral orals" (42) in which
students publicly presented exhibitions, "tangible demonstrations of
their knowledge and competence rather than accumulating 'seat time'

(credits) or grades on multiple choice tests" (30). CPESS also enlisted the collaboration of "parents (or grandparents, aunts, older siblings)" in the school's operations and decision making (an approach that has been pioneered in the lower schools by James Comer of Yale University) (22).

At CPESS these innovations, which are usually identified with progressivism, served a solidly traditional emphasis on intellectual habits of mind. The school's curriculum was organized around "five major 'intellectual habits'—habits that should be internalized by every student, and used no matter what they are studying about, both in school and especially out of it!" (41). The five habits condense the moves of intellectual culture into a set of templates:

1. Concern for evidence (how do you know that?)
2. Viewpoint (who said it and why?)
3. Cause and effect (what led to it, what else happened?)
4. Hypothesizing (what if, supposing that)
5. Who cares? Knowing and learning take on importance only when we are convinced it matters, it makes a difference (41).

Asking why academic work should indeed "matter" to a fifteen-year-old, Meier recognizes the wisdom of not getting bogged down in the old conflict between vocational and liberal justifications for learning. For CPESS students a subject or issue might matter "because it will help get us ahead, get into a good college, hold a well-paying job," or because "it will also help save the world" (41). A school can keep both liberal and vocational justifications for education in play, making the tension and debate between them a focus of school discussion.

This creation of "a strong school culture" (24), in which the moves of the intellectual game are clarified, seems ultimately to have been the key to CPESS's success. As Meier describes it, it is an atmosphere in which intellectual issues matter and "the clash of ideas" (11) is central rather than marginal or nonexistent. Again Meier's crucial assumption is that becoming a literate person is like joining a social club, though one bent on expanding rather than restricting its membership. For most American students, joining such a club entails a profound change in their social affiliations and the way they think about themselves, a fact that explains why curricular prescriptions for more classic texts or more cultural literacy facts are inevitably superficial.

As Meier puts it in a passage I quoted earlier, the essential key for club members is learning "to say 'I've got a theory!'" and, for that to happen, "somewhere, young people need to join, if only part-time, the club we belong to. That's more critical than the particulars of what they learn" (157). In a talk entitled "Changing Our Habits of Schooling," Meier observes that most schools have been settings "in which few had reason to imagine themselves as members of the club that teachers belonged to. Children need to be members of a community that encourages youth to roam imaginatively across genders, nationalities, races, periods of history, and universes. Only in a community in which children and adults belong to the same club does such an imaginative life thrive." Meier adds that "seeing oneself as members of the same club is not a matter of liking or not liking one's teachers," but of wanting to be the kind of person they are: "It goes deeper. Young children select from the wide range available to them whom they will sound like, walk like, and so forth," and Meier mentions her brother, who, when he went to baseball games, "was watching as a make-believe ball player, an aspiring member of that club."[11] Schools fail when they do not inspire such emulative "watching" of the academic game, when the student body remains a youth club divorced from the adult club.

Meier knows that most students "resist membership" in the club of intellectuals—"either out of fear of rejection or because to join such a club means to reject their own community or peer clubs. Or because they just don't 'get it' yet, or 'who wants it!'" (158). Schools fail either because they do not represent the intellectual life at all, or they represent it only intermittently, as a set of dissociated courses and teachers—the mixed message curriculum—rather than as a connected conversation that students can understand and enter. Again, the crucial element is organization: changing "our accepted organization of schooling," Meier writes, is a prerequisite for "creating environments where all kids can experience the power of their ideas" (4). The organization of

CPESS involves an unusual degree of collaboration and coordination, primarily among the faculty, but also including parents. Meier notes that in the conventional schools in which she and her staff had previously worked, "we had grown accustomed to closing our [classroom] doors and secretly doing what we wanted," a separatism that is often seductive to progressive educators who are alienated from the established institution and have the freedom to do their own classroom thing (24). But the CPESS model also differs from traditional programs in which "core" subjects are so isolated that they obscure the critical conversation that gives them meaning. At CPESS Meier and her staff taught together in interactive courses, frequently airing their disagreements openly rather than keeping them hidden. Meier observes that since "our adult debates are not hidden from our students" (58), a "climate of diversity and disagreement" arises that "becomes enormously powerful over time" and draws students in (59).

This positive view of disagreement provided CPESS with a creative way of dealing with vexed political issues and their much disputed place in classrooms. For Meier bringing debates about politics into the curriculum is preferable either to teaching one political view exclusively or teaching a variety of views in isolation from one another, practices that conceal the adult conversation from students:

> Few young people [she writes] imagine that adults have intense discussions around ideas, that what they are studying is influenced by what their teachers read and debate: arguing over the impact of voluntary versus forced migrations, what constitutes "our" canon, hearing each other out on words like "Eurocentric" and "Afrocentric," and considering how the concepts we introduce help or hinder our capacity to imagine "the other." Such discussions surprise visitors to our school, but above all they influence our students for whom these matters would otherwise be "academic" (118).

Meier notes that "staunch 'lefties' occasionally berate us at CPE for not removing books with the 'wrong' beliefs, and they're not always satisfied with our solution: write an attack and we'll post it or even include it in the back of the book." As Meier writes, "ignoring the clash" of values—like that between religion and secularism—"won't resolve it. These questions are the stuff of a good democratic debate for the minds and hearts of Americans" (81).

Finally, in creating a *public* sphere of intellectual discussion and disagreement in the school, CPESS developed what is arguably a better model of "staff development" than the one that has become most popular in which a master teacher (or college professor) talks with teachers about how to teach or showcases "best practices." Meier writes that "because our adult debates are not hidden from our students, there is no sharp dividing line between 'staff development' activities and student educational activities" (58). In other words, teachers learn to teach not by watching or getting advice from master teachers, but by visiting "each other's classes, to reflect on their own and their colleagues' practice, and give each other feedback and support" in the process of the planning and teaching of their courses (56). Taking a page from Meier's model, college and high school teachers need to collaborate in designing courses together and adapting them for teaching at their different sites.[12]

MUST BIGNESS BE BAD?

I have saved for last my one point of disagreement with Meier, on the issue of school size. Meier argues that in order to be effective, the kind of learning community she promotes and developed at CPESS has to be small: "Only in small schools can we reasonably speak of immersing students in a culture that adults have played a significant role in shaping" (113). "In schools," she maintains, "big doesn't work no matter how one slices the data. . . . Small school size is not only a good idea but an absolute prerequisite for qualitative change in deep-seated habits." "Only in a small school can deep ongoing discussion take place in ways that produce change and involve the entire faculty" (107–8). Only in small schools can "the accountability we owe to parents and the public" be "a matter of access, not of complex governing bodies or monitoring arrangements" (112).

I do not dispute the claim—which is now widely accepted by educators and public officials—that for many students to become motivated

and to do their best work, they need to be in small groups for a significant portion of the school or college day. Nor do I dispute Meier's claim
that the reforms she and her associates instituted at CPESS would have
been impossible to implement in a large school. I want to argue, however, that the small vs. big dichotomy is another of those educational
polarities that we are too quick to see as mutually exclusive. Like the
dualisms that oppose traditional and progressive methods or academic
and personal discourse, the choice between small vs. large schools (or
small vs. large classes) is one that we should resist. It is possible, after
all, for students to spend considerable time in classes of twelve to
twenty-five while at other times working in larger groups. Though a
major proportion of students' experience should be in small classes,
not all classes need to be small all the time, nor do all schools.

Precisely because of what Meier herself so well points out—the
magnitude and power of the youth culture that competes for students'
attention with schooling—it's hard to imagine educational success on
a mass democratic scale that tries to fight bigness with smallness. To
put the point another way, the more we cut the process of education
into smaller units, the harder we make it for that process to maintain
consistency and quality control and to represent itself intelligibly to students. The smaller we make the units of education, the more we increase curricular fragmentation and decrease the amount of common
focus that is necessary for intellectual clarity. The incoherence of the
mixed-message curriculum that I examined in chapter 3 results from
chopping the curriculum into small courses that do not communicate
and therefore can't discover their latent common ground.

Like most of today's categorical arguments for educational smallness, Meier's seem to have arisen in reaction to bad versions of bigness. I believe that for school culture to gain the clarity that will enable it to counteract the youth culture "that has been developed for
adolescents only," we need to rethink bigness in more imaginative
ways. The very size and public reach of popular films, music, and
sports, and the tremendous sense of commonly shared culture they
produce, contributes to the excitement and interest generated by these
media mega-spectacles. When it comes to education, however, we assume that large size has to mean alienation rather than excitement.

It should be possible for schools to learn from the media's success at mega-communication without replicating the media's worst aspects. Large assembly meetings could coexist with small classes the way the best college lecture courses combine with small discussion sections. Indeed, in many cases, the quality of discussion in small classes would itself improve if larger meetings provided the common intellectual reference point that those small classes now lack. Chicago's North Side College Prep has instituted such a weekly all-school colloquium based on general intellectual and cultural issues. North Side is a magnet school that attracts mostly high-achieving students, but its all-school colloquium is potentially adaptable to the student bodies and problems of more troubled schools. New electronic technologies should also help us reimagine school and class size, for a wired classroom can be both small and big at the same time, physically small while connecting with larger groups.[13]

At times, Meier's small-is-beautiful bias betrays a certain romantic localism, as in her contribution to a recent Boston Review Symposium, published as a book under the title *Will Standards Save Higher Education?* In reacting against standardized testing, Meier tends to confuse common intellectual standards with standardization. Thus she questions whether "it is possible and desirable to agree on a single definition of what constitutes a well-educated eighteen year old and demand that every school be held to the same definition."[14] This attack on "single definitions" seems strange coming from Meier, since in *The Power of Their Ideas* she herself advances a single definition of the well-educated student. As I noted above, Meier calls the "five major 'intellectual habits'" central to the CPESS curriculum "habits that *should be internalized by every student*" at CPESS, "*and used no matter what they are studying about, both in school and especially out of it!*" (41; emphasis mine). I do not often find myself on the same side as the conservative Abigail Thernstrom in any dispute, but Thernstrom seems to me quite right in a response included in *Will Standards Save Higher Education?* when she wonders if Meier would "label the insistence that kids learn to read abhorrent 'standardization.'" Does Meier, Thernstrom asks, "really want to argue about the worth of learning geometry or the importance of understanding why we fought a civil war?"[15]

But however we may feel about Meier's localist bias, it does not vitiate the value of her educational ideas and her example. Meier is a great educator and educational thinker because she has synthesized the best lessons of both progressivism and traditionalism. She understands that the problem of education has to be thought through from the viewpoint not of the already educated, but of the clueless student for whom the very words "education" and "academic" are opaque. But she also understands that such students have the ability to join an intellectual community that makes sense to them. In the demystification of academia that we need, thinkers and teachers like Deborah Meier will lead the way.

How to Write an Argument

WHAT STUDENTS AND TEACHERS *REALLY* NEED TO KNOW

1. Enter a conversation just as you do in real life. Begin your text by directly identifying the prior conversation or debate that you are entering. What *you* have to say won't make sense unless your readers know the conversation in which you are saying it.

2. Make a claim, the sooner the better, preferably flagged for the reader by a phrase like "My claim here is that. . . ." You don't actually have to use this exact phrase, but if you couldn't do so you're in trouble.

3. Remind readers of your claim periodically, especially the more you complicate it. If you're writing about a disputed topic—and if you aren't, why write?—you'll also have to stop and tell the reader what you are *not* saying, what you don't want readers to take you as saying. Some of them will take you to be saying it anyway, but you don't have to make it easy for them.

4. Summarize the objections that you anticipate will be made (or that have in fact been made) against your claim. This is done by using such formulas as "Here you will probably object that . . . ," "To put the point another way . . . ," or "But why, you may ask, am I so emphatic on this point?" Remember that your critics, even when they get mean and nasty, are your friends: you need them to help you to clarify your

claim and to indicate why what you're saying is of interest to others besides yourself. Remember, too, that if naysayers didn't exist, you'd have no excuse for saying what you are saying.

5. Say explicitly why you think what you're saying is important and what difference it would make to the world if you are right or wrong. Imagine a reader over your shoulder who asks, "So what?" Or "Who cares about any of this?" Again, you don't actually have to write such questions in, but if you were to do so and couldn't answer them you're in trouble.

6. Write a meta-text into your essay that stands apart from your main text and puts it in perspective. An effective argumentative essay really consists of two texts, one in which you make your argument and a second one in which you tell readers how and how not to read it. This second text is usually signaled by reflexive phrases like "Of course I don't mean to suggest that . . . ," "What I've been trying to say here, then, is that . . . ," etc. When student writing is unclear or lame, the reason often has less to do with jargon, verbal obscurity, or bad grammar than with the absence of this layer of meta-commentary, which explains why the writer thought it was necessary to write the essay in the first place.

7. Remember that readers can process only *one* claim at a time, so resist the temptation to try to squeeze in secondary claims that are better left for another essay or paragraph, or for another section of your essay that's clearly marked off from your main claim. If you're a professional academic, you are probably so anxious to prove that you've left no thought unconsidered that you find it hard to resist the temptation to try to say everything all at once. Remember that giving in to this temptation to say it all at once will result in saying nothing that will be understood while producing horribly overloaded paragraphs and sentences like this one, monster-sized discursive footnotes, and readers who fling your text down and reach for the *TV Guide*.

8. Be bilingual. It is not necessary to avoid Academicspeak—you sometimes need the stuff to say what you want to say. But whenever you do have to say something in Academicspeak, try also to say it in

conversational English as well. You'll be surprised to discover that when you restate an academic point in your nonacademic voice, the point will either sound fresher or you'll see how shallow it is and remove it.

9. Don't kid yourself. If you couldn't explain it to your parents the chances are you don't understand it yourself.

INTRODUCTION: IN THE DARK ALL EGGHEADS ARE GRAY

1. John Gardner, quoted in Ellie McGrath, "Welcome Freshmen," *Time* (September 10, 2001): 64.
2. On star high schools, see Jay Matthews, *Class Struggle: What's Wrong (and Right) with America's Best Public High Schools* (New York: Times Books, 1998).
3. See Gerald Graff, "Life of the Mind Stuff," in *Beyond the Culture Wars: How Teaching the Conflicts Can Revitalize American Education* (New York: W. W. Norton, 1992), 86–104.
4. I am indebted to Michael Bérubé for this formulation.
5. Howard Becker, in conversation. Becker's own work and career refute the belief that social science writing has to obfuscate in order to make an impact. See Becker's useful guide, *Writing for Social Scientists: How to Start and Finish Your Thesis, Book, or Article* (Chicago: University of Chicago Press, 1986).
6. Steven Pinker, "Some Remarks on Becoming a 'Public Intellectual.'" Paper presented at the MIT Communications Forum "Public Intellectuals and the Academy," December 2, 1999. Posted January 5, 2000: http://media-in-transition.mit.edu/articles/pinker.html.
7. Gregory Jay, unpublished talk delivered at session on "Academic Criticism and the Public Media," Modern Language Association Annual Convention, December 1991.
8. Donald (now Deirdre) McCloskey, "The Neglected Economics of Talk," *Planning for Higher Education* (Summer 1994): 12.

9. John Stuart Mill, "On Liberty," in *Utilitarianism, Liberty, Representative Government* (London: Dent & Sons, 1951), 129. The internal connection between controversy and thought is well developed by Michael Billig, in *Arguing and Thinking: A Rhetorical Approach to Social Psychology*, rev. ed. (New York: Cambridge University Press, 1996).

10. See the arguments, for example, of Pierre Bourdieu, Jean-Claude Passeron, Monique de Saint Martin et al., in *Academic Discourse*, trans. Richard Teese (New York: Oxford University Press, 1994), and Samuel Bowles and Herbert Gintis, in *Schooling in Capitalist America: Educational Reform and the Contradictions of Economic Life* (New York: Basic Books, 1976).

CHAPTER 1: THE UNIVERSITY *IS* POPULAR CULTURE, BUT IT DOESN'T KNOW IT YET

1. George Santayana, *The Middle Span* (New York: Charles Scribners Sons, 1945), 162.

2. William James, "The Ph.D. Octopus," in *Essays, Comments, and Reviews* (Cambridge: Harvard University Press, 1987), 67–74; first published in 1903.

3. On the habit of exaggerating the specialization of academic research, see my essays, "The Charge That Research Is Narrow and Opaque Is Decades Out of Date," *Chronicle of Higher Education* (October 21, 1992): A56; "The Scholar in Society," in *Introduction to Scholarship in Modern Languages and Literatures*, ed. Joseph Gibaldi (New York: Modern Language Association, 1992), 343–62.

4. Karen W. Arenson, "Campuses Across America Are Adding 'Sept. 11 101' to Curriculums," *New York Times* (February 12, 2002): A13.

5. Ellen Willis, "My Sokaled Life," *Village Voice* (June 25, 1996): 20–1.

6. For standard sources, see Laurence Veysey, *The Emergence of the American University* (Chicago: University of Chicago Press, 1965); Frances Oakley, *Community of Learning: The American College and the Liberal Arts Tradition* (New York: Oxford University Press, 1992); Helen Lefkowitz Horowitz, *College Life: Undergraduate Cultures from the End of the Eighteenth Century to the Present* (Chicago: University of Chicago Press, 1987).

7. On undergraduate cluelessness in the earlier part of twentieth century, see Horowitz, *College Life*, and my *Professing Literature: An Institutional History* (Chicago: University of Chicago Press, 1987), 98–118; I am indebted to Ned Laff for calling my attention to the discrepancy between rapidly changing intellectual paradigms and the continuity of student alienation.

8. Mike Rose, *Lives on the Boundary: A Moving Account of the Struggles and Achievements of America's Educational Underclass* (New York: Penguin Books, 1989), 188.

9. Julie Lindquist, "Hoods in the Polis," *Pedagogy* 1, 2 (Spring 2001): 267.

10. Deborah Meier, *The Power of Their Ideas: Lessons for America from a Small School in Harlem* (Boston: Beacon Press, 1995), 155–7. The account to which Meier refers is by Kenneth Freeston; on the clublike nature of academic lit-

eracy, Meier also cites Rose's *Lives on the Boundary* and Frank Smith's *Reading Without Nonsense* (New York: Teachers College Press, 1985); see also Smith's *Joining the Literacy Club: Further Essays into Education* (Portsmouth, N.H.: Heinemann, 1988).

11. Jim Benton, private correspondence.

12. Joseph Harris, *A Teaching Subject: Composition Since 1966* (Upper Saddle River, N.J.: Prentice Hall, 1997), 102.

13. Harris, 105.

14. Kurt Spellmeyer, quoted by Carol Severino, who makes a similar argument in "Where the Cultures of Basic Writers and Academia Intersect: Cultivating the Common Ground," *Journal of Basic Writing*, 11, no. 1 (Spring 1992): 7.

15. Zdenek Salzmann, *Language, Culture, and Society: An Introduction to Linguistic Anthropology*, 2d ed. (Boulder, Colo.: Westview Press, 1998), 172.

16. Salzmann, 172–3; for the argument that "diglossia" is preferable to "code switching" as a model for teachers of African American students, I am indebted to Vershawn A. Young and his University of Illinois at Chicago Ph.D. dissertation in progress.

17. Deborah Meier, *The Power of Their Ideas*, 164.

18. Joseph M. Williams, private correspondence.

19. I am indebted to Gregory Jay for suggesting the volleyball analogy.

20. E. D. Hirsch, *Cultural Literacy: What Every American Needs to Know* (New York: Houghton Mifflin Co., 1987), 130.

21. Barbara Herrnstein Smith, "Cult Lit: Hirsch, Literacy, and the National Culture," in *The Politics of Liberal Education*, Darryl J. Gless and Smith, eds. (Durham, N.C.: Duke University Press, 1992), 75–94.

22. Nicholas D. Kristof, "The Veiled Resource," *New York Times* (December 11, 2001): A27.

23. David K. Cohen, Milbrey McLaughlin, and Joan E. Talbert, eds., *Teaching for Understanding: Challenges for Policy and Practice* (San Francisco: Jossey-Bass, 1993).

24. Enrico Fermi, quoted by William Mullen in "U. of C. Celebrates Genius, Leadership of Enrico Fermi," *Chicago Tribune* (September 30, 2001): sec. 4, 1.

25. See Stanley Fish, "Anti-Professionalism," in *Doing What Comes Naturally: Change, Rhetoric, and the Practice of Theory in Literary and Legal Studies* (Durham, N.C.: Duke University Press, 1989), 215–46; Bruce Robbins, *Secular Vocations: Intellectuals, Professionalism, Culture* (London: Verso, 1993).

26. Victor Villanueva, Jr., "Whose Voice Is It Anyway? Rodriguez' Speech in Retrospect," *Living Languages*, eds. Nancy Buffington, Clyde Moneyhun, and Marvin Diogenes (New York: Blair Press, 1997), 115.

27. Elaine Maimon, quoted by Susan Peck MacDonald, *Professional Academic Writing in the Humanities and Social Sciences* (Carbondale, Ill.: Southern Illinois University Press, 1994), 17.

28. Lisa Delpit, *Other People's Children: Cultural Conflicts in the Classroom* (New York: The New Press, 1995), 32–3 and passim.

29. William Labov, "The Logic of Nonstandard English," in *The Politics of Literature: Dissenting Essays on the Teaching of English*, Louis Kampf and Paul Lauter, eds. (New York: Random House, 1972), 208.

30. Labov, 212–3.

31. Hubert B. Herring, "Orientation Is Given the Old College Try," *New York Times* (August 23, 2001): A18.

32. Richard Hofstadter, *Anti-Intellectualism in American Life* (New York: Random House, 1963).

33. Maureen Dowd, "Grilled Over RATS," *New York Times* (September 13, 2000): A31.

34. Jonathan Chait, "Presumed Ignorant," *New Republic* (April 30, 2001): 46.

35. Stephen S. Hall, "The Smart Set," *New York Times Magazine* (June 4, 2000): 52.

36. Stephen Holden, "Got Game. And Pen. And Mentor," *New York Times* (December 19, 2000): B31.

CHAPTER 2: THE PROBLEM PROBLEM AND OTHER ODDITIES OF ACADEMIC DISCOURSE

1. Howard Gardner, *The Unschooled Mind: How Children Think and How Schools Should Teach* (New York: Basic Books, 1991), 172.

2. Wayne C. Booth, Gregory G. Colomb, and Joseph M. Williams, *The Craft of Research* (Chicago: University of Chicago Press, 1995), 59–63.

3. Booth, Colomb, and Williams, 48–60.

4. Vivian Gornick, *Fierce Attachments: A Memoir* (New York: Farrar Straus Giroux, 1987), 108. Gornick's book was called to my attention by Ann Merle Feldman.

5. Gornick, 109.

6. Plato, *Phaedrus and the Seventh and Eighth Letters*, trans, Walter Hamilton (London: Penguin Books, 1973), 95–103; Jacques Derrida, "Plato's Pharmacy," in *Dissemination*, trans. Barbara Johnson (Chicago: University of Chicago Press, 1981), 102–12.

7. Robert Scholes, *The Crafty Reader* (New Haven: Yale University Press, 2000), 22–24.

8. Scholes, 25.

9. Mina P. Shaughnessy, *Errors and Expectations: A Guide for the Teacher of Basic Writing* (New York: Oxford University Press, 1977), 240.

10. Booth, Colomb, and Williams, *The Craft of Research*, 95.

11. David Bartholomae, as quoted by Mike Rose, *Lives on the Boundary: A Moving Account of the Struggles and Achievements of America's Educational Underclass* (New York: Penguin Books, 1989), 189. Bartholomae's comment is in "Inventing the University," *Cross-Talk in Comp Theory: A Reader*, ed. Victor

Villanueva, Jr. (Urbana, Ill.: NCTE, 1997), 607. "Inventing the University" was first published in 1985.

12. Rose, *Lives on the Boundary*, 189.

13. Jane Tompkins, *A Life in School: What the Teacher Learned* (New York: Addison-Wesley, 1996), 65.

14. Shaughnessy, *Errors and Expectations*, 240–41.

15. Basil Bernstein, *The Structuring of Pedagogic Discourse*. Vol. IV. *Class, Codes and Control*, 2d ed. (London: Routledge & Kegan Paul, 1990), 94–130.

16. Shirley Brice Heath, *Ways With Words: Language, Life, and Work in Communities and Classrooms* (New York: Cambridge University Press, 1983), 398.

17. Rosina Lippi-Green, *English With an Accent: Language, Ideology, and Discrimination in the United States* (New York: Routledge, 1997), 111–2.

18. William Labov, "The Logic of Nonstandard English," in *The Politics of Literature: Dissenting Essays on the Teaching of English*, eds. Louis Kampf and Paul Lauter (New York: Random House, 1972), 208.

19. William Graves Perry, *Forms of Intellectual and Ethical Development* (New York: Holt, Rinehart and Winston, 1970).

CHAPTER 3: THE MIXED-MESSAGE CURRICULUM

1. For two of the most prominent, see Ernest Boyer, *College: The Undergraduate Experience in America: The Carnegie Foundation for the Advancement of Teaching* (New York: Harper & Row, 1987); Allan Bloom, *The Closing of the American Mind: How Higher Education Has Failed Democracy and Impoverished the Souls of Today's Students* (New York: Simon and Schuster, 1987); for a more recent restatement of the complaint, see Frank H. T. Rhodes, "A Battle Plan for Professors to Recapture the Curriculum," *Chronicle of Higher Education* (September 14, 2001): B7–10.

2. See Graff, "Other Voices, Other Rooms," in *Beyond the Culture Wars: How Teaching the Conflicts Can Revitalize American Education* (New York: W. W. Norton, 1992), 105–24; for a more succinct version of my argument, see Graff, "Colleges Are Depriving Students of a Connected View of Knowledge," *Chronicle of Higher Education* (February 15, 1991): A48.

3. Brent Staples, *Parallel Time: Growing Up in Black and White* (New York: Pantheon Books, 1994), 211–2.

4. Kathleen McCormick, *The Culture of Reading and the Teaching of English* (Manchester and New York: Manchester University Press, 1994), 97.

5. McCormick, 121.

6. McCormick, 124.

7. Howard Gardner, *The Unschooled Mind: How Children Think and How Schools Should Teach* (New York: Basic Books, 1991), 155–8.

8. A prime case is American studies programs in universities, which were intended by their founders to integrate departments of literature, social sci-

ence, and history, but instead became their own parallel universes. On the fate of American studies, see my "The Promise of American Literature Studies," *Professing Literature: An Institutional History* (Chicago: University of Chicago Press, 1987), 209–25.

9. W. B. Carnochan, *The Battleground of the Curriculum: Liberal Education and the American Experience* (Stanford: Stanford University Press, 1993); also on the McCosh-Eliot debate, see Graff, *Professing Literature*, 61–2.

10. David Carkeet, "How Critics Write and How Students Write," *College English* 37, no. 6 (February 1976): 601.

11. David Richter, ed., *Falling into Theory: Conflicting Views on Reading Literature* (Boston: Bedford Books, 1994), vii.

12. John Taylor Gatto, radio interview with David Cayley, in *The Education Debates*, ed. David Cayley (transcripts of the Canadian Broadcasting Corp., Toronto, Ontario, 1998–99), 107.

13. Art Young, *Teaching Across the Curriculum*, 3d ed. Prentice Hall Resources for Writing (Upper Saddle River, N.J.: Prentice Hall, 1999), 1–2.

14. See Graff, *Professing Literature*, 6–12 and passim; "Burying the Battlefield," *Beyond the Culture Wars*, 125–43.

15. Frank H. T. Rhodes, "A Battle Plan for Professors to Recapture the Curriculum," B8.

16. See Graff, "Turning Conflict into Community," *Beyond the Culture Wars*, 171–96.

17. Jane Tompkins and Graff, "Can We Talk?" in *Professions: Conversations on the Future of Literary and Cultural Studies*, ed. Donald E. Hall (Urbana, Ill., and Chicago: University of Illinois Press, 2001), 21–36.

18. Faith Gabelnick, Jean MacGregor, Roberta Matthews, and Barbara Leigh Smith, *Learning Communities* (San Francisco: Jossey-Bass, 1990); for more recent assessments, see the special issue on learning communities of *Peer Review*, journal of the Association of American Colleges and Universities (Summer/Fall, 2001).

19. Gabelnick et al., 64.

20. On this all too familiar cycle of futility, see Graff, "Curricular Reform Blues," *ADE Bulletin* 108 (Fall 1994): 23–6.

21. For a cogent critique of the isolationist scholarly temperament, see David Damrosch, *We Scholars: Changing the Culture of the University* (Cambridge: Harvard University Press, 1995); for a satiric though affectionate look at the communal culture of the academic conference circuit, see Damrosch's *Meetings of the Mind* (Princeton: Princeton University Press, 2000).

CHAPTER 4: TWO CHEERS FOR THE ARGUMENT CULTURE

1. Deborah Tannen, *The Argument Culture: Moving from Debate to Dialogue* (New York: Random House, 1998), 3. Page references to this book are henceforth given in the text.

2. George Lakoff and Mark Johnson, *Metaphors We Live By* (Chicago: University of Chicago Press, 1980).

3. Tannen, "Agonism in the Academy: Surviving Higher Learning's Argument Culture," *Chronicle of Higher Education* (March 31, 2000): B7.

4. Sharon James McGee, in conversation.

5. Michael Sandel, "The Right to Judge a Nominee's Ideology," *New York Times* (January 14, 2001): Wk 17.

6. Elbow's distinction is developed in "Methodological Doubting and Believing: Contraries in Inquiry," in *Embracing Contraries: Explorations in Learning and Teaching* (New York: Oxford University Press), 257–64.

7. Alex S. Jones, "A Time for Fairness and Ferocity," *New York Times* (December 19, 2000): A35.

8. Tannen, *The Argument Culture: Stopping America's War of Words* (New York: Ballantine Books, 1999).

9. I am indebted to Naomi De-Malach for reminding me of this important point.

10. Monty Python, "The Argument Clinic," transcribed from "The Second [In Sequence, Not in Quality] Monty Python's Flying Circus Videocassette" (Paramount Pictures, 1970, 1972, 1992).

11. Steve Benton, letter to the editor, *Chronicle of Higher Education* (May 5, 2000): B15.

12. Jeffrey Wallen, "Professional Discord," *College English* 64, no. 3 (January 2002): 348. Wallen is rightly challenging my own occasionally idealized invocations of academic conference culture.

13. Joseph Harris, *A Teaching Subject: Composition Since 1966* (Upper Saddle River, N.J.: Prentice Hall, 1997), 119.

14. Arthur Powell, Eleanor Farrar, and David K. Cohen, *The Shopping Mall High School: Winners and Losers in the Educational Marketplace* (Boston: Houghton Mifflin, 1985), 67–8.

15. Michael Billig, *Arguing and Thinking: A Rhetorical Approach to Social Psychology*, rev. ed. (New York: Cambridge University Press, 1996), 1–3. Another rhetorician who argues along similar lines is James Crosswhite, in *The Rhetoric of Reason: Writing and the Attractions of Argument* (Madison: University of Wisconsin Press, 1996).

16. Andrea A. Lunsford and John J. Ruszkiewicz, *Everything's an Argument* (Boston: Bedford Books, 1998), iii. A partial list of recent writing texts that more or less assume that "everything's an argument" would include Lunsford and Ruszkiewicz, *The Presence of Others: Voices and Images that Call for Response*, 3d ed. (Boston: Bedford Books, 1999); Tilly Warnock, *Writing Is Critical Action* (Glenview, Ill.: Scott, Foresman and Co., 1989); David J. Klooster and Patricia L. Bloem, *The Writer's Community* (New York: St. Martin's Press, 1995); John C. Bean, *Engaging Ideas: The Professor's Guide to Integrating Writing, Critical Thinking, and Active Learning in the Classroom* (San

Francisco: Jossey-Bass, 1965); Judith Summerfield, *Negotiations: A Reader for Writers* (New York: McGraw-Hill, Inc., 1992); Herbert W. Simons, *Persuasion in Society* (London: Sage, 2001); and Ann Merle Feldman, Nancy Downs, and Ellen McManus, *In Context: Participating in Cultural Conversations* (New York: Longman, 2002).

17. Lunsford and Ruszkiewicz, *Everything's an Argument*, 5. On the issue of debate versus winning, Elaine Showalter points out that a rich literature on how to negotiate disagreements productively "is widely available in the legal and corporate world that so many academics disdain or distrust." This "literature of negotiation," Showalter writes, "is not just about winning. . . . It explains, step by step, how to separate people from problems, how to listen, how to identify shared interests, how to develop a process of principled dialogue and negotiation" ("Taming the Rampant Incivility in Academe," *Chronicle of Higher Education* [January 15, 1999]: B5). Showalter mentions Roger Fisher and Scott Brown's *Getting Together: Building Relationships as We Negotiate* (New York: Penguin Books, 1989) and Fisher, Elizabeth Coppleman, and Andrea Kupfer Schneider's *Beyond Machiavelli: Tools for Coping with Conflict* (Cambridge: Harvard University Press, 1994). To her list I would add Fisher and William Ury's *Getting to Yes: Negotiating Agreement Without Giving In*, 2d ed. (New York: Penguin Books, 1991).

18. Robert Hughes, *Culture of Complaint: The Fraying of America* (New York: Oxford University Press, 1993), 79–84.

19. Jed Perl, "American High," *New Republic* (May 31, 1999): 50.

CHAPTER 5: PARALYSIS BY ANALYSIS?

1. Bob Dylan, "Love Minus Zero—No Limit"; "The Gates of Eden"; transcribed from recordings.

2. Stephen Jay Gould, "The Brain of Brawn," *New York Times* (June 25, 2000): A16.

3. Mihaly Csikszentmihali, *Flow: The Psychology of Optimal Experience* (New York: Harper and Row, 1990).

4. Phil Jackson with Hugh Delehanty, *Sacred Hoops: Spiritual Lessons of a Hardwood Warrior* (New York: Hyperion, 1995), 4.

5. Gould, "The Brain of Brawn," A16.

6. The Editors of *Golf Digest*, "Foreword" to Tiger Woods, *How I Play Golf* (New York: Warner Books, 2001), 8.

7. Ted Williams, *The Science of Hitting* (New York: Simon and Schuster, 1971).

8. Percy Bysshe Shelley, "A Defense of Poetry," in *Critical Theory Since Plato*, ed. Hazard Adams (New York: Harcourt Brace Jovanovich, 1971), 511; Shelley, "To a Skylark," *English Poetry and Prose of the Romantic Movement*, rev. ed., ed. George Benjamin Scott (Chicago: Scott, Foresman, 1950), 130–2; William Wordsworth, "The Tables Turned," in *English Poetry and Prose of the Romantic Movement*, 259; Friedrich Schiller, *Naive and Sentimental Poetry*, trans. Julius A. Elias (New York: Frederick Ungar, 1966).

9. George Santayana, "Penitent Art," *Essays in Literary Criticism of George Santayana*, ed. Irving Singer (New York: Charles Scribners Sons, 1956), 235, 238.

10. The classic Frankfurt School critique of instrumental rationality is Theodore W. Adorno and Max Horkheimer's *Dialectic of Enlightenment*, trans. John Cumming (New York: Seabury Press, 1972).

11. W. H. Auden, "In Memory of W. B. Yeats," in *The Collected Poetry of W. H. Auden* (New York: Random House, 1945), 50. On romantic aesthetics and the logic of "guilt by association," see my *Literature Against Itself: Literary Ideas in Modern Society* (Chicago: University of Chicago Press, 1979; 2d ed., Ivan R. Dee, 1995).

12. Charles Dickens, *Hard Times*, ed. Kate Flint (London: Penguin Classics, 1995; first published 1854), 9–12.

13. Sandra Stotsky, *Losing Our Language: How Multicultural Classroom Instruction Is Undermining Our Children's Ability to Read, Write, and Reason* (New York: The Free Press, 1999); Rita Kramer, *The Ed School Follies: The Miseducation of America's Teachers* (New York: The Free Press, 1991); Diane Ravitch, *Left Back: A Century of Failed School Reforms* (New York: Simon and Schuster, 2000).

14. John Dewey, *Experience and Education* (New York: MacMillan, 1938), 73–88.

15. Lawrence Cremin, *The Transformation of the School: Progressivism in American Education, 1876–1957* (New York: Random House, 1961), 237. Though the distortions of Dewey have indeed been "incredible," Christopher Lasch argues persuasively that Dewey could have foreseen these distortions of his doctrine but failed to guard against them (see Lasch, *The New Radicalism in America, 1889–1963* ([New York: Knopf, 1965], 161).

16. Hughes Mearns, quoted by David Myers, in *The Elephants Teach: Creative Writing Since 1880* (Englewood Cliffs, N.J.: Prentice Hall, 1996), 113.

17. Cremin, *The Transformation of the School*, 207.

18. Jane Tompkins, *A Life in School: What the Teacher Learned* (New York: Addison-Wesley, 1996), 30. Further page references to this book henceforth are given in the text.

19. James Thurber, *Let Your Mind Alone: And Other More or Less Inspirational Pieces* (New York and London: Harper & Bros., 1937).

20. Saul Bellow, *Herzog* (New York: Viking, 1965), 166.

21. Jules Feiffer, *The Explainers* (New York: McGraw-Hill, 1960).

22. Saul Bellow, *Ravelstein* (New York: Viking, 2000), 203.

23. Sarah Boxer, "Trash Tropes and Queer Theory: Decoding the Lewinski Scandal," *New York Times* (August 5, 2001): Wk 7. Boxer's article was occasioned by the appearance of Lauren Berlant and Lisa Duggan, eds., *Our Monica, Ourselves: The Clinton Affair and the National Interest* (New York: New York University Press, 2001).

24. Unsigned, "Don't Mean Diddly," *New Yorker* 70, no. 20 (July 11, 1994): 4.

25. "Don't Mean Diddly," 4.

26. Brian Hall, "The Group," *New York Times Book Review* (June 6, 1999): 23.

27. David Denby, *Great Books: My Adventure with Homer, Rousseau, Woolf, and Other Indestructable Writers of the Western World* (New York: Simon and Schuster, 1996), quoted by Hall, 23.

28. Harold Rosenberg, "Everyman a Professional," in *The Tradition of the New* (New York: Horizon Press, 1959), 61.

29. Wallace Stevens, "Not Ideas About the Thing But the Thing Itself," in *Collected Poems* (New York: Alfred Knopf, 1954), 534.

CHAPTER 6: UNLEARNING TO WRITE

1. Henry Louis Gates, *Loose Canons* (New York: Oxford University Press, 1992), 38.

2. Jeffrey Williams, "The New Belletrism," *Style* 33, no. 3 (Fall 1999): 429.

3. Williams, 415.

4. H. Aram Veeser, ed., *Confessions of the Critics* (New York: Routledge, 1996); Lennard A. Davis, *My Sense of Silence: Memoirs of a Childhood with Deafness* (Urbana, Ill.: University of Illinois Press, 1990); Davis, *The Sonnets* (Albany: State University of New York Press, 2001).

5. For two sketches of such a history, see Graff, "The Charge That Research Is Narrow and Opaque Is Decades Out of Date," *Chronicle of Higher Education* (October 21, 1992): A56; "The Scholar in Society," in *Introduction to Scholarship in Modern Languages and Literatures*, ed. Joseph Gibaldi (New York: Modern Language Association, 1992), 343–62.

6. Frederick C. Crews, *The Pooh-Perplex: A Freshman Casebook* (New York: Dutton, 1963), 65. Crews has updated his satire on academic schools in *Postmodern Pooh* (New York: North Point Press, 2001); he honors my "teach the conflicts" theory as one of his targets.

7. Michael Bérubé, *Marginal Forces, Cultural Centers: Tolson, Pynchon, and the Politics of the Canon* (Ithaca, N.Y.: Cornell University Press, 1992), 315.

8. Bérubé, 314.

9. Bérubé, 300.

10. George Orwell, "Such, Such Were the Joys," *A Collection of Essays* (New York: Harcourt Brace Jovanovich, 1993), 131–2.

11. W. B. Scott, *Parodies, Etcetera, and So Forth*, Gerald Graff and Barbara Heldt, eds. (Evanston, Ill.: Northwestern University Press, 1985; first published by Ardis Publishers, 1978) 45, 49–50.

12. Henry James, "The Art of Fiction," *The House of Fiction: Essays on the Novel by Henry James*, ed. Leon Edel (London: Rupert Hart-Davies, 1957), 33.

13. Norman Maclean, "Episode, Scene, Speech, and Word: The Madness of Lear," in *Critics and Criticism: Ancient and Modern*, ed. R. S. Crane (Chicago: University of Chicago Press, 1952), 595–6.

14. Norman Maclean, *A River Runs Through It and Other Stories* (Chicago: University of Chicago Press, 1976), 1.

15. Wayne C. Booth, *The Rhetoric of Fiction* (Chicago: University of Chicago Press, 1961), 364–65.

16. *Beyond the Fringe,* transcribed from the recording.

17. On the cult of opposition to "the Organization Man" in the 1950s, see Andrew Hoberek, *White Collar Culture: Work, Organization, and American Fiction, 1943–1959* (Ph.D. diss., University of Chicago, 1997).

18. Gerald Graff, *Poetic Statement and Critical Dogma* (Evanston, Ill.: Northwestern University Press, 1970; rpt. University of Chicago Press, 1980), xiii.

19. Mark Twain, *Adventures of Huckleberry Finn,* eds. Gerald Graff and James Phelan (Boston: Bedford Books, 1995), 151.

20. William P. Germano, *Getting It Published: A Guide for Scholars and Anyone Else Serious About Serious Books* (Chicago: University of Chicago Press, 2001), 40.

21. Richard E. Miller, "The Arts of Complicity: Pragmatism and the Culture of Schooling," *College English* 61, no. 1 (September, 1998): 21. See also Miller's *As If Learning Mattered: Reforming Higher Education* (Ithaca, N.Y.: Cornell University Press, 1998).

22. James Nehring, *"Why Do We Gotta Do This Stuff, Mr. Nehring?" Notes from a Teacher's Day in School* (New York: Ballantine Books, 1989), 124.

23. Miller, "The Arts of Complicity," 25.

24. Henry Giroux, "Liberal Arts Education and the Struggle for Public Life: Dreaming About Democracy," in Gless and Smith, eds., *The Politics of Liberal Education* (Durham, N.C.: Duke University Press, 1992) 127.

25. David Kaufer and Gary Waller, "To Write Is to Read Is to Write, Right?" in C. Douglas Atkins and Michael L. Johnson, eds., *Writing and Reading Differently: Deconstruction and the Teaching of Composition and Literature* (Lawrence, Kans.: University of Kansas Press, 1985), 87.

CHAPTER 7: SCHOLARS AND SOUND BITES: THE MYTH OF ACADEMIC DIFFICULTY

1. T. S. Eliot, "The Metaphysical Poets," in *Selected Prose of T. S. Eliot,* ed. Frank Kermode (New York: Harcourt Brace Jovanovich, Farrar Straus and Giroux, 1975; first published 1922), 65. Italics in original.

2. George Steiner, "An Academic Comes of Age in 'The Sleepless City,'" *Chronicle of Higher Education* (February 6, 1998): B6.

3. Jerry Coyne, "Of Vice and Men—A Natural History of Rape," rev. of Randy Thornhill and Craig Palmer, *Biological Bases of Sexual Coercion, New Republic* (April 3, 2000): 28.

4. Jane Tompkins and Gerald Graff, "Can We Talk?" in *Professions: Conversations on the Future of Literary and Cultural Studies,* ed. Donald E. Hall (Urbana, Ill., and Chicago: University of Illinois Press, 2001), 23.

5. Graham Robb, "Bosom Buddies" (rev. of Caleb Crain, *American Sympathy: Men, Friendship, and Literature in the New Nation*), *New York Times Book Review* (June 3, 2001): 18.

6. Bruce Robbins, *Secular Vocations: Intellectuals, Professionalism, Culture* (London: Verso, 1993), 87–91.

7. Patricia Nelson Limerick, unpublished manuscript.

8. Eve Kosofsky Sedgwick, *Epistemology of the Closet* (Berkeley: University of California Press, 1990), 29.

9. Sedgwick, 52.

10. William Safire, "King of Chutzpah," *New York Times* (November 30, 1998): A23.

11. Sedgwick, *Epistemology of the Closet*, 55.

12. Fredric Jameson, *The Political Unconscious: Narrative as a Socially Symbolic Act* (Ithaca, N.Y.: Cornell University Press, 1981), 9.

13. Jameson, 10.

14. Deirdre McCloskey disagrees, arguing that "the person who made up this memorable phrasing of it is burning right now in hell" (McCloskey, *Economical Writing*, 2d ed. [Prospect Heights, Ill.: Waveland Press, 2000]), 37; elsewhere McCloskey advises writers: "*Don't keep outlining what you are going to say.* Just say it" ("Bush," *Eastern Economic Journal* 27, no. 3 [Summer 2001]: 370). Italics in original.

15. Many would argue, of course, that academic writing is unlikely to improve as long as publish-or-perish requirements force professors to churn out books and articles that presumably would not see print otherwise. I have yet to meet a fellow academic, however, who confessed to having published something solely because tenure or promotion standards required it. The truth may be even more grim: we publish this stuff because we actually believe in it! Nevertheless, it would indeed be highly beneficial to reduce the present crassly *quantitative* publication requirements, as has been recently proposed by a group of scholars, campus administrators, publishers, and librarians in a statement reported by the *Chronicle of Higher Education:* "To assure quality," the group urges "a reduced emphasis on quantity" (Denise K. Manger, "Seeking a Radical Change in the Role of Publishing," *Chronicle of Higher Education* [June 16, 2000]: A17). Unfortunately, the competitive nature of the higher education system has prevented universities from considering such a policy. Like superpowers who fear that reducing their nuclear arsenals would weaken them against rivals, university administrators feel they can't unilaterally "disarm" by reducing their publication requirements when their competitors do not.

On the other hand, universities may be forced to rethink their book-publishing requirements on faculty if the economic recession prevents presses from publishing many academic books at all. Modern Language Association president Stephen Greenblatt has called needed attention to this issue in an open letter to language and literature departments. Given the pressures that have caused presses to "cut back on the number of books they publish annually in certain fields," and given the fact that "books are not the only way of judging scholarly achievement," Greenblatt asks if departments should "continue to insist that only books and more books will do" (Stephen Greenblatt, open letter to members, May 28, 2002, Modern Language Association of America).

16. Zachary Karabell, *What's College For? The Struggle to Define American Higher Education* (New York: Basic Books), 73.

17. Alan Sokal, "A Physicist Experiments With Cultural Studies," *Lingua Franca* 6. no. 4 (1996): 62–4.

18. Lee Siegel, "The Gay Science: Queer Theory, Literature, and the Sexualization of Everything," *New Republic* 219, no. 19 (1998): 30.

19. Dinesh D'Souza, *Illiberal Education: The Politics of Race and Sex on Campus* (New York: Free Press, 1991), 178; David Lehman, *Signs of the Times: Deconstruction and the Fall of Paul de Man* (New York: Poseidon Press, 1992); John M. Ellis, *Against Deconstruction* (Princeton, N.J.: Princeton University Press, 1989).

20. J. Hillis Miller, *The Ethics of Reading: Kant, de Man, Eliot, Trollope, James, and Benjamin* (New York: Columbia University Press, 1987), 38.

21. Stanley Fish, "Short People Got No Right to Live: Reading Irony," *Daedalus* (Winter 1983): 175–91; Tompkins, "Me and My Shadow," *New Literary History* 19, no. 1 (1987): 169–76; Gates, "What's Love Got to Do With It? Critical Theory, Integrity, and the Black Idiom," *New Literary History* 18, no. 2 (1987): 345–62; W. J. T. Mitchell, "The Good, the Bad, and the Ugly: Three Voices of Value," *Raritan* 6, no. 2 (1986): 63–76.

22. Terry Eagleton, "The Ballad of English Literature," *Against the Grain: Selected Essays* (London and New York: Verso, 1986), 185.

23. Hilary Putnam, "The Meaning of Meaning," *Mind, Language and Reality: Philosophical Papers*, vol. 2 (New York: Cambridge University Press, 1975), 227.

CHAPTER 8: WHY JOHNNY CAN'T ARGUE

1. Deborah Meier, *The Power of Their Ideas: Lessons for America from a Small School in Harlem* (Boston: Beacon Press, 1995), 11.

2. Paul Grice, *Studies in the Way of Words* (Cambridge, Mass.: Harvard University Press, 1989).

3. I acquired Ellen's paper at a workshop for college and high school teachers. As elsewhere here when quoting from student writing, I have changed the student's name.

4. See my earlier discussion of Basil Bernstein's distinction between elaborated and restricted codes in chapter 2.

5. The "So what?" problem has been acutely discussed by University of Chicago

compositionist Joseph M. Williams, who writes extensively on "problem formation" as the key enabling step in writing persuasive arguments. (I referred to Williams's work earlier in my discussion of "the problem problem.") Williams observes that when student writers are unaware that they need to pose a problem near the beginning of an essay, they end up either merely summarizing their reading or asserting their opinions in a vacuum. In either case, Williams notes, the writing will lack motivation and prompt readers to ask, "So what, if we don't know that?" (Joseph M. Williams, "Problems into Problems," unpublished essay).

CHAPTER 9: OUTING CRITICISM

1. Mike Rose, *Lives on the Boundary: A Moving Account of the Struggles and Achievements of America's Educational Underclass* (New York: Penguin Books, 1989), 191.

2. Chris Baldick, *The Social Mission of English Criticism 1848–1932* (New York: Oxford University Press, 1983), 4–5.

3. Howard Gardner has frequently objected to anti-intellectual curricular misapplications of his influential work on Multiple Intelligences:

   I have been angered and hurt by assertions . . . that my theory is a license to do whatever one wants; a way to insinuate self-esteem as the central goal of education; a claim that everyone is equally smart; an argument against assessments, standards, hard work, or discipline.

   Exactly the opposite is the case. I believe in rigorous curricula, clear standards of performance, the highest possible demands to be made on individuals, self-esteem as the result of disciplined achievements (Howard Gardner, "Commentary," *St. Louis Post Dispatch* [December 26, 1995]: T77).

   Gardner warns that these conclusions about the need for curricular rigor and standards "do not follow from MI theory either" (77), but he makes clear where his own preferences lie: "In the end," he writes, "we want students to develop *a single, powerful mind,* housing strands of knowledge that can be integrated and synthesized" (emphasis mine) ("Anti-Babel Standards," *Education Week* XIV, no. 1 [September 7, 1994]: 56). Italics added.

   Gardner has insisted that the multiple intelligences theory is an empirical account of human cognitive capacities from which no particular curricular prescriptions necessarily follow. In his words, the theory "is a claim about the organization of the mind/brain; it is not, and was never intended to be a recipe for education" ("Commentary," T77).

4. Michael W. Smith and Peter Rabinowitz, *Authorizing Readers: Resistance and Respect in the Teaching of Literature* (New York: Teachers College Press, 1998), 80. I find the same difficulty in the examples of "good" student discourse presented by James D. Marshall, Peter Smagorinski, and Smith in

The Language of Interpretation: Patterns of Discourse in Discussions of Literature (Urbana, Ill.: NCTE Research Report No. 27, 1995).

5. Kenneth A. Bruffee, *Collaborative Learning: Higher Education, Interdependence, and the Authority of Knowledge* (Baltimore: Johns Hopkins University Press, 1993).

6. Robert Scholes, *Textual Power: Literary Theory and the Teaching of English* (New Haven: Yale University Press, 1985), 33. As Jonathan Culler points out, we see a text *as* literary by applying a "rule of significance," whereby we read the text "as expressing a significant attitude to some problem concerning man and/or his relation to the universe" (*Structuralist Poetics: Structuralism, Linguistics, and the Study of Literature* [Ithaca, N.Y.: Cornell University Press, 1975]), 115.

7. Scholes, *Textual Power*, 31.

8. Scholes, 38.

9. Scholes, 24.

10. Scholes, 34–5.

11. Mark Twain, *The Adventures of Huckleberry Finn: A Case Study in Critical Controversy*, eds. Gerald Graff and James Phelan (Boston: Bedford Books, 1995); William Shakespeare, *The Tempest: A Case Study in Critical Controversy*, eds. Graff and Phelan (Boston: Bedford Books, 2000); David Richter, *Falling into Theory: Conflicting Views on Reading Literature* (Boston: Bedford Books, 1994).

12. Another set of texts that is organized around broad public issues is Greenhaven Press's Opposing Viewpoints Series (Greenhaven Press; P. O. Box 289009; San Diego, Calif. 92198–9009).

13. Graff and Phelan, "Why Study Critical Controversies," in Twain, *Adventures of Huckleberry Finn*, 3; Twain's "Notice" appears on p. 27 of this edition. In warning against looking for "a moral" in his narrative, Twain would have been thinking not of academic close reading practices, which had not yet come into existence when he wrote, but of the sanctimonious American moralism that is satirized so extensively in the novel itself.

14. Van Wyck Brooks, *The Ordeal of Mark Twain* (Cleveland: World Publishing Co., 1965; first published, 1920).

CHAPTER 10: THE APPLICATION GUESSING GAME

1. On Chicago's MAPH, see Allison Schneider, "Master's Degrees, Once Scorned, Attract Students and Generate Resources," *Chronicle of Higher Education* (May 1999): A12–3; Jenny Adams, "Jumping into the Culture Wars," *University of Chicago Magazine* (October 1997): 25–9. In *The Employment of English: Theory, Jobs, and the Future of Literary Studies* (New York: New York University Press, 1998), Michael Bérubé discusses the prospects of expanded MA degree programs as one solution to the crisis in the academic job mar-

ket and also makes a compelling case for using the MA as the much-needed link between high school and college teaching (81–6).

2. Richard and Margot Jerrard, *The Grad School Handbook: An Insiders Guide to Getting in and Succeeding* (New York: Perigee Books, 1998), 111.

3. Jerrard, *The Grad School Handbook*.

4. Eve Kosofsky Sedgwick, *Epistemology of the Closet* (Berkeley: University of California Press, 1990), 198.

5. Stanley Fish, *Professional Correctness: Literary Studies and Political Change* (New York: Oxford University Press, 1995), 74. Ironically, Fish's book is an attack on the premise MAPH is based on, that academic humanists can become public intellectuals and influence their society without ceasing to act as academics. Clearly this attack will be correct if humanists communicate their ideas poorly, though Fish's example shows they do not have to.

6. Gerald Graff and Andrew Hoberek, "Hiding It from the Kids (With Apologies to Simon and Garfunkel)," *College English* 62, no. 2 (November 1999): 242–54.

CHAPTER 11: HIDDEN INTELLECTUALISM

1. Michael Warner, "Tongues Untied: Memoirs of a Pentecostal Boyhood," *Voice Literary Supplement* (February 1993): 13–4.

2. George Orwell, "The Art of Donald McGill," *A Collection of Essays* (New York: Harcourt Brace, 1993), 104–16.

3. Thomas McLaughlin, *Street Smarts and Critical Theory: Listening to the Vernacular* (Madison, Wis.: University of Wisconsin Press, 1996), 29.

4. McLaughlin, 26.

5. McLaughlin, 29.

6. Graff, "Hidden Meaning, or Disliking Books at an Early Age," *Beyond the Culture Wars: How Teaching the Conflicts Can Revitalize American Education* (New York: W. W. Norton, 1992), 64–85.

7. Richard Hofstadter, *Anti-Intellectualism in American Life* (New York: Random House, 1963).

8. David Riesman with Nathan Glazer and Reuel Denney, *The Lonely Crowd: A Study of the Changing American Character* (Garden City, N.Y.: Doubleday, 1953).

9. Hofstadter, *Anti-Intellectualism in American Life*, 34.

10. Peter Guralnick, *Last Train to Memphis: The Rise of Elvis Presley* (Boston: Little, Brown & Co., 1994), 327.

11. Mark Edmundson, "My First Intellectual," *Lingua Franca* (March 1999): 55.

12. On the theory of mental discipline, see my *Professing Literature: An Institutional History* (Chicago: University of Chicago Press, 1987), 30–1; 72–4.

13. Terry Eagleton, *Literary Theory: An Introduction* (Minneapolis: University of Minnesota Press, 1983), 29.

14. McLaughlin, *Street Smarts and Critical Theory*, 152–53.
15. McLaughlin, 153.
16. McLaughlin, 155. John Trimbur makes a similar argument to McLaughlin's about students' insights into the study of literature. Trimbur quotes from a student whose paper, he says, perceptively registers the contradictions and tensions between high and popular culture. He suggests that such a student is "neither naive nor clueless when it comes to considering why he has so persistently been called upon to study literature." Trimbur is right to credit his student with insight into a cultural contradiction, but the terms "culture" and "contradiction" come not from the student but from Trimbur's reformulation of his words. In fairness, Trimbur does acknowledge that teachers need "to raise [the student's] contradictory experience to consciousness and to reinterpret it" (John Trimbur, "Taking English," in *When Writing Teachers Teach Literature: Bringing Writing to Reading*, eds. Art Young and Toby Fulwiler [Portsmouth, N.H.: Boynton Cook Publishers, 1995], 20–2).
17. Julie Lindquist, "Hoods in the Polis," *Pedagogy* I, no. 2 (Spring 2001): 264.
18. Steve Benton, "Concealed Commitment," *Pedagogy* I, no. 2 (Spring 2001): 251–9.
19. Ned Laff, private correspondence.
20. John Brereton, private correspondence.

CHAPTER 12: A WORD FOR WORDS AND A VOTE FOR QUOTES

1. David Cayley, ed., *The Education Debates* (transcripts of the Canadian Broadcasting Corp., Toronto, Ontario, 1998–99), 45.
2. John Dewey, *Experience and Education* (New York: MacMillan, 1938), 67ff.
3. Ira Berkow, *To the Hoop: The Seasons of a Basketball Life* (New York: Basic Books, 1997), 138; for another meditation on words and basketball, see former New York Knick star and current broadcaster Walt ("Clyde") Frazier, *Word Jam: An Electrifying, Mesmerizing, Gravity-Defying Guide to a Powerful and Awesome Vocabulary* (New York: Troll Communications, 2001). Frazier writes of his realization on becoming a broadcaster that "the more words I knew, the more confident and effective I would be." Carrying pocket dictionaries and workbooks with him wherever he went, Frazier also made lists: "lists of power words that made my speech provocative and created vivid images, lists of words that alliterated and devastated" (8). Frazier's book is properly aimed at children and adolescents who need to be convinced that using "power words" is cool. (On Frazier's book, see Harvey Araton, "Frazier Gets Assists Doling Out Words," *New York Times* [February 27, 2001]: C16.)
4. Joseph Harris, *A Teaching Subject: Composition Since 1966* (Upper Saddle River, N.J.: Prentice Hall, 1997), 46. Page references to this book henceforth are given in the text.

5. Wayne C. Booth, Gregory G. Colomb, and Joseph M. Williams, *The Craft of Research* (Chicago: University of Chicago Press, 1995), 103–4.
6. Booth, Colomb, and Williams, 102.

CHAPTER 13: WRESTLING WITH THE DEVIL

1. Donald C. Jones, "Engaging Students in the Conflict: Academic Discourse, Its Variations, and Its Instruction," *Composition Studies* 28, no. 1 (Spring 2000): 95. Page references to this essay are henceforth given in the text.
2. For a reconstruction of that debate and another from the 1991 meeting, see David Bartholomae, "Writing with Teachers: A Conversation with Peter Elbow," 479–88; Peter Elbow, "Being a Writer vs. Being an Academic: A Conflict in Goals," 489–500; David Bartholomae and Peter Elbow, "Interchanges: Responses to Bartholomae and Elbow," 501–9; all in Victor Villanueva, ed., *Cross-Talk in Comp Theory: A Reader* (Urbana, Ill.: NCTE, 1997).
3. Lynn Z. Bloom, "Textual Terror, Textual Power: Teaching Literature Through Writing Literature," in *When Writing Teachers Teach Literature: Bringing Writing to Reading*, ed. Art Young and Toby Fulwiler (Portsmouth, N.H.: Boynton Cook Publishers, 1995), 80. Other contributors to this collection who also object to the privileging of expository argument in literature courses and urge its replacement by creative writing include Charles Schuster and Carl R. Lovitt. I respond to these and other similar arguments in an afterword to the collection (324–33).
4. Bloom, 78–79.
5. Patricia Bizzell, *Academic Discourse and Critical Consciousness* (Pittsburgh: University of Pittsburgh Press, 1992), 125.
6. Bizzell, 218–19.
7. Mark Twain, *Adventures of Huckleberry Finn*, eds. Gerald Graff and James Phelan (Boston: Bedford Books, 1995), 27.
8. J. D. Salinger, *The Catcher in the Rye* (Boston: Little, Brown, 1951), 17.
9. Salinger, 18.
10. Salinger, 19.
11. Gerald Graff, *Beyond the Culture Wars: How Teaching the Conflicts Can Revitalize American Education* (New York: W. W. Norton, 1992), 64–68.

CHAPTER 14: DEBORAH MEIER'S PROGRESSIVE TRADITIONALISM

1. Deborah Meier, *The Power of Their Ideas: Lessons for America from a Small School in Harlem* (Boston: Beacon Press, 1995), 20. Page references to this book are henceforth given in the text.
2. To refute this nostalgia, Meier cites the statistical research of Richard Rothstein in his Century Foundation Report, *The Way We Were? The Myths and Realities of America's Student Achievement* (New York: Century Foundation Press, 1998). For other debunkings of the alleged decline in performance of American students, see Leon Botstein, *Jefferson's Children: Educa-*

tion and the Promise of American Culture (New York: Doubleday, 1997), 22–23 and passim, and my own *Beyond the Culture Wars: How Teaching the Conflicts Can Revitalize American Education* (New York: W. W. Norton, 1992), 87–92.

3. Meier, private correspondence. CPESS is a public pilot school, which Meier (in correspondence) calls "an attempt to demonstrate that charters were not needed." At the same time, Meier defends school choice *if* it can be made to promote community rather than free marketeering:

> We need to examine whether public chartering is part of a trend towards everybody-out-for-themselves or is a wider way of looking at community. It could be either. The question is, what kind of public policy could make charters a vehicle for democratic life rather than a vehicle for running away from democratic life? . . . The geographic neighborhood school can be a way of isolating us from our fellow citizens, or it can be a way of creating strong communities. In that sense, these labels sometimes hide what's really happening underneath them. . . . Some schools of choice, I think, are simply vehicles for creating class segregation within cities, and enabling people to go to private schools with a public subsidy (Interview with David Cayley, in *The Education Debates*, ed. David Cayley [transcripts of the Canadian Broadcasting Corp., Toronto, Ontario, 1998–99], 40–41).

See also Meier, "Choice Can Save Public Education," *The Power of Their Ideas*, 81.

4. Paul Goodman, *Compulsory Miseducation and the Community of Scholars* (New York: Vintage Books, 1966).

5. Meier, radio interview with David Cayley, *The Education Debates*, 45.

6. William Damon, quoted by Ethan Bronner, "Rethinking America's Schools of Hard Knocks," *New York Times* (May 30, 1999): 3.

7. John Dewey, *The School and Society* (Chicago: University of Chicago Press, 1990; first published, 1900, 1902), 15.

8. Dewey, 152.

9. Jane Tompkins, *A Life in School: What the Teacher Learned* (New York: Addison-Wesley, 1996), 147. For another writer who makes a case for teachers getting out of their students' way, see Donald Finkel, *Teaching with Your Mouth Shut* (Portsmouth, N.H.: Heinemann Boynton Cook, 2000).

10. William Ayers, *A Kind and Just Parent: The Children of Juvenile Court* (Boston: Beacon Press, 1997), 78.

11. Meier, "Changing Our Habits of Schooling," Marianne Amerel Memorial Lecture (East Lansing, Mich.: The Holmes Group, 1993), 12–3.

12. For an example of a kind of staff development project in which teachers at different levels work together in course design and delivery teams—a kind of *vertical* learning community—see Gerald Graff, "Working with the

Schools: Project Tempest," *Publications of the Modern Language Association,* 115, no. 7 (December 2000): 1968–71.

13. Herbert W. Simons, a professor of rhetoric and communications at Temple University, has experimented with an adaptation of the talk-show format in a program of public debates he has developed there called the "Temple Issues Forum," which has a student arm, the Temple Debate and Discussion Club. Simons argues that the talk-show format is more successful than the single-person lecture in engaging the interest of today's young people. Simons's is the kind of thinking that is needed for imagining educational bigness in more arresting ways. "The Temple Issues Forum," unpublished talk delivered at the Rhetoric Society of America Conference, May 2002.

14. Meier, "Educating a Democracy," in *Will Standards Save Higher Education?,* ed. Deborah Meier (Boston: Beacon Press, 2000), 7.

15. Abigail Thernstrom, "No Excuses," in *Will Standards Save Higher Education?,* 37.